The European Union and Military Force

The Common Security and Defence Policy maps out how the EU – established primarily to be an economic organisation – can purposefully prepare for and apply the use of military force. In this insightful work, Per M. Norheim-Martinsen argues that, since the EU is not a state but nevertheless does embody some non-intergovernmental characteristics, neither EU studies nor strategic studies is sufficient for fully understanding the Policy itself. Combining the two fields, the author utilises the instrumentality and clarity of the strategic approach, while retaining an understanding of the unique character of the EU as a strategic actor. In so doing, he provides a fruitful conceptual framework for analysing the development of the CSDP, how it functions in practice and how it will continue to evolve in the face of the challenges which lie ahead. This book will appeal to scholars and advanced students of European studies, international relations and strategic studies.

PER M. NORHEIM-MARTINSEN is a Senior Research Fellow at the Fafo Institute for Applied International Studies in Oslo. He has a PhD from the University of Cambridge, and has previously held positions in the Norwegian Defence Research Establishment (FFI) and the Norwegian Military Academy.

The European Union and Military Force

Governance and Strategy

PER M. NORHEIM-MARTINSEN

CAMBRIDGE
UNIVERSITY PRESS

CAMBRIDGE UNIVERSITY PRESS
Cambridge, New York, Melbourne, Madrid, Cape Town,
Singapore, São Paulo, Delhi, Mexico City

Cambridge University Press
The Edinburgh Building, Cambridge CB2 8RU, UK

Published in the United States of America by Cambridge University Press, New York

www.cambridge.org
Information on this title: www.cambridge.org/9781107028906

First published 2013

Printed and bound in Great Britain by the MPG Books Group

A catalogue record for this publication is available from the British Library

Library of Congress Cataloguing in Publication data
Norheim-Martinsen, Per M.
    The European Union and military force : governance and
    strategy / Per M. Norheim-Martinsen.
        pages cm
    Includes bibliographical references and index.
    ISBN 978-1-107-02890-6
    1. European Union.   2. Strategic culture–European Union
    countries.   3. European Union countries–Military policy–Decision
    making.   4. Civil-military relations–European Union
    countries.   5. European Union countries–Strategic
    aspects.   6. European Union countries–Defenses.   I. Title.
    UA646.N635 2013
    355'.03354–dc23
    2012018817

ISBN 978-1-107-02890-6 Hardback

Contents

Abbreviations and acronyms

ACT	NATO Allied Command Transformation
AMIS	African Union Mission in Sudan
AMM	Aceh Monitoring Mission
ASEAN	Association of Southeast Asian Nations
AU	African Union
CA	Comprehensive Approach
CAR	Central African Republic
CCC	Capabilities Commitment Conference
CCM	Civilian Crisis Management
CDM	Capability Development Mechanism
CIC	Capabilities Improvement Conference
CIS	Communications and Information Systems
C4ISR	command, control, communications, computers, intelligence, surveillance and reconnaissance
CFSP	Common Foreign and Security Policy
CHG	Civilian Headline Goal
CHOD	Chief of Defence Staff
CIMIC	Civil–Military Cooperation
CIVCOM	Committee for Civilian Aspects of Crisis Management
CivMilCell	Civil–Military Planning Cell
CJTF	NATO Combined Joint Task Force
CMC	Crisis Management Concept
CMCO	Civil–Military Coordination
CMPD	Crisis Management and Planning Directorate
CoC	Code of Conduct
COIN	Counterinsurgency
CONOPS	Concept of Operations
COREPER	Committee of Permanent Representatives
CPCC	Civilian Planning and Conduct Capability
CPI	Comprehensive Planning Initiative
CRCT	Crisis Response Coordinating Team

CRT	Civilian Response Team
CSDP	Common Security and Defence Policy
CTG	Counter-Terrorism Group
CTM	Core Team Meeting
DAC	Deployable Augmentee Cadre
DCI	NATO Defence Capabilities Initiative
DG-E	Directorate General for External and Politico-Military Affairs
DG-Relex	Directorate General for External Relations
DRC	Democratic Republic of Congo
D-SACEUR	Deputy Supreme Allied Commander Europe
EBA	European Border Agency
EBAO	Effects-Based Approach to Operations
EBB1/2	European Bulletin Board (Government and Industry Contracts)
EBO	Effects-Based Operations
ECAP	European Capability Action Plan
ECSC	European Coal and Steel Community
EEAS	European External Action Service
EDA	European Defence Agency
EDC	European Defence Community
ELMA	European Union Military Staff Lessons Learned Application
ELPRO	European Union Military Staff Lessons Learned Process
EMP	Euro-Mediterranean Partnership
EMU	European Monetary Union
ENP	European Neighbourhood Policy
EPC	European Political Cooperation
ESS	European Security Strategy
EU	European Union
EUBG	European Union Battlegroup
EUMC	European Union Military Committee
EUMM	European Union Monitoring Mission in Georgia
EUMS	European Union Military Staff
EUPM	European Union Police Mission in Bosnia-Herzegovina
Eurogendfor	European Gendarmerie Force
EUSG	European Union Staff Group in NATO-SHAPE

EUSR	European Union Special Representative
FHQ	Force Headquarters
FOC	Full Operational Capacity
FSO	Full Spectrum Operations
FYROM	Former Yugoslav Republic of Macedonia
GAERC	General Affairs and External Relations Council
GAM	Free Aceh Movement
HLG	Headline Goal
HR-CFSP	High Representative for the Common Foreign and Security Policy
IAEA	International Atomic Energy Agency
IED	Improvised Explosive Device
IEMF	European Union Interim Emergency Multinational Force in the DR Congo
IMPP	United Nations Integrated Mission Planning Process
INTDIR	Intelligence Directorate of the EU Military Staff
IPU	Integrated Police Unit
ISAF	International Security Assistance Force in Afghanistan
JHA	Justice and Home Affairs
KFOR	Kosovo Force
LOI	Letter of Intent
MAD	Mutually Assured Destruction
MI6	British Secret Intelligence Service
MILREP	Military Representative
MINURCAT	United Nations Mission in the Central African Republic and Chad
MIP	Mission Implementation Plan
MONUC	United Nations Organization Mission in DR Congo
NAC	North Atlantic Council
NATO	North Atlantic Treaty Organisation
NATO-SHAPE	NATO Supreme Headquarters Allied Powers Europe
NBG	Nordic Battlegroup
NCW	Network Centric Warfare
NDC	Nordic Defence Cooperation
NGO	Non-governmental organisation
NRF	NATO Response Force
NSS	US National Security Strategy
NTM-I	NATO Training Mission in Iraq

OAE	NATO Operation Active Endeavour
OCCAR	Organisation for Joint Armament Cooperation
OHQ	Operations Headquarters
OHR	Office of the High Representative in Bosnia and Herzegovina
OpCen	Operations Centre
OPLAN	Operation Plan
OSCE	Organisation for Security and Cooperation in Europe
Policy Unit	Policy Planning and Early Warning Unit
POP	Policy Option Paper
PSC	Political and Security Committee
PSO	Peace Support Operation
QMV	Qualified Majority Voting
R&D	Research and Development
RMA	Revolution in Military Affairs
RRF	Rapid Reaction Force
RRM	Rapid Reaction Mechanism
SAC	NATO Strategic Airlift Capability
SALIS	NATO Strategic Airlift Interim Solution
SAP	Stability and Association Process
SEDE	European Parliament Subcommittee on Security and Defence
SFOR	Stabilisation Force (Bosnia-Herzegovina)
SIAC	Single Intelligence Analysis Capacity
SITCEN	Joint Situation Centre
SSR	Security Sector Reform
TCA	Trade and Cooperation Agreement
TEU	Treaty on European Union
TFEU	Treaty on the Functioning of the Union
UAV	Unmanned Aerial Vehicle
UN	United Nations
UNAMID	African Union/United Nations Hybrid Operation in Darfur
UNIFIL	United Nations Interim Force in Lebanon (I and II)
UNMIK	United Nations Interim Administration Mission in Kosovo
UNOMIG	United Nations Observer Mission in Georgia
WEU	Western European Union
WEAG	Western European Armaments Group

Preface

The reason for writing this book was that I wanted to understand how a non-state civilian actor such as the EU can purposefully prepare for and apply the use of military force. I wanted to present a way to understand the EU's Common Security and Defence Policy (CSDP), how it has evolved and how it works in practice. More importantly, I wanted to offer a robust and inclusive conceptual framework for understanding how it will continue to evolve in the years to come.

The book comes at a time when the CSDP seems to have lost much of the dynamic that characterised it during its first ten years. Today, Europe is more concerned with saving the Eurozone than with launching expensive military operations in faraway regions. But the CSDP is not dead. It is evolving, sometimes in leaps but more often slowly, cumulatively, as it has since its very origins in the creation of the European Coal and Steel Community (ECSC) as essentially a project for peace back in 1951. This is why this book is not primarily a book about the Lisbon Treaty or the crisis of the Eurozone. It is essentially a book about continuity, and the incremental evolution of the norms, ideas, expectations and practices that underpin European security governance.

For some time now, the academic debate on the EU as a security policy actor has been stuck in the notion that the nation state can no longer provide security on its own, while the EU does not yet have the means to fill the resulting gap. At the same time, scholars have realised that cooperation in the CSDP does go beyond mere intergovernmental bargaining, even though it falls short of supranational integration. Indeed, the CSDP has been allowed to develop over the past ten years within something of a theoretical vacuum. In the field of EU studies a number of more or less fitting labels, including partial or composite actorness, (still) civilian power, or normative power, have been introduced to get to grips with the changing character of the EU as an international actor. Traditional strategic studies, on the other hand, have remained focused on the state and national constraints on security and defence, and have failed, therefore, to pursue explanations of how the CSDP has evolved.

Coming from a military background, I wanted to utilise the instrumentality and clarity of the strategic approach, while retaining an understanding of the unique character of the EU as an international actor. The aim has been to reduce the theoretical gap between EU and strategic studies by combining the concept of security governance with an analysis of the EU as a strategic actor. This book demonstrates how a security governance approach can be used as a tool for identifying alternative mechanisms that can help explain outcomes that are inconsistent with, or only partly explained by, realist or intergovernmental approaches. When combined with the concept of strategic actorness, it provides a fruitful conceptual framework for a nuanced analysis of what the EU has accomplished so far with the CSDP, how it works in practice, and the challenges ahead.

It is worth pointing out that this book is certainly not a defence script for a military EU. Rather I have wanted to avoid the normative perspectives that have permeated parts of the CSDP research agenda for some time now. This book is simply an attempt to understand one of, or perhaps the most, important and ambitious political project of our time.

The principal argument of the book is that, by placing a broad understanding of a Comprehensive Approach at the heart of what might be described as an emerging European strategic culture, the EU as a collective found a commonly acceptable reference point for the evolving CSDP. This has, in turn, created growing expectations of civil–military integration at all levels. The book shows that by striking a balance between the influence of state, individual and institutional actors, the EU has, in several areas, been able to lead a proactive and efficient foreign and security policy, without losing the legitimacy of the consensus mechanism. Yet institutional developments have not led to an integrated civil–military organisation. The same has been the case with capability developments and operations, which have sustained a separation of civil and military instruments, and, therefore, in many ways, failed to take advantage of the EU's inherent comparative advantage as a comprehensive strategic actor.

I would like to thank a number of colleagues and friends for their input and support during the writing of this book. Sven Biscop,

Paul Cornish, Helene Sjursen and all of my former colleagues at the Norwegian Defence Research Establishment (FFI) have to be mentioned explicitly in this regard. However, my greatest intellectual debt is to Geoffrey Edwards whose challenging yet always friendly advice has been a constant source of inspiration throughout my short academic career.

Much of the research for this book is based on interviews with people who are or have been in close contact with the issues and events discussed. Most of the interviews were contributed on a non-attributable basis, but I would like to take the opportunity to thank all those who gave their time in speaking to me. Any errors of fact or judgement remain, of course, mine alone.

Finally, this book could not have come about without the unflinching support from and encouragement by my family, which grew from two to four during the course of writing it. My deepest gratitude, therefore, goes to my loving wife Siw, for putting up with my absent-mindedness, and sometimes frustration, during periods of intensive research, and to my dear children, Sverre and Julie, for putting everything into perspective.

1 | Introduction: CSDP, strategic actorness and security governance

A strategic approach may be necessary to produce conditions of stability which will make possible continuing peace; but other, more positive measures, are needed to create peace itself.

Sir Michael Howard (1983a)

Some 50 years after the Treaty of Rome set out a framework for lasting peace through integration on a continent that had fostered two devastating wars in less than 30 years, the EU has developed into a regional institution with military ambitions that extend well beyond Europe. Since the birth of the Common Security and Defence Policy (CSDP) in Saint-Malo in 1998, the Union has carried out more than 20 crisis management operations, six of them military.[1] It has also endorsed the 2003 European Security Strategy (ESS) and its 2008 update, which in many ways represented the missing link that sought to give the CSDP a sense of purpose and direction (European Council 2003d, 2008c). Since military force is often seen as indicative of statehood, these developments raise questions regarding our understanding of the EU as an international actor. A number of labels have subsequently been introduced to describe the nature of the EU's actorness or power, including partial or composite actorness, (still) civilian power, soft power or normative power. However, rather than explicitly or implicitly using statehood as a yardstick or focal point for studying the CSDP, or having to resort to the kind of normatively laden 'labelling' that has dominated parts of the debate on the CSDP, this book adopts the concept of a *strategic actor* to allow an independent assessment of how any actor, state or non-state, may purposefully prepare for and apply the use of military force. The question that it sets out to answer, therefore, is whether the EU, since it falls short of statehood yet has moved beyond being merely an intergovernmental organisation, has become a *strategic actor*; i.e. one that (1) has the capacity to formulate common security interests, and (2) can

1

generate relevant capabilities, which (3) it has the resolve to use to promote common interests.

In answering this question, realist and intergovernmental theories, which are still viewed by many as providing valid explanations for the lack of inter-state cooperation on issues such as security and defence, or so-called 'high politics', arguably fall short (see e.g. Gegout 2002; Hyde-Price 2004; Matlary 2009; Moravcsik 1993, 1998; Rynning 2003). To proponents of these theories the rapid and far-reaching evolution of the CSDP represents in many respects an anomaly, or as Jolyon Howorth remarks (2007: 235): 'For realists, ESDP [now CSDP] continues to defy the rules of the international game.' This raises the question: what approaches *are* appropriate for understanding the CSDP? One approach that has been applied to other areas of EU policy is the concept of *governance*. So far security and defence have been kept firmly outside the orbit of a so-called 'governance turn in EU studies', since in this particular domain states are often seen to remain the dominant, if not only actors. However, an evolving scholarship on *security governance* has opened up new avenues of research that may also benefit the study of the CSDP (see Norheim-Martinsen 2010).

By venturing down some of these avenues, and seeing them in relationship with strategic actorness, this book forges a conceptual link between traditional strategic studies, on the one hand, and the insights of the so-called governance turn in EU studies, on the other. That way we are able to utilise the instrumentality and clarity of the strategic approach in *structuring* the analysis, while retaining an understanding of the unique character of the EU in how we *approach* it.

This first chapter proceeds by discussing the two key concepts employed by the book: strategic actorness and security governance. It then clarifies the conceptual relationship between the two, before showing how they provide the structure for the rest of the book.

Conceptions of the EU as an international actor

The idea of the EU as an international actor has always been a question of whether the EU can be seen as something more than the sum total of its Member States. The famous quip about the EU as an 'economic giant, a political dwarf and a military worm', suggests that it certainly is an economic actor, but that it lacks the ability to be(come) an assertive actor in the military domain.[2] Indeed, security and defence have been contested issues throughout the history of the European integration project. In 1952, the treaty on the European Defence Community (EDC) was signed after an initiative by French Defence Minister René Pleven, but the treaty was never ratified by the French Parliament and, therefore, never came into force (see Dinan 1994: 8). Although several subsequent initiatives were launched throughout the Cold War period, security and defence remained predominantly NATO's domain. It was only when the Common Foreign and Security Policy (CFSP) was included in the Treaty on European Union (TEU), agreed in Maastricht in 1991, that the 'progressive framing of a common defence policy' (TEU, art. J.4) became a stated objective of the EU.[3]

At least prospectively, this added a new dimension to the European integration project that would take it in the direction of an international actor without the usual reservations, i.e. that it had economic clout but lacked 'hard power'. The move towards a closer political union spurred, on the one hand, a renewed theoretical debate concerning the question of whether 'actorness' could be bestowed on an international institution in the first place, and whether it is feasible to talk about 'partial actorness' or 'composite actorness' short of statehood (Allen and Smith 1990; Bretherton and Vogler 2006; Engelbrekt and Hallenberg 2008; Ginsberg 1989, 1999, 2001; Peterson and Sjursen 1998; Piening 1997; Rummel 1990; Sjöstedt 1977; Smith 2001; Taylor 1979). On the other hand, since up to the early 1990s the actual impact of the European Community (EC) clearly had not matched its ambitions, Christopher Hill (1993) took a more pragmatic approach to the actor question. He conceptualised the EU's international role as a function of what it had been talked up to do and what it was actually able to deliver (Hill 1993). This he referred to as a 'capability–expectations gap', which he saw as having three main components: the ability to agree, resource allocation, and the instruments at the EU's disposal (Hill 1993: 315). Hill argued that if the EU was to be a more credible international actor, the gap had to be closed, which meant that European foreign policy had to be demonstrated in actual behaviour rather than aspirations or prospects (see also Hill 1998, 2004). As a non-static concept by which EU foreign policy can be monitored, Hill's capability–expectations gap has remained a helpful conceptual tool for the study of the EU's impact and role in international relations (see Hill and Smith 2011 in particular). Taking a similar pragmatic approach, this book seeks to contribute to this tradition by focusing specifically on the acquisition and use of military force and how this affects the overall role of the EU as an international actor.

However, the plans for a prospective military role for the EU represented a move that, to some minds, meant that the very image that it projected to the outside world had to be redefined. As the CSDP was realised, there was a reappraisal of a 20-year-old debate concerning the EU's status as a 'civilian power' by a number of commentators questioning whether the Union could still remain one even if it acquired military capabilities (Smith 2000; Stavridis 2001; Telo 2006). The term 'civilian power', introduced by Francois Dûchene (1972), was initially subjected to heavy criticism by, amongst others, Hedley Bull (1982, 1983), but gained salience together with the growing acceptance of notions of 'soft power' in the early 1990s (see Nye 1990, 2004; Nye and Keohane 2001). At this time, the EU debate was mirrored by a parallel debate on Germany as a civilian power in view of the gradual re-employment of its armed forces abroad after reunification (see Maull 1990, 2000).[4]

With the addition of a military dimension to the EU in 1999, some argued that the Petersberg tasks, which were taken over from the Western European Union (WEU) and describe the functional parameters for the kind of military tasks that the EU might carry out, were still within the remit of a civilian power, since collective defence and nuclear capability remained the privilege of NATO (Joergensen 1997; Smith 2000). Others argued that the Union retained essential characteristics of a civilian power and that the turn to military force did not fundamentally change this perception (Cornish and Edwards 2001). Still others argued that the military dimension muddled the Union's 'distinct profile' as an actor with a civilian international identity (Whitman 2006; Zielonka 1998).

Over the years, the debate has maintained its distinctly normative character, as the CSDP has shown more practical results. For example, in a revision of the notion of 'normative power' that he introduced as a term that could capture the EU's ideational impact on international affairs, Ian Manners backs away from his original conclusion that the EU can be both a normative power and a military power (Manners 2002, 2006).[5] Having observed developments under the CSDP between 2002 and 2006, he argues that although 'it is tempting to think that the EU can have-its-cake-and-eat-it-too in militarizing its normative power', it is, at the same time, 'unfeasible that either Turkey or Russia

would be as receptive to norm diffusion if they believed that EU battle groups or combat forces would soon be peace-making in Kurdish
areas or Chechnya' (Manners 2006: 183, 194). Manners, therefore,
warns against treating the acquisition of military capabilities as being
unquestionably positive for the EU, since it may harm other instruments of power.

Regardless of any normative judgements that could be passed on
developments towards a heavier military role, it is not feasible to
imagine that the EU has remained or can remain unaffected by these
developments. They do, on the one hand, sit uneasily with the 'old'
image of the EU as a limited civilian power, and, since military force
is associated with statehood, it tends to invoke fear among those who
do not want to see a federal Europe in the making. On the other hand,
using statehood as an implicit yardstick tends to produce too easy
dismissals of the potential salience of the CSDP, especially by those
who choose to compare it to, for example, the military might of the
United States. None of these perspectives appears particularly helpful.
Instead, this book adopts the concept of *strategic actorness* to ensure
an independent assessment of how any actor, state or non-state, may
purposefully prepare for and apply the use of military force.

The EU as a strategic actor

The traditional research trajectory through which the use of military
force has been studied has been strategic studies, a field that today,
to the regret of some, has become a marginalised subfield of security
studies (see e.g. Betts 1997). Strategic studies, as Hew Strachan has
pointed out, 'flourish more verdantly in schools of business studies
than in departments of international relations', but, as he goes on to
say: 'Strategic studies are not business studies, nor is strategy ... a
synonym for policy' (Strachan 2005: 34). Betts' and Strachan's call
for the reinstatement of the theories and models of strategic studies as a useful trajectory through which to study the connections
between security and military force comes across as pertinent advice,
insofar as security itself has become a notoriously elusive term due
to the proliferation of 'new' threats in the post-Cold War security
environment.

The current state of security studies is the result of a 20-year-old
debate between those who have wanted to restrict the use of the term

to traditional threats and those who have argued for an expansion into various new domains, such as human rights, environmental issues, etc. (Ayoob 1995; Buzan *et al.* 1998; Haftendorn 1991; Katzenstein 1996b; Krause and Williams 1997). There are, indeed, good reasons to limit the use of the term security. While many realists claim that widening it diverts the focus away from the more serious threats (Deudney 1990; Freedman 1998; Walt 1991, 1998), others argue that the act of *securitisation* elevates issues, such as, for example, immigration, to a state of emergency, which allows policy-makers to bypass normal principles of a democratic society, such as legality, transparency, parliamentary scrutiny, etc. (see e.g. Huysmans 1995, 1998; Waever 1995, 1998, 2005). The general expansion of the security research agenda is still largely irreversible, insofar as policy-makers, not academics, define what they regard as security (Kolodziej 2000: 20). Or, to paraphrase Alexander Wendt: security is what states, and a growing number of other actors, make of it.[6] However, because of the current state of security studies, the strategic approach may help us in our assessment of the various security measures taken by different actors in their efforts to further what is perceived to be in their best interests, especially in the context of the 'hazy continuum' of contemporary peace operations where the use of military force is often hard to relate to any specific threat (Moore 2003).

If we take Clausewitz's traditional definition of strategy – 'the use of engagements for the object of the war' – as a starting point, it may at first sight seem somewhat narrow for a contemporary security environment, in which the term war is rarely used, and military force, at least when applied alone, is perceived by many as obsolete in the face of the security challenges of the day (Clausewitz 1976 [1832]: 128).[7] Yet, as Colin Gray argues, Clausewitz's original definition easily lends itself to an 'expansion of domain so as to encompass policy instruments other than the military' (Gray 1999a: 17). As he goes on:

The cardinal virtue of the Clausewitzian definition of strategy is that it separates those things that must be separated. Anyone who reads, understands and accepts the Clausewitzian definition will never be confused about what is strategic and what is not ... Armed forces in action, indeed any instrument of power in action, is the realm of tactics. Strategy, in contrast, seeks to direct and relate the use of those instruments to policy goals. Clausewitz, therefore, is crystal-clear in distinguishing between action and effect and between instrument and objective.[8]

The essence of strategy, therefore, boils down to the extent to which any instruments of power – military or non-military – further a perceived political end. Military power is not strategic per se. It is the linking of military power to political purpose that is strategic. Hence, the EU's perceived focus on 'soft power' or non-military instruments is not necessarily less strategic than the manifestly more militaristic approach demonstrated, for example, by the United States. Strategy is about ends and means, or specifically how they are linked. Accordingly, we can conceptualise a strategic actor as one that (1) has a capacity to formulate common security interests (ends), and (2) can generate relevant capabilities (means), which (3) it has the resolve to use to promote common interests.[9]

The first appeal of this definition is the way it reflects the central ends–means quality of strategy. It indicates, for example, that capabilities are not objective entities, but must be seen to reflect certain security interests and how they ought to be pursued. Secondly, by focusing on the relationship between ends and means rather than the character of the means (i.e. civilian or military) as the defining factor of actorness, the categorisation, and hence the problems of accommodating different forms of power projection inherent to the ongoing debates on what kind of actor or power the EU is, are avoided. Thirdly, the definition is parsimonious, which is a central criterion by which theoretical concepts are measured (see Underdal 1983).[10] And finally, the three criteria – ends, means and resolve – allow an assessment of developments within the CSDP against three more or less clearly identifiable benchmarks. Accordingly, it is possible to use the concept to monitor the CSDP, while at any given point in time being able to come up with some conclusions regarding the status of the EU as a strategic actor. In line with Hill's abovementioned conceptualisation of an international actor, strategic actorness is, therefore, treated as a matter of 'level of' rather than 'either/or'.

However, to most people the very notion of actorness would also rest with some minimum intuitive qualities, or some form of ideational presence or personality. András Szigeti singles out 'identity' as one such quality, arguing that being an actor 'presupposes that the given institution has an independent, non-elusive and fairly permanent identity that is not merely the sum of the identities of its constituents' (Szigeti 2006: 22). Likewise, Giovanni Grevi argues that, 'in the case of the EU – a collective international actor bringing together 27 member states – the claim to "actorness" depends crucially on its internal institutional and normative features' (Grevi 2009). Also within the strategic studies tradition, the idea that an actor, whether a state or another polity, acts within the context of its identity(/ies), history, norms, ideas, etc., has been subject to a 30-year-old debate on *strategic culture*, a concept that has received renewed interest in the EU context (Cornish and Edwards 2001, 2005; Heiselberg 2003; Hyde-Price 2004; Longhurst and Zaborowski 2004; Martinsen 2004; Matlary 2006; Meyer 2006; Norheim-Martinsen 2007; Rynning 2003).

The EU debate has largely circled around whether the EU has a strategic culture or not, which is a question that seems to defy a contemporary understanding of strategic culture, and, therefore, does not benefit from how strategic culture can be used as an analytical tool. The key point is that strategic culture cannot be treated as a criterion for a strategic actor, since all behaviour is ultimately cultural behaviour.[11] Instead strategic culture ought to be treated as a precondition or a set of boundaries within which any strategic actor operates. Given this premise, studying certain elements of an EU strategic culture may, therefore, help identify some fundamental parameters that may constrain or facilitate a strategic actor's room for manoeuvre. We shall, therefore, return to this issue in Chapter 2 of the book.

In any case, the very notion of being a strategic actor requires the presence of something more. This something may come in the shape of a dominant or hegemonic power that is able to impose its will on the organisation and give it a sense of purpose or direction (see e.g. Foot *et al.* 2003). This has arguably been the case in NATO, which as the intergovernmental organisation par excellence, nevertheless, has proven capable of strategic action due to the hegemonic role of the United States in the Alliance (see e.g. Layne 2000). The EU lacks a hegemonic United States. Many would argue that, being an intergovernmental organisation, it lacks even a minimum sense of political leadership (see e.g. Toje 2008b). However, the abovementioned something may also come in the shape of some shared normative, institutional and/or other feature that set it apart from a traditional alliance or organisation. We must identify and test these to be able to show that the EU, in the area of security and defence, has moved beyond formal intergovernmental constraints and may, thus, be capable of strategic action. This requires an approach that allows us to investigate mechanisms and processes other than those that follow from a purely intergovernmental approach. In the current literature the concept of *governance* appears a particularly appropriate one for the subject matter at hand.

The governance turn in EU studies

Since the 1990s, various notions of governance have become a central approach in studies of the EU (see e.g. Bulmer *et al.* 2007; Christiansen and Piattoni 2003; Hooghe and Marks 2001; Jachtenfuchs 2001; Jachtenfuchs and Kohler-Koch 2004; Kohler-Koch and Eising 1999; Marks *et al.* 1996; Tallberg 2003b). This so-called 'governance turn in EU studies' follows a general trend in *International Relations theory* away from a focus on states and hierarchical modes of policy-making towards horizontal networks within and beyond the state (Hix 1998; Pierre and Peters 2000; Rosenau and Czempiel 1992). Its origins are found within the field of political science and public policy analysis, where it describes the setting, application and enforcement of rules that guide the distribution of public goods (see e.g. Powell 1990; Scharpf 1993). It is held that this can be accomplished, often more effectively than in hierarchical systems, through policy coordination in horizontal networks or markets. Today, governance has become a widely used catchphrase to describe the dispersion of authority and increased complexity of social and political interaction that follows in a globalising international system (Hewson and Sinclair 1999; Karns and Mingst 2004).

Governance typically involves 'various actors, including both public and private institutions and organisations, civil society and individuals acting in the framework of institutions' (Raik 2006: 80). It may include 'any form of coordination of interdependent social relations', ranging from centralised state control to self-regulation (Jessop 1999: 351). However, it is often contrasted to government, or conceptualised as a *move* from government to governance, pointing towards a relative weakening of the state as the primary actor in international relations. In this view, the transfer of authority to the regional or international level does not necessarily 'represent a substitution of the state as central authority by international institutions, which would suggest centralisation at a new level, but typically marks the dispersion of political authority between governments and their international organizations' (Krahmann 2003a: 12). As such, the governance perspective does not represent a fundamental break with state-centric approaches, but focuses instead on the interaction, formal and informal, of various actors, both private and public, at different levels within and beyond the state. It has been argued, therefore, that governance is particularly well-suited for describing the functioning of the EU, since 'the governing of the Union takes place without a single authority and in the framework of a complex and multi-layered set of rules and norms' (Raik 2006: 81).

Essentially, the governance turn in EU studies has marked a shift away from the traditional integration theories towards treating the EU as an evolving, yet fairly stable, policy-making system (Wallace 2005). Instead of looking at the EU as a product of functional spill-over or intergovernmental bargaining, the governance approach in its most extreme form 'treats the shape of the system as an independent variable explaining its policies' (Raik 2006: 81). This constitutes an important shift of focus, which has generated new insights into other domains of EU policy. But because of the general exclusion of security and defence from the governance research agenda, studies of the CSDP have so far not been able to profit from these insights.

However, a growing literature on 'security governance', which has sought to extend the general governance turn in International Relations to include also traditional 'high politics' (Kirchner 2006; Kirchner and Sperling 2007a, 2007b; Krahmann 2003a, 2003b, 2005; Schroeder 2006, 2011), seems to suggest that a similar expansion of the governance turn in EU studies may be pertinent. A co-written article from 2004, in which a team of scholars set out the governance of European security in five general features, presents itself as an appropriate starting point (Webber *et al.* 2004). Indeed, the Europeanisation of security accomplished through EU-led initiatives is one of three cases that are examined to demonstrate the utility of security governance for understanding security in post-Cold War Europe. The other two issues are the transformation of NATO, and what the authors refer to as the relationship between forms of inclusion and exclusion in governance (see also Webber 2007). The five features of security governance refer to:

I. heterarchy, or the existence of multiple centres of power;
II. interaction of multiple actors, both public and private;
III. formal and informal institutionalisation;
IV. relations between actors that are ideational in character; and
V. collective purpose

(Webber *et al.* 2004: 4–8)

It could – and should – certainly be pointed out that the features are not very clearly defined, that they tend to float into each other, and that they, therefore, need to be refined and rooted more explicitly in theory if security governance is to serve as a concept from which to launch an alternative approach to studying the CSDP. But, as a first step, the article does present ample empirical evidence to suggest that the 'growing complexity and diffusion in the security governance of Europe ... operates within the EU itself' (Webber *et al.* 2004: 15–16). A similar case is made by Michael E. Smith who shows how EU foreign policy cooperation has evolved from an intergovernmental forum for coordination towards what he refers to as a typical *governance system* (Smith 2004: 38–49). Smith concludes that the establishment of the CFSP marked a final step in this process, because it prepared the Union for:

setting goals, devising specific policies (or norms) to reach them, implementing such policies, providing the necessary resources to carry out the policies, and establishing some form of policy assessment or oversight to ensure that goals are being met and actors are fulfilling their obligations. (Smith 2004: 49)

In doing so, Smith implicitly alludes to well-established criteria for an international actor, while explicitly tying them to governance. He then presents wide empirical evidence to support his thesis that, in the establishment of the CFSP and the way that it has developed, the EU 'demonstrates that institutions can be designed and developed to encourage international cooperation in ways that go beyond transaction-costs approaches, or beyond bargaining' (Smith 2004: 12). However, Smith cautiously excluded the CSDP from his research agenda, arguing that, at the time his research was conducted, the military dimension of the CFSP was still underdeveloped. That is no longer the case.

Rather this book proceeds on the basis that there is today sufficient indicative evidence to extend the governance turn in EU studies to also cover the CSDP. The five features of security governance listed above present themselves as an appropriate starting point for merging some of the more promising questions and theories of the general governance turn in international relations into one EU security governance research programme.[12] Indeed, when it comes to research on the CSDP, such issues as, for example, the impact of 'Brusselsization' on the CSDP, the role of individual entrepreneurship in the 'Solana era', the socialising effects of institutions, and the presence of a European strategic identity or culture, are often treated in isolation from each other, and would benefit from a more integrated approach. Accordingly, the next section shows first how the five features fit with developments under the CSDP. The chapter then moves on to discuss the theoretical underpinnings and implications of security governance for the book's analysis of the EU as a strategic actor.

Towards heterarchy

The first feature of security governance is *heterarchy*, or the growth of multiple centres of power and coordinated actions taken in response to common and increasingly complex security challenges. It reflects the central proposition in the governance literature that the hierarchical mode of policy-making associated with government must be supplanted by an understanding of how actors other than government as such take part in increasingly complex and decentralised policy-making processes. At the international level, the distinction between government and governance is highly relevant since a central governmental authority is lacking. This is hardly a novel observation, but it may be useful to view the growth of some order, routinised arrangements and convergence of interests that add up to a certain capacity to govern, as a *move* from government to governance in European security (Krahmann 2003a). This does not imply that states are not still the primary actors even in an emerging European security governance structure, but simply that their role is supplemented in particular by new institutionalised actors with some degree of autonomy. This has been the case with NATO, which has essentially reconstituted itself as a proactive security organisation in place of the traditional alliance it used to be (Asmus 2002; Cornish 1997), but even more so with the EU, which has, with the creation of the CSDP, not only added a new security hub separate from NATO, but also brought into the equation several more or less autonomous sub-actors, such as the European Commission and various other bodies, such as the European Defence Agency (EDA). In fact, the story of the CSDP can rather convincingly be depicted as the evolution from an intergovernmental bargain towards a highly institutionalised polity with a growing desire for autonomy.

The origins of the CSDP, or perhaps more correctly the changing preconditions that made an idea, which had been floated on several occasions since the first attempt to establish the European Defence Community (EDC) in 1952, suddenly appear feasible, are traced back to the end of the Cold War and a chain of events that allowed the idea of the CSDP to take root. These events included the removal of the Soviet threat, German reunification, and the eruption of hostilities in the Balkans from 1991 onwards (Howorth 2007: 23). Yet much of the remainder of the 1990s was essentially marked by hesitation and scepticism towards a prospective CSDP on the part of key Member States, especially Britain. It seems a fair judgement, therefore, that the 'external shocks' model, coupled with a focus on inter-state bargaining and domestic policy changes (see Biscop 1999; Howorth 2000, 2005), explain well the (lack of) progress up until the official turning point in Saint-Malo in 1998 (Schroeder 2006: 2–3). In fact, there was no EU security policy to talk about, either on paper or in practice, before this point. However, in the period that followed, although the European security and defence project was subject to some setbacks, most notably the 2003 Iraq crisis, it is an equally fair judgement that the initial scepticism towards the idea was overtaken by the weight of the process.[13] Today, it is more or less taken for granted that the EU should have some sort of a military role. It appears also that after most of the current institutional apparatus was in place around 2000, more recent developments should be seen as unfolding within an emerging yet fairly stable policy-making system, rather than as steps as such in an ongoing integration process (Smith 2004; Wallace 2005).

In a gradually more confident EU, we may even observe the contours of a 'third way' in the sense that the CSDP, rather than being merely a response to the call for Europe to share the security burden, offers an alternative security approach – and the growing confidence to pursue it (see e.g. Biscop 2007). This is perhaps most clearly observed in the growing will to pursue autonomy from NATO, whether in the conduct of autonomous operations or in the establishment of autonomous capabilities. For example, apart from the still ongoing EUFOR operation in Bosnia, the Berlin Plus framework for EU–NATO cooperation has not been used for any CSDP operations since operation *Concordia* in Macedonia in 2003. Instead, the EU has made repeated moves towards creating some autonomous capabilities, such as its own operational headquarter capacity (the OpCen) placed within the CivMilCell of the

EU Military Staff (EUMS), despite the fact that a similar proposal was scrapped in 2003 because it was deemed an unnecessary duplication of already existing capabilities (i.e. NATO-SHAPE).[14] So, although there remains considerable resistance towards a truly autonomous CSDP among some Member States, the very idea – unheard of only five years ago – is clearly becoming more accepted.

As a result, governments in Europe today have the choice of channelling their strategic resources through either NATO or the EU or both. These institutions are, in turn, judged on their ability to innovate and adapt to the challenges of a rapidly changing security environment. This is reflected, for example, in the repeated efforts to create new structures, such as the NATO Combined Joint Task Forces (CJTF) and the EU Battlegroups (EUBG), which compete for relevance and resources in a gradually tighter security 'marketplace'.[15] It seems that it has taken the EU some time to fully appreciate the wider conceptual space for alternative security approaches that the removal of the old threat scenario has brought about. However, now that it is apparently coming to grips with this reality to which the growing desire for autonomy seems to testify, one may perhaps also expect to see signs of a more distinctly 'European' CSDP. This would also highlight the comparative advantage of each organisation, and ultimately ensure the continued relevance of and need for both the EU and NATO in the future European security architecture.

Moreover, while Webber *et al.* show that the overall European security order in the period after the end of the Cold War has become less hierarchical, partly due to the EU's newfound role, it can also be argued that this is a key feature of the CSDP itself. The Franco-British relationship is often seen as *the* key to the CSDP, in the same way as the Franco-German relationship is traditionally seen as the key to European integration at large (see e.g. Gegout 2002; Matlary 2009). But there are certain traits indicating that such bilateral or multilateral relationships may play less of a role once a political process gains a certain momentum. The traditional realist understanding of the international system as made up of great and lesser powers carries merit only up to a certain point, when alternative channels of influence than sheer state power need to be taken into consideration. This is particularly true of the CSDP; claims to 'Europeaness' seem to carry more and more weight in debates about what kind of strategic direction the EU should take.[16] This is a process that draws its support from various institutional actors in Brussels as well as the smaller Member States, rather than being controlled top-down by a handful of large powers. It is, therefore, necessary to take into consideration multiple actors within the CSDP framework, not merely as an interesting yet assumingly less important feature of a more complex European security environment, but as genuine factors that influence the way the CSDP evolves. As such, the second feature of security governance is an implicit and necessary result of the first.

The interaction of multiple actors

While states remain primary actors in European security, their role both when it comes to security policy-making and delivering security is increasingly being challenged by multiple public and private actors. This proliferation of security actors within and beyond the state can be observed, for example, in the growing involvement of aid workers, judges, police officers, customs officers and private contractors in post-conflict reconstruction, but also in various aspects of war-fighting. Another dominant trend is that defence industries have become denationalised and compete in a global marketplace, where governments have become customers rather than simply employers. Today, governments as niche providers of services, such as mine clearance, transport and logistics, and personnel security, compete with private actors in a global security marketplace, where cost-efficiency and effectiveness have become the guiding principles (see e.g. Avant 2004; Markusen 2003). Finally, a rapidly expanding number of human rights organisations, charities and think tanks monitor the security policies of states, while offering independent advice and policy options based on experience and expertise that governments may often lack. Although these developments represent general traits of the current global security environment, it is also arguably a quite specific feature of the EU – that it has sought to accommodate various processes of fragmentation in the monitoring, delivery and coordination of its security policy.

For example, the Union has for years sought to integrate long-term conflict prevention tools with short-term crisis management capabilities, both civilian and military, but with increasing emphasis on the latter. Indeed, the resulting turf-battle between the Commission and the Council is well known to and commented upon by many who take an interest in EU security policy (Christiansen 2001; Dijkstra 2008;

Duke and Vanhoonhacker 2006). However, from a security governance point of view, this illustrates the fact that, within the EU security
policy apparatus, there exists a number of actors, supranational and
intergovernmental, that compete and, more or less successfully, integrate their approaches in a sort of micro version of the broader security marketplace.

A similar trend is also evident in the way Europe's defence industries
have developed. Having traditionally been protected from international
competition, several European defence companies have been forced to
merge into multinational corporations in order to survive in a global
market. As such, they have assumed a similar central role to the one
they used to have at the national level, as key players on the regional
level. The EU represents, in turn, the regional actor that has been most
active in facilitating international cooperation on military acquisitions,
most notably in its support for projects such as the Eurofighter and the
A-400-M transport aircraft, the Commission's persistent attempts to
create a more competitive European defence industrial market, and
the establishment of a European Defence Agency (EDA). The latter is
yet another example of a semi-independent EU actor that produces
advice for Member States and monitors their conduct.[17]

Indeed, whereas monitoring security policies and producing policy
options are tasks that used to be carried out exclusively by states, such
prerogatives are being shared today by a host of different actors. Within
the EU institutional set-up, there are several bodies, including the Policy
Planning and Early Warning Unit (Policy Unit), the European Union
Military Staff (EUMS) and the EU Joint Situation Centre (SITCEN),
that are well placed to offer strategic advice and options on issues
on which the Member States lack information or expertise.[18] The EU
also has its own security research institute, the EU-ISS in Paris, which
together with several think tanks and policy centres scattered around
Europe, constitutes, in the words of Ian Manners (2006: 191–192), a
'transnational advocacy' for CSDP.

In fact, when Solana was tasked to produce the European Security
Strategy (ESS) in 2003, he was able to draw upon both a consid-
erable in-house expertise and the intellectual resources of a large
European security research community. By then the Member States
had grown accustomed to receiving advice from Solana and the Policy
Unit, and could leave the drafting to a small, centrally placed team in
Brussels, who could in turn draw upon various resources to produce a

comprehensive document, instead of going for the usual, more elaborate procedure of leaving it to an Intergovernmental Conference (IGC) (Bailes 2005: 8).[19] This not only shows the flexibility of governance structures, but also illustrates that the obvious institutional expansion that has occurred has been accompanied by a growing trust in these institutions on behalf of most of the EU Member States. It also draws attention to the role of political entrepreneurship in the European integration project, as personified by such grand visionaries as Jean Monet and Robert Schuman. Indeed, Solana is often given a central role in the development of the CSDP, but exactly what role he played is often not specified. Given also the general proliferation of individual agents of foreign and security policy in the EU, as reflected in the appointment of an expanding number of EU Special Representatives and policy coordinators, and the establishment of the European External Action Service (EEAS), it seems vital that the role of individual agency is accommodated in contemporary approaches (see Hermann *et al.* 2001; Norheim-Martinsen 2008).[20]

Formal and informal institutionalisation

A central premise in the security governance literature is that institutions play a key role in European security. Institutions are not considered to be constricted to mere bargaining arenas in which rational actors may produce cooperative outcomes, as posited, for example, by neo-liberal institutionalists (see e.g. Keohane 1984; Keohane and Martin 1995). When interacting in institutionalised settings, actors tend to develop shared ideas and a common understanding of the organisation's purpose and legitimate scope of action, which is, in turn, sustained and enforced as they develop an allegiance to the institution and the cause. In other words, when a certain level of institutionalisation has been reached, the institution itself and the people who inhabit it may be expected to gain an increasingly independent and autonomous role (see e.g. DiMaggio and Powell 1991; March and Olsen 1989; Smith 2004).

A key feature of the CSDP is that it has been accompanied by a vast number of committees and sub-units that today constitute a significant institutional nexus, made up of hundreds of permanent representatives and seconded personnel. This has not only led to a considerable increase in the overall body of work being carried out, but also to new tensions between national capitals and centralising tendencies in Brussels. This perceived shift of weight has been referred to by various commentators as 'Brusselsization' (Allen 2004; Nuttall 2000) or 'supranational inter-governmentalism'; i.e. 'the phenomenon whereby a profusion of agencies of inter-governmentalism take root in Brussels and ... gradually create a tendency for policy to be influenced, formulated and even driven from within that city' (Howorth 2007: 30).[21] The underlying premise is that, through interaction and socialisation, the people involved at EU level institutions cease to be mere agents of national interests and tend to develop some sort of collective *esprit de corps* that supports a distinctly trans-European perspective on the CSDP. In fact, upon his appointment as High Representative for CFSP (HR-CFSP), Javier Solana saw it as a central task to establish something of an institutional strategic culture, seemingly well aware of the fact that a 'strategic culture that fosters early, rapid and when necessary, robust intervention', the objective he later incorporated into the European Security Strategy (ESS), had to start from within (European Council 2003d: 11).

Relations between actors that are ideational in character

The first three features of security governance presuppose that political processes are subject to other, more indirect, sources of influence than sheer state power. As such, they rest ultimately upon the assumptions of a fourth feature of security governance. That is, the central message conveyed in the security governance literature that institutions act as socialising agents and not merely as arenas for coordinated action suggests that there exist certain collectively held *ideas* and *norms* that structure the relations between the actors involved whenever they interact in institutionalised settings. Such ideational ties between actors are a consequence of the lack of formal regulations in a non-hierarchical structure. The underlying premise is that ideas matter in international politics. But since ideas do not 'float freely', they need to be interpreted and reproduced by international institutions, which, in turn, project them as appropriate norms of legitimate behaviour (see Desch 1998; Parsons 2002; Risse-Kappen 1994). It can even be argued that relationships between actors in certain international sub-systems, such as the EU, are, in fact, conditioned by ideational factors *rather than* material ones.

In the period after 11 September 2001, the long-standing debate about the merits of Euro-Atlantic approaches (encapsulated within NATO) and Europeanist approaches (encapsulated within the EU) has come to be framed largely in terms of convergence on the interpretation of threats, but divergence on the means to tackle them (see Biscop 2004; Duke 2004; Kagan 2003; Toje 2005). Acting European seems to have become an end in itself for an EU all the more eager to show autonomy, as described above. This may not be considered the most rational way of boosting European security since it necessarily leads to duplication of structures and capabilities that are shared amongst largely the same Member States. However, to the extent that certain collectively or institutionally held norms, in a given setting, do matter over material factors (e.g. improving military capabilities), institutions such as the EU may appear to act irrationally in a traditional ends–means understanding of the term. This is due to the fact that institutions are sometimes valued on the basis of a 'logic of appropriateness' rather than a 'logic of consequences', whereas they may embrace certain practices simply because they are seen to enhance the legitimacy of the institution or its participants (March and Olsen 1989).

The EU is arguably one such institution that to a large extent has internalised a set of collective European norms that supplement or even supplant national norms. With the way that the CSDP has evolved, we also see how national norms of sovereignty and self-reliance, which have traditionally constrained security and defence relations between states, have been gradually softened by the emergence and internalisation of norms at the EU level (see e.g. Davidson *et al.* 2002; Manners and Whitman 2000; Rieker 2006). In other words, the possibility that institutions through norm diffusion may shape interests, and even the identities upon which these interests are based, suggests 'the possibility of the formation of a distinct polity', not replacing national identities or interests but overlapping with them to create a policy realm or space in which states 'reconstitute their behaviours and interests in terms of European norms rather than national ones' (Smith 2004: 37). Indeed, there are strategic relationships between the EU and the outside world, as seen for example in the Western Balkans, where bilateral relations between states have largely been replaced by a common EU approach, which has compliance with European norms rather than fulfilment of national interests as its central objective, although the one does not necessarily exclude the other.[22] So, although the CSDP is obviously not recognised by *either* materially or ideationally characterised relationships, as if these two represented ontological categories that were somehow in competition, the emergence of a distinctive European ideational dimension does arguably represent a prominent feature of the CSDP that needs to be investigated further.

A collective purpose

The fifth feature of security governance is the most problematic, empirically and conceptually, since our intuitive notion of *purposefulness* admittedly does not, at the outset, seem to fit very well with the rather arbitrary way in which the European security architecture has evolved since the end of the Cold War. However, purposefulness can be understood in terms of both structure and process. In terms of structure, governance systems condition the behaviour of actors 'by prescribing rules of entry, norms of interaction and constraints on behaviour', while as process, 'governance is concerned with policy outcomes and the manner in which actors interact to achieve and define these' (Webber *et al.* 2004: 8). Within governance systems, policy outcomes may meet the objectives of a majority of actors but not necessarily all of them, or they may be shaped by actors who have a specific interest in some outcome or who are in a position to influence the process one way or the other, and allegiances and influence may change over time. In short, what you see is not always what you get.

Hence, this last feature also describes well the fits-and-starts mode in which the CSDP itself has evolved, by some referred to as a form of 'glorified adhockery' (Everts and Keohane 2003: 178). Despite the apparent lack of a 'game plan', the CSDP appears to be underpinned by certain conceptions, 'expressly articulated within a European institutional context, of an appropriate security order – one shared on both sides of the Atlantic' (Webber *et al.* 2004: 18). Going back to the foundations of the European integration project, the very purpose of the original European Coal and Steel Community (ECSC) was to establish a secure Europe, a task that the EU has carried out by consolidating the new order ('deepening') and by seeking to extend it ('widening') to its neighbouring regions. Making conflict prevention a central feature of the EU's external purpose and eventually adding military capabilities to its civilian instruments is hardly surprising when viewed in a broader perspective.

Still, although the development of the CSDP could rather broadly be seen to serve a collective purpose, the process certainly gives ample room for various options en route – to which its short history testifies. As regards critical junctures in the process, the preferences of the larger Member States have undoubtedly played a decisive role (see e.g. Gegout 2002; Matlary 2009). But an exclusive focus on state preferences tells us little about what goes on in between the history-making grand summits and meetings, which often only formalise practices that have evolved over time. Also, policy outcomes rarely reflect the sum total of actors' fixed preferences, but result rather from social interactions where preferences are likely to change through mechanisms of learning, bargaining, persuasion, etc. One prominent development in this regard has been the consolidation of a European security discourse or strategic narrative (Howorth 2004), which appears to have built up underneath a desire to act distinctly European, i.e. recognised by more autonomy, a comprehensive security approach, constraints on the use of force and neutrality when choosing to intervene.[23] The more specific and commonly accepted this narrative gets, the more the chance of rhetorical entrapment grows (see Risse 2000; Schimmelfenning 2003), whereas similar effects can also be observed in the way that institutional practices tend to create precedence. Institutions such as the EU are learning organisations in the sense that they evolve by establishing ad hoc solutions, such as the framework nation command option used in operation *Artemis* in the DR Congo. Temporary solutions have, as in this example, then been formalised in the establishment of several national headquarters, which, in turn, has strengthened the EU's autonomy from NATO.[24] This outcome is far from the prospect envisioned in the Berlin Plus agreement, and probably not what the British had in mind when deciding to move along with the CSDP together with the French in Saint-Malo back in 1998.

In the broadest sense, then, a collective purpose would be a fitting overall description of how the CSDP has evolved in response to the first four features of security governance. Once a polity has reached a stage where these four features kick in, the sense of collective purpose seems to grow stronger also, together with the chance that lock-in effects and precedents will come into play. Rather than intentionally serving a purpose, developments and events unfolding are seen in a 'most favoured' light, so that they are made to serve a collective purpose – put rather crudely that the EU should play a (or the) central role in European (perhaps also global) security, drawing on its key strengths as a civilian power, and on the development of a military capacity.

The promise of the security governance approach

What the previous section shows is that the five features of security governance provide a fitting description of how the CSDP has evolved. It also draws attention to mechanisms and processes that essentially modify the formal status of the CSDP as an intergovernmental policy area. For the sake of argument, we can, therefore, conclude that the EU has 'moved from government to governance' (Krahmann 2003a) also when it comes to 'hard politics', and that the 'governance turn in EU studies' (Hix 1998) can and probably should be extended to cover also the CSDP. However, governance is not a unified theory, nor even a unified approach. It is rather a term used to describe a capacity to govern, although naturally it is disposed to policy areas that are difficult to control or coordinate because they cut through multiple policy areas (e.g. environmental issues), and/or transcend the boundaries of normal government (e.g. activities of international corporations). Governance is also often used normatively, as in for example 'promoting good governance', where it says something about the quality of policy-making systems, including governments, and the decisions they produce. According to Kirchner and Sperling (2007a: 8), there are at least four ways in which security governance has been employed: as a general theory, a theory of networks, a system of international and transnational regimes, and a 'heuristic device for recasting the problem of security management'. In recent years, Kirchner and Sperling have done a considerable service to the latter conception of the term. Other volumes have explored the EU's capacity to shape global security governance structures (Kirchner and Sperling 2007b; Wagnsson *et al.* 2009). Yet others have explored how the EU has responded to changing patterns of internal and external security governance (Schroeder 2011).

This book neither uses the term security governance normatively, nor does it readily fit in any of the categories above. Instead it employs a specific understanding of security governance as a means of identifying key processes and mechanisms *beyond* the formal intergovernmental traits of the CSDP, which are deemed to enhance and sustain the

EU's *capacity to govern* or act in – i.e. not simply coordinate national policies across – this domain. The implicit assumption is that those approaches that limit themselves to looking merely at the intergovernmental dynamics of the CSDP are not able to explain fully how it works. They are not necessarily 'wrong', but they do obscure alternative lines of enquiry that would deepen our knowledge of the EU. As is often pointed out, the value of the governance approach rests not so much with the way it competes with alternative approaches, but more with its ability to emphasise the strengths of existing theories and perspectives (Webber *et al.* 2004: 4). We shall, therefore, move on to discuss some of the implicit theoretical assumptions on which security governance rests, and highlight some theories that may further help explore some of the issues and questions raised in the discussion above.

First of all, security governance is a product of a changing (European) security environment, which provides the necessary context from which the five features draw their descriptive power. These changes include the replacement of inter-state conflict as the major security threat in Europe with new threats, such as international terrorism, proliferation of weapons of mass destruction (WMDs), civil wars and regional conflicts that threaten to spill over into Europe, and organised crime (Arquilla and Ronfeldt 2001; Barcelona Report 2004; Biscop 2004; Kaldor *et al.* 2007; Smith 2000). These new threats have largely blurred the division into external and internal security, while challenging the ability of states to deal with them alone (Bigo 2001; Borchert 2006; Pastore 2001). The end of the Cold War also opened up new opportunities for states to cooperate with other state and non-state actors, which helps explain the general proliferation of transnational security cooperation and institutions in this period (Krahmann 2005; Roper 2000).

The challenge that the new security environment essentially poses to the idea of the state as the central, if not only player, represents a shift of focus that is also only partly accommodated by some of the key alternative approaches that have been applied to explain or understand developments in European security. Security regimes, for example, are seen to evolve out of the convergence of state interests, a process which can be helped by international institutions, but which is still strictly state-driven (Jervis 1982; Krasner 1983; Rittberger 1995). Even security communities, which have been subject to renewed interest since the end of the 1990s (Adler 1997; Adler and Barnett 1998; Buzan *et al.* 1998; Deutsch 1957; Williams and Neumann 2000), are based on the assumption that states are the primary source of insecurity to one another: shared norms and identities may modify or even remove this feeling of insecurity, but states, nevertheless, remain the key players defining international security, while institutions merely strengthen and preserve the 'tightness' of one security community.[25]

It is also worth mentioning that security and defence have been kept firmly outside the scope some of the classical integration theories. Functionalist or neo-functionalist mechanisms of functional and political spillover have proved their strength in addressing the forces behind integration in socio-economic policy areas (Burley and Mattli 1993; Haas 1958; Lindberg 1963; Schmitter 1969; Tranholm-Mikkelsen 1991). But economic incentives carry only limited explanatory power when applied to 'high politics', where objectives such as national sovereignty and independence tend to outweigh *economic* gains.

Therefore, when compared to other approaches, security governance's key asset is that, while not disregarding the state as a key actor in international security structures, it opens up to theories that are more sympathetic to alternative channels of influence than those that look at traditional state sources of power in classical hierarchical systems. As a first theoretical building block of a security governance research programme, the governance literature suggests that *network analysis* can 'offer valuable insights into the structure and function of the multiple, diverse and frequently overlapping control and coordination arrangements that together make up global and security governance structures' (Krahmann 2005: 22; Rosenau 1995).

Network approaches are useful, because they allow us to pursue power relations within heterarchic structures, and draw attention to how actors both within and between organisations interact irrespective of formal organisational boundaries and procedures. As such, they are able to accommodate both formal and informal processes, as well as actors whose formal source of influence is unclear, as would be the case, for example, with some of the semi-independent agencies that are located on the side (or even inside) of the EU's formal organisation, such as the European Defence Agency (EDA) and the Joint Situation Centre (SITCEN).[26] Network approaches offer convincing explanations of how power within organisations often comes from the degree to which an actor is at the centre of many relationships or processes other than formal placement. Indeed, access to and the ability to process information and offer advice may be a stronger source of influence than being a small state with a formal right to vote amongst 26 others. Although the main focus of network analysis is on how the structure of ties affects social outcomes, and not on the influence of individual agents of power, network approaches are also conscious of how change agents and opinion leaders often play a significant role in the adoption of innovative practices (see e.g. Rogers 2003). To this end, network analysts identify a number of mechanisms that facilitate or restrict actors' influence within a governance structure, including relative placement in the structure, direct or indirect access to decision-making, access to and control of information, control of and ability to set the agenda, independence, and trust received from other actors in the network (see e.g. Carrington *et al.* 2005; Freeman 2004; Scott 1991; Wellman and Berkowitz 1988). The relative performance of a governance structure can also be measured by looking at such indicators as the openness, reach and cohesion of actors within a network. As such, the insights of network analysis can help better our understanding of the internal dynamics of the CSDP by focusing on such questions as who are the most powerful or influential actors, and by showing what material and other resources a certain actor can mobilise to increase his or her influence within a particular governance structure. These tools could also aid further investigation into the relationship between state, individual and institutional agency in the CSDP, which is a matter that has received only marginal attention so far (Merand 2008; Tallberg 2008).

There is also a particular need for theorising the impact of institutionalisation on the CSDP. Security and defence have been rapidly growing policy areas in the EU, which involves an increasing number of permanent representatives, as well as seconded officers, diplomats and civil servants who are often seen to develop some degree of collective *esprit de corps* (see Duke 2005; Howorth 2007; Meyer 2006). This has led to an alleged shift of weight from national to EU institutions, a process often referred to as 'Brusselsization', i.e. the tendency for security and defence policy to be formally and/or informally, influenced, formulated and, to some extent, driven from within the EU's different institutional structures (see Howorth 2007: 30). However, the actual salience and impact of such a shift is a matter that needs to be substantiated further. As the need for these centralised institutions in the implementation of the CSDP grows – i.e. for strategic and operational planning, early warning, contingency planning, policy analysis, etc. – their role as effective implementers also needs to be evaluated.[27] New institutionalist theories, as Michael E. Smith (2004) has demonstrated in the case of the CFSP, would be particularly helpful for identifying the mechanisms through which central institutions also shape the CSDP.

However, new institutionalism is not one theory, but denotes rather a renewed interest in the role of institutions and institutionalisation in the understanding of human actions within organisations or society as a whole. The upsurge in the field owes much to the works of James March and Johan P. Olsen (1984, 1989, 1995, 2005), who essentially re-introduced and further developed the ideas of 'old' institutionalism, which had been discredited, due to their lack of theoretical underpinnings, by the 'behaviouralist intermission' in International Relations theory from the interwar period onwards (see Hollis and Smith 1990; Peters 1999). Although there exists a number of subfields to new institutionalism, it roughly contains three major strands of theory – rational institutionalism, historical institutionalism and sociological institutionalism (see Hall and Taylor 1996; Immergut 1998). It is the latter two in particular that appear most helpful in the exploration of the issues that have been sketched out for this book.

Historical institutionalists, on the one hand, focus on the historical legacy of institutions and argue that some decisions made in the past tend to create precedents that shape and constrain actors' choices at a later stage, a concept often referred to as 'path dependency' (Krasner 1984; Pierson 2000). As such, they point to a central mechanism that explains some of the lock-in effects that tend to come into play once an institution achieves a certain momentum. However, historical institutionalists have devoted little attention to explaining how institutions affect behaviour (Hall and Taylor 1996: 950). Sociological institutionalists, on the other hand, link up with a long research tradition in sociology, represented by scholars such as Emile Durkheim, Max Weber and Talcott Parsons, which has yielded numerous theories of how institutions affect the behaviour of actors through mechanisms of social interaction. The more recent sociological thread in new institutionalism owes much to scholars such as March and Olsen (1984, 1989, 1995, 2005) and Paul DiMaggio and Walter Powell (1991). In short, the theoretical landscape of new institutionalism contains a range of well-documented mechanisms that explain institutional change and behaviour, including path dependencies, positive feedback loops, social learning, adaptation, persuasion, compliance, professional and organisational cultures, etc. (see also Smith 2004: 35). Moreover, given the strategic orientation of the book, new institutionalism shares many of its central claims with the sociological school of strategic studies, which has, in turn, benefited from recent theoretical developments inside the sociological institutionalist school in particular (see Egnell 2006).[28]

Finally, the (security) governance turn owes much of its intellectual debt to the wider constructivist turn in International Relations theory (Adler 1997; Checkel 1998; Cronin 1999; Farrell 2002; Hall 1999; Hopf 1998; Katzenstein 1996a, 1996b; Kier 1997; Legro 1995; Onuf 1998; Parsons 2002; Wendt 1992, 1995, 1998, 1999).[29] Despite its critics (see e.g. Hyde-Price 2006; Moravcsik 1999; Smith 1999), social constructivism today has a well-established record of showing how ideas and norms condition the behaviour of states through mechanisms of normative appropriateness. There is also a particular strand of constructivism that employs the concept of Europeanisation to explain how states (both members and non-EU members) adapt and change their behaviour to fit with norms at the EU level through a number of mechanisms, such as, for example, elite socialisation and bureaucratic adaptation (Cowles *et al.* 2001; Davidson *et al.* 2002; Featherstone and Kazamias 2001; Manners and Whitman 2000; Olsen 2002). However, it appears that often, and especially when it comes to 'hard politics', references to shared norms and ideas tend to be given first when states' actions seem to conflict with the national interest. Yet the story of the EU, and especially the CSDP, is very much a 'despite of' one, which should warrant further exploration of this common ideational realm.

The promise of the security governance approach rests with the fact that it thrives on a number of established theoretical insights that when applied together can generate a better understanding of the CSDP. For example, combining the insights of sociological institutionalism and network analysis allows us to explain how actors within an organisation change their behaviour, but also if and why they have actual influence over policy-making. If combined, new institutionalism can fill some of the holes in constructivist thinking, such as how norms are created and gain prevalence inside institutional structures.

The criticism often launched against constructivism, that it favours structure over agency (Checkel 1998), is effectively met by also explicitly looking at individual actors' roles inside institutional structures. Finally, the broad theoretical foundations of security governance are able to accommodate key theories and concepts in the strategic studies tradition, including models of civil–military coordination, strategic culture and interoperability. These traditional concepts are, in turn, updated to a new reality and allowed to benefit from theoretical insights developed in other fields of research.

Hence, a conceptual link is forged between traditional strategic concepts, on the one hand, and the insights of the so-called governance turn in EU studies, on the other. That way we are able to utilise the instrumentality and clarity of the strategic approach in *structuring* the analysis, while retaining an understanding of the unique character of the EU in how we *approach* it. However, before we move on with the analysis, we need to spend some time clarifying what exactly this somewhat unlikely conceptual marriage between strategic actorness and security governance entails.

Strategic actorness and security governance

First, the relationship between security governance and strategic actorness is not a causal one, at least not in a narrow neo-positivist meaning of causation. It would be difficult, or at least impractical, to isolate a static (set of) independent variable(s) from security governance that will make it possible to draw a causal link to strategic actorness. Nor would it produce the kind of answers we are looking for. Causal theorising involves asking whether x causes y, and then measures correlation between the independent and dependent variable(s) and the corresponding causal effects. However, in this book we are more interested in the conditions that make y possible. This objective is better served by a *constitutive* understanding of the relationship between security governance and strategic actorness. According to Alexander Wendt (1998; 1999: 83–84), constitutive theorising involves asking 'how possible' and 'what' questions in order to reveal 'conceptually necessitating' conditions for a phenomenon to take place; for example, the existence of the rules and norms of diplomacy can be seen as constitutive for inter-state bargaining. Similarly, security governance can be seen as constitutive for strategic actorness;

i.e. without it (or some other alternative explanation) strategic actorness is inconceivable.[30]

Second, the previous section identified a number of *mechanisms* through which security governance can affect EU strategic actorness. Social mechanisms represent a useful middle ground between social laws and description (Hedström and Swedberg 1998; Merton 1957). They operate 'at an analytical level below that of an all-encompassing theory' (Checkel 2005: 4), and make it possible to arrive at less general and abstract theories. They are, as Jeffrey Checkel (2008: 2) notes, highly useful scientific tools, employed today by rationalists, constructivists, quantitative and qualitative researchers, and scholars engaged in new research on case studies in particular. This broad scope makes it possible to synthesise insights and findings across different theories, as long as it is clear what a social mechanism is. Although several definitions exist (see e.g. Checkel 2005; Hedström and Swedberg 1998), a minimum definition of a mechanism is, according to John Gerring (2007b: 178), 'the pathway or process by which an effect is produced or a purpose accomplished'. Or more generally, mechanisms connect things and reduce, therefore, 'the lag between input and output, cause and effect' (Checkel 2005: 4). In our case, adopting a number of potential social mechanisms from established theories has the advantage that they are firmly rooted in theory and have been tested in other empirical environments.

The mechanisms are, in turn, put to the test by tracing key processes relevant to each of the three criteria for strategic actorness. As an oft-used method in social sciences, process tracing typically involves consulting archival records and secondary sources, alone or in combination with interviews (George and Bennett 2005; Gerring 2007a). However, the CSDP is a notoriously closed policy field, in the sense that it tends to produce an enormous amount of official 'output', in the shape of strategic options, joint actions and various semi-official 'food for thought' papers, framework papers and action plans, but keeps deliberations closed to outsiders, and does not make minutes of Council and various Committee meetings available for public access (see Smith 2004: 13–14). Given the data access, several accounts have charted the official decisions of the EU pertaining to foreign, security and defence policy (e.g. Ginsberg 1989; Schneider and Seybold 1997). Such quantitative approaches may tell us something about an increase or decrease in cooperative behaviour between EU Member States, but they tell us little about the relative importance of each decision, the decisions that never were, or the institutional processes that make each grand yes-vote possible. Indeed, informal processes and procedures are often as important as the formal ones, which leaves the researcher with little choice but to resort to qualitative interviews simply to understand what goes on 'behind closed doors'.

The research for the book is, therefore, based on more than 40 interviews with key EU and national actors, conducted in three main rounds – May 2003, May 2006 and June 2009 – but supplemented with fresh interviews and observations following the entry into force of the Lisbon Treaty on 1 December 2009. This has allowed a close scrutiny of developments in the CSDP over a period of eight years. Due to the often sensitive character of the subject matters discussed, most of the interviews were carried out on a non-attributable basis. Sometimes, interviewees would also share unofficial documents, such as background papers or works in progress that (may or may not) have become publicly available (in a different form) at some point, but which offered insight into the process through which the final product came about. Referencing these documents has been problematic, given the need to respect the confidentiality under which the information was obtained, but I have sought to be as open as possible.

Structure of the book

To recap the chapter, the question that this book sets out to answer is whether the EU, in view of its adoption of a security and defence policy, has become a *strategic actor*, which is conceptualised in three interconnected criteria – ends, means and resolve. However, since the very notion of a strategic actor would be incompatible with the formal intergovernmental character of the CSDP, *security governance* is introduced as an alternative approach that can also incorporate the informal mechanisms and processes that make a seemingly ungovernable policy area governable. The rationale for exploring these two concepts is essentially rooted in empirical observations rather than driven by a desire to develop and test yet another set of theoretical concepts, adding to the already existing 'forest of terms' that has emerged to describe what the EU has or has not become over the course of more than ten years of the CSDP. Indeed, the strength of both concepts is that they draw upon established research traditions, which together make it possible to draw out essential traits of a strategic actor that differs in form and function from the study objects that have normally been subjected to the scrutiny of scholars in the strategic studies and governance research traditions.

As this first chapter has shown, the five features of security governance do not only resonate well with key elements of the CSDP. The concept of governance is also able to accommodate and benefit from some of the traditional models in strategic studies, such as the integrated model of civil–military relations introduced by the sociological school of strategic studies already in the 1960s (Janowitz 1960). A closer look at these traditional models may, in fact, generate new insights into issues that the EU is battling with today, which tend to be regarded by contemporaries as new and unique to the Union, but which, in fact, often are not. The debate around the eventual presence (or not) of an EU strategic culture is yet another issue that tends to be detached from its 'real' roots in strategic studies, but which can, when used with care, generate essential insights into some of the elements that facilitate and constrain the CSDP. The issue of strategic culture is, therefore, treated in depth in Chapter 2.

Chapters 3 to 6 then move on to discuss each of the three criteria for strategic actorness, including the institutional ability of the EU to bring together ends and means in the planning for and carrying out of operations. To put them in the proper strategic context, each of the four chapters are introduced and discussed with a reference to Sir Michael Howard's four dimensions of strategy – the social, the logistical, the technological and the operational (Howard 1983b). This is not only an acknowledgement of one of the most important pieces on strategy written over the last 50 years. Each dimension serves the purpose of framing the discussion of a cluster of issues that are regarded as essential to strategic analysis. Indeed, Howard wanted to convey the close interconnectedness of the four dimensions, as well as the catastrophic implications of forgetting or disregarding any of them. The four dimensions thus serve as a constant reminder and guideline for what is, indeed, essential for a strategic actor.

Accordingly, Chapter 3 draws attention to the social dimension of strategy as an essential factor behind the analysis of the first criterion for a strategic actor: the capacity to formulate common security interests or ends. This is, if we recap the two first features of security governance, an area characterised by multiple actors interacting in a heterarchical structure. Using a network approach, the chapter, therefore, explores the relationship between the state, and individual and institutional agency in the CSDP, seeking to uncover the way that actors within and beyond the Member States ultimately affect the EU's ability to generate efficient and legitimate security policies.

Chapter 4 addresses the role of central EU institutions as 'movers' – or the logistical dimension that links interests (ends) with capabilities (means). The purpose of the chapter is to critically assess the results of the third feature of security governance, i.e. the massive institutional expansion of the Council Secretariat to support the CSDP. The question asked is whether the EU has ultimately been able to develop a civil–military organisation 'fit for purpose'. To this end, the chapter draws upon a combination of new institutionalist theory and two ideal strategic models for organising the civil–military interface: the so-called 'normal' or stovepipe model (Huntington 1957), and the 'constabulary' or integrated model (Janowitz 1960).

Chapter 5 addresses the second criterion for a strategic actor, the ability to generate relevant capabilities for stated objectives. This is an area that, in accordance with the fourth feature of security governance, has been subject to important changes in the ideational or normative relations that regulate defence acquisitions and planning in Europe today. Indeed, the purpose of the chapter is not to simply compare military hardware or national defence budgets, but to assess the role that the EU – directly and indirectly – has played in the development of both civilian and military capabilities to support the CSDP. Taking the concept of *broad interoperability* as a point of departure, the chapter discusses the relative character of capabilities and the potential for obtaining comparative advantage through innovation, although not necessarily along the technological dimension, which for many years remained the key determinant for the outcome of wars.

Chapter 6 directs attention to the operational dimension of strategy, which relates directly to our third and final criterion for a strategic actor, the resolve to engage in operations that promote common interests. This is also the ultimate test case for a collective purpose behind the CSDP, to recap the fifth and final feature of security governance. Operations or missions constitute a source of success or failure, pride or shame, and determine ultimately how a state or institution – whatever is considered to constitute the 'we' – is perceived both by its own constituents and its surroundings. The chapter, therefore, takes a comprehensive view on the more than 20 civilian and military operations that the EU has carried out under the auspices of the CSDP to assess how they have affected the EU itself, its relations with the outside world, and its ability to generate lessons learned from operational experience.

Finally, Chapter 7 concludes that approaching the EU as a strategic actor from a governance perspective allows us to see the whole picture in a way that looking at a multitude of factors, which before have been treated in isolation, does not. The analysis shows that the implicit and explicit benchmarks that the EU has set for itself, most notably the ambitions and claims to becoming a comprehensive strategic actor, have only partly been fulfilled. This has important implications for the future of the CSDP, and for the future of European security governance at large.

2 | *European strategic culture and the Comprehensive Approach*

Once upon a time, there were nasty states who didn't like each other much, even fighting bloody wars. Then the EU Fairy showed them the way to cooperate, first on coal and steel, afterwards on other things as well. Today, Euro-people look back in wonder on their ignorant and aggressive forefathers, and they live happily ever after.

> The EU founding myth according to Peter van Ham (2005: 39)

Like any strategic actor, the EU does not and cannot operate outside a fairly stable ideational context or culture that constrains and facilitates certain actions. Ideational relations between the various actors involved in the CSDP are, as explained in Chapter 1, also a key defining feature of the EU as a security governance structure. It is necessary, therefore, to address this element first to be able to understand developments within the three criteria for strategic actorness. After 40 years of NATO dominance, the end of the Cold War spurred some essential changes to the European security environment that together pushed in the direction of a heavier security role for the EU. At the same time, the EU carried forward a strong awareness of its origins as a project for peace, having risen from the ashes of two world wars. This necessarily put some constraints on the way that defence aspects were to be accommodated in the EU framework. In other words, the CSDP was conceived, evolved and continues to evolve inside a quite specific context; or what, in the strategic literature, is often referred to as a *strategic culture*.

Having been subject to debate in academic circles for some time, the idea of a common European strategic culture 'that fosters early, rapid and when necessary, robust intervention' was elevated to a policy objective in the 2003 European Security Strategy (ESS) (European Council 2003d: 11). It is still too early to judge if this objective has been met – if, indeed, a strategic culture is something that can be purposely shaped to fit some desired end-state. However, the document itself remains a source of ambition and a benchmark against which the Union's security policy is still measured (Biscop 2007; Biscop and Andersson 2008; Deighton and Mauer 2006; European Council 2008c). It also showed that the EU need not be very different from a state in the way that it uses strategic narratives as a way to legitimise, expand or restrict the scope of its actions. As such, the document had a reach far beyond the short-term political context in which it was conceived. It was in itself a significant step in the constant reaffirmation and incremental evolution of a European strategic culture, as is argued in this chapter.

However, before moving on to analyse the ESS, it is necessary to revisit briefly both the recent academic debate on an *EU* strategic culture, and the overall strategic culture research tradition, to avoid some of the loopholes and conceptual difficulties that *cultural* studies tend to entail. The chapter then moves on to analyse the ESS as a key expression of a nascent *strategic narrative*, and a readily observable component in the shaping of a European strategic culture. Hereunder, the notion of a Comprehensive Approach to security is identified as a natural – or culturally conditioned – focal point around which the CSDP was to be shaped. The chapter concludes that the Comprehensive Approach has subsequently become a strategic *end* in itself for the EU, and that it, therefore, represents a central reference point for further analysis of the EU's performance as a strategic actor.

Is there a European strategic culture?

Going back some 30 years, the strategic culture debate has evolved in step with scholarly developments and changes in the security environment, proving its endurance in the recent revival of the concept as part of the contemporary European security debate (Cornish and Edwards 2001, 2005; Heiselberg 2003; Howorth 2007; Hyde-Price 2004; Longhurst and Zaborowski 2004; Martinsen 2004; Matlary 2006; Meyer 2006; Norheim-Martinsen 2007; Rynning 2003; Toje 2008a). The appeal of the concept rests with its inherent potential for incorporating a range of more or less elusive ideational factors, such as history, norms, identity, values and ideas, in explanations of why certain states – and, more recently, institutions – act the way they do. Herein we also find strategic culture's weak spot: the term means different things to different people. Or as Colin Gray remarks (2006: 9):

'The ability of scholars to make a necessarily opaque concept like strategic culture even less penetrable is truly amazing.'

Indeed, to some the idea of a European strategic culture represents
something of a contradiction in terms, because the persistence of heavily ingrained *national* strategic cultures would seem to render it impossible (Hyde-Price 2004; Matlary 2006; Rynning 2003). To others, the
idea that national strategic cultures may coexist with a European one
seems wholly uncontroversial (Cornish and Edwards 2001, 2005;
Howorth 2007). However, the bottom line is that if the EU uses military force or other instruments in pursuit of some notion of collective
European security interests, it does so de facto within some kind of
context or (a) strategic culture(s). It makes little sense, therefore, to
state that the EU has or has not acquired a strategic culture. What
this chapter argues is simply that the concept of strategic culture lends
itself as the most fruitful theoretical platform from which to discuss
the ideational boundaries that necessarily constrain and shape military
(and civilian) developments inside the EU. As such, strategic culture
is, as explained in Chapter 1, not to be regarded as a criterion for
strategic actorness, but represents rather a *constitutive* factor of security governance that facilitates and/or constrains strategic actorness.
A more principled reason for taking up the discussion is, nonetheless,
that the issue of a European strategic culture continues to attract controversy, and tends to be treated somewhat detached from its roots in
the strategic literature.

Going back to the origins, the term *strategic culture* was first coined
by Jack Snyder, who argued that strategic cultures are the product
of each state's unique historical experience, which is reaffirmed and
sustained as new generations of policy-makers are socialised into a
particular way of thinking (Snyder 1977). Criticising the rational actor
models of the time, Snyder questioned the predominant assumption
that the Soviet Union and the United States would share nuclear strategic thinking, which among other truisms at the time had laid the basis
for the MAD (Mutually Assured Destruction) strategy. This shift of
focus 'from rational man to national man' was immediately picked up
by a number of scholars in the late 1970s and early 1980s, who agreed
that factors, such as historical experience, political culture and geog-
raphy, do act as constraints on strategic thinking (Booth 1979; Gray
1981; Lord 1985; Pipes 1977). However, as Snyder later summed it up
(1990: 3): 'some of the early American literature on strategic culture

exaggerated past US-Soviet differences, and exaggerated the likelihood that such differences would persist in the future'. Incidentally, similar criticisms can be launched against the persistent propensity to make comparisons across the Atlantic, this time between Western Europe – with the EU as the most pertinent expression of what is typically European – and the United States.[1] The resulting stereotyping of Europe as weak and the United States as strong has helped obscure questions, such as whether comparisons between two such vastly different entities are even feasible, whether US standards represent sensible yardsticks against which to measure European power, or whether transatlantic differences are rooted merely in material preconditions or in more fundamental differences of identity and culture.[2] As a timely reminder, therefore, one should bear in mind that strategic culture, despite some of its later uses, was originally intended as a tool to explain the persistence of the way that a given strategic community thinks and acts; it was not intended as a comparative tool.

As a reaction to the inherent danger of ending up with 'caricatures of culture', a second generation of strategic culture scholars, having observed the differences between what policy-makers say and what they actually do, voiced a general scepticism towards the feasibility of studying culture at all (Campbell 1992; Klein 1988, 1989). According to them, strategic culture was not expected to have much effect on strategic behaviour at all. Again, similar sentiments are mirrored in the debate about a European strategic culture. Some scholars remain sceptical of the actual impact of an EU strategic culture, since it seems to them to be reflected mostly in rhetoric (Rynning 2003). And whereas some tend to downplay the role of 'symbolic victories' such as the 2001 Laeken Council, at which the CSDP was declared operational (Duke 2002; Lindley-French 2002b), others conclude more favourably (Andréani *et al.* 2001; Cogan 2001; Howorth 2002). The point is that there might be a considerable gap between the usually upbeat tone of EU declarations and actual improvements, material or otherwise, in strategic capacity, as is perhaps best conceptualised in Hill's 'capability–expectations gap' (Hill 1993, see discussion in Chapter 1).

Some of these apparent inconsistencies were picked up by a third generation of scholars, who essentially parted ways on the question of whether *behaviour* was to be defined inside or outside of the term. If behaviour was separated from culture, as Alistair Iain Johnston (1995) argued, one would be able to draw up a falsifiable theory of strategic culture, which could be pitted against other alternative explanations (see also Kier 1997; Legro 1995).[3] Yet Johnston's attack on previous strategic culture scholars resulted in a protracted discussion with Colin Gray, who argued that strategic behaviour must irrevocably be part of strategic culture, since culture represents the context for *all* things strategic (Gray 1999b).[4] In a more recent paper Gray also rather tellingly deems the failure to agree on a definition of strategic culture as 'rather foolish since there is general agreement on the content of the subject and, roughly, on how it functions'. Including or excluding behaviour from the definition is, as he goes on, 'a burning issue for theory builders but otherwise not really of any great significance' (Gray 2006: ii).

At the heart of the matter remains the fact that strategic culture is a notoriously elusive concept, the appeal *and* curse of which rests with its inherent inclusiveness and all-encompassing nature. However, it can be argued that some elements of a strategic culture can be studied with more precision than others. Going beyond the Johnston/Gray debate, Kerry Longhurst (2000), for example, offers a distinction between unobservable and observable components of strategic culture. In the first category we find the 'foundational elements' of strategic culture, or the core values that gives it 'its basal quality and characteristics' (Longhurst 2000: 305). As unobservables, or a priori qualities, these are the factors that seem prone to the kind of caricatures of culture for which earlier strategic culture studies have been criticised. Ole Waever (1998) raises a similar concern with regard to analyses of Europe as a security community. He argues that the origins of peaceful Europe seem 'terribly over-determined', and that 'thus, a study of "security communities" should not focus on origins but try to grasp the clashing social forces that uphold and undermine "expectations of non-war"' (Waever 1998: 71, 75). These clashing social forces parallel, in turn, what Longhurst refers to as the 'actual *observable* manifestations of the strategic culture – "the self-regulating *policies* and *practices*" which give active meaning to the foundational elements by relating and promoting them to the external environment' (Longhurst 2000: 305, my emphasis).

In a similar vein, Iver B. Neumann and Henrikki Heikka (2005) discuss strategic culture as the product of the dynamic interplay between *discourse* and *practice*. Drawing on sociological studies of culture, they argue that discourse is the vehicle through which strategic culture reveals itself, while practice is the socially recognised forms of behaviour that stems from it and ultimately defines the strategic culture in question (see Schatzki *et al.* 2001; Swidler 2001). This discursive turn in strategic culture studies can, in turn, be related to a growing interest in the role of *strategic narratives* (Arquilla and Ronfeldt 2001; Freedman 2006; Kaldor *et al.* 2007). Lawrence Freedman (2006: 22–23) contends, for example, that:

> Culture, and the cognition which it influences, is rarely fixed but in a process of development and adaptation … It is in this context that the concepts of narratives – compelling story lines which can explain convincingly and from which inferences can be drawn – becomes relevant. Narratives are designed or nurtured with the intention of structuring the responses of others to developing events. They are strategic because they do not arise spontaneously but are deliberately constructed or reinforced out of ideas and thoughts that are already current … Narratives are about the ways that issues are framed and responses suggested.

In a contemporary security environment, Freedman goes on, the role of strategic narratives has become even more salient, since the wars of ideas that take place in the media and the public domain are often as important as the ones on the ground. Security strategies, strategy papers, Defence White Papers and the like, as the most deliberate expressions of strategic narratives, represent not merely, or perhaps even primarily, strategic guidelines, but documents for public consumption, deliberate efforts to legitimise future actions, and reconcile with or signal difference to the 'other' as part of shaping one's own strategic identity. In his book *Writing Security*, David Campbell (1992), for example, shows how the United States has continuously and actively used narrative descriptions of 'the other' to consolidate an American 'self' that needs to be kept secure.

Strategic narratives are, as such, not merely rhetorical, but represent 'speech acts' – i.e. sentences or locutions with a certain force (see Austin 1955; Buzan *et al.* 1998; Waever 1995). Sometimes they even contain the power to change, insofar as by saying something, or performing a speech act, an option that was not there before is created. Repeating the statement can, in turn, reinforce an idea, build up a sense of common identity or cause, or even command certain actions by way of rhetorical entrapment (see Risse 2000; Schimmelfenning 1999, 2003). In methodological terms then, strategic narratives represent a key *mechanism* through which strategic cultures reproduce, expand or limit the cultural boundaries for what a strategic actor can or is expected to do (see discussion in Chapter 1).

This does *not* imply that an actor is in a position to use narratives freely to change or create a certain strategic culture, which seems to be indicated by the call of the ESS for one that specifically 'fosters early, rapid and when necessary, robust intervention'. Strategic narratives are essentially conservative, since they need to be constructed out of ideas that are recognisable to and considered legitimate by their recipients (Freedman 2006). Insofar as (strategic) narratives are 'compelling storylines' and not 'the truth', they may be challenged by competing narratives if or when the EU were to 'lose its aura of progressivism', as Mark Gilbert warns (2008) in his excellent analysis of how a commonly shared progressive conception of the European integration project has produced an over-simplified, unhistorical and somewhat teleological version of contemporary European history. A strategic narrative, as any narrative, is ultimately reliant on its credibility and legitimacy as such – and, indeed, whether it is reflected in actual *practice*. It is then, and only then, we may talk about a strategic culture.

With this in mind, the chapter moves on to analyse the ESS as essentially a strategic narrative intended to 'sell' the burgeoning CSDP as an inherent and natural part of an evolving EU. Accordingly, attention is predominantly directed to the overall and more enduring storyline that the document conveys and its implications for the CSDP, rather than to the more contextually dependent details of the document.

Beyond constructive ambiguity

Until 2003, the CSDP had been successfully clouded in 'constructive ambiguity' (Heisbourg 2000, 2004). The relatively loose shape and direction of the project, as reflected in the, to some, irreconcilable goals of European autonomy *and* the strengthening of the Atlantic Alliance, gave ample room for coordinative narratives at the national level that supported the fleeting CSDP but still agreed with the rather different aspirations of French Europeanism, British Atlanticism and German federalism respectively (Howorth 2004). However, as the evolving crisis in Iraq made it obvious just how fragile the political unity on which the CSDP rested was, it eventually became clear that 'constructive ambiguity was no longer an option' (Howorth 2004: 228). Therefore, although the need for a firmer policy platform on which to base the CSDP had been obvious for some time, it was the Iraq crisis that triggered the process that led to the adoption of the document titled *A Secure Europe in a Better World: European Security Strategy* at the Brussels European Council on 12 December 2003.

The ESS thus served the specific purpose of mending relations between US Secretary of Defence Donald Rumsfeld's infamously branded 'old' and 'new' Europe, and the rift that had emerged between Europe and the United States. However, in hindsight the ESS was, in the words of Alyson Bailes (2005: 1), a 'conceptual and procedural turning point [and] an important stage in the developing self-awareness and ambition of the EU as a player in the global arena'. As shown in Chapter 3 of this book, the *process* by which the ESS came about is a particularly telling example of how a security governance structure can produce surprising results by going outside of formal procedures. In the end, the ESS was drafted and adopted in less than seven months, truly a remarkable feat in light of the cumbersome intergovernmental procedures that often formally underpin the CSDP. This was made possible by a combination of a favourable political climate at the time, a sense of urgency, and the fact that Solana and his team were there to pick up the task and carry it through efficiently without breaking the trust of the Member States.

As became clear when President Sarkozy in 2007 signalled a major revision of the ESS as part of his plans for the upcoming French Council Presidency (second half of 2008), this combination of factors was something that could not easily be reproduced (*Financial Times* 2007). Instead, the EU Member States mandated a *review* of the implementation of the ESS in December 2007. This resulted in a round of high-level seminars, which gave a small group of senior academics and practitioners the opportunity to offer their views on the future parameters of the EU's security and defence policy. The method was, as such, not dissimilar to the one that produced the ESS in 2003, but this time the impact was more sobering. Rather than resulting in the bold new security strategy that President Sarkozy had signalled, the December 2008 European Council adopted a rather more conservative *Report on the Implementation of the European Security Strategy*. Apart from adding a number of threats to the list, the document essentially reaffirmed the key elements of the 2003 ESS, making clear that it 'remains fully relevant' and that the report 'does not replace the ESS, but reinforces it' (European Council 2008c: 3). Since it did not have the attention that the Iraq crisis had ensured in 2003 either, the document was almost immediately forgotten and never received a fraction of the comments and analysis that the 2003 ESS attracted. That the latter did receive so much attention is probably also the main reason why it has proved so enduring and alive in the minds of both academics and practitioners.[5]

Because of the special political circumstances in which it came about, the ESS was naturally followed by a trail of analyses (Bailes 2004, 2005; Berenskoetter 2004; Biscop 2004; Duke 2004; Toje 2005) that compared it with the US National Security Strategy (NSS) issued by the Bush Administration the year before (US Government 2002). Christoph Heusgen, then Director of the Policy Planning and Early Warning Unit, is also reported to have admitted that the title and acronym of the ESS was chosen deliberately because comparisons with the US version were not only inevitable but also what the Member States intended with the document (quoted in Toje 2005: 120). Consequently, as Simon Duke (2004: 461) points out, the existence of the NSS was exploited in the ESS, which used, in the words of Alyson Bailes (2005: 32), 'the concomitant language to signal subtle differences as well as togetherness'. The NSS still represents, therefore, a natural reference point when discussing the ESS, although it is important to bear in mind that the two documents, despite their tacit connection, had different purposes. For example, whereas the NSS served as 'a reference and justification for action policy choices' (Haine and Lindström quoted in Duke 2004: 460), the ESS served as a reference and justification for having a common security and defence policy in the first place. Also, whereas the publication of the NSS is a more or less frequent enterprise, allowing the reader to assess the evolution of a national strategy – the NSS was followed by new versions in 2006 and 2010 (US Government 2006, 2010) – the ESS was a first, though obviously not appearing in a strategic void, yet being 'too late' in the sense that the CSDP was already well under way. As such, the ESS had not only to define where the CSDP was going, but also its status as of 2003. That is, it had to reconstruct the rationale for the CSDP, until then based on 'constructive ambiguity', a notion that simply did not hold water as the project was taking shape.

Creating a purpose for the CSDP

A strategy paper ought to define actual goals and set up priorities to achieve policy objectives, while describing which means can be used, and under what conditions, to fulfil those objectives (Toje 2005: 121). However, it also serves as a premeditated justification or rationale for situations where ultimately external use of force can be used. It is a tool for building a preparedness for and acceptance of these situations in the minds of constituents as well as the outside world. Accordingly, a strategy paper typically starts with a general description of the security environment, which in turn sets the pace and direction for the rest of the document; i.e. a paper that starts from the assumption that one is at war will necessarily invoke a greater sense of urgency than one that places itself in a less threatening security environment. As part of this exercise, a strategy paper typically offers an interpretation of how the status quo has emerged and the role that the state or organisation has played in getting there.

Whereas the 2002 NSS took as its point of departure the end of the Cold War, 'a decisive victory for the forces of freedom', the ESS – somewhat surprisingly given the centrality of this event for the creation of the CSDP – virtually leapfrogged over the Cold War. Instead, it went back to what Frank Schimmelfenning (2003: 265–278) refers to as the 'founding myth' of European integration, the historical responsibility for creating lasting peace among democratic European states (however, see Gilbert 2008). As such, the ESS essentially restored an idea that had played a minor role in the integration process during the Cold War, by placing it at the heart of the forces that had 'transformed relations between our states, and the lives of our citizens', with the result that Europe has never been 'so prosperous, secure or free' (ESS: 1).[6] Having successfully escaped the legacy of two devastating world wars, the logic goes, Europe should now 'be ready to share in the responsibility for global security and in building a better world' (ESS: 1).

The reference to the founding myth can be seen as an attempt at pinning the CSDP to the one uniting experience that the European states have in common, while offering an alternative to national strategic cultures. However, a question that has been frequently asked is whether it represents a strong enough rationale on which to build a shared and strong European strategic culture. Adrian Hyde-Price (2004) argues that the unprecedented effect that the experience of war has traditionally had on national strategic cultures is exactly why such a common European strategic culture is unlikely to emerge. In a similar vein, Peter van Ham (2001, 2005: 39) argues that the founding myth 'breaks a pattern since historically war and violence have played a major part in state-formation'. Or, as he goes on to state: 'Without war "we" hardly know who "we" are'. Consequently, the absence of robust EU military operations may help us appreciate 'why the EU lacks confidence and status in the military arena' (van Ham 2005: 40).[7] The NSS, again offering a striking contrast, described a state at war again, only ten years after declaring victory in the Cold War.[8] The war references were subsequently toned down in the 2006 and 2010 versions, but the rhetoric, as exemplified by the identification of terrorism as 'the enemy', nevertheless signified a strikingly different strategic outlook than the ESS.[9] While the United States continues to see a world replete with dangers, the EU rather sees security challenges that need to be taken seriously in order to avoid a situation where Europe '*could* be confronted with a very radical threat indeed' (ESS: 5, emphasis added).

In fact, the ESS presents a rather different rationale for a security strategy. Insofar as an important function of such a document is to preserve or strengthen a strategic culture, the peaceful starting point for the ESS represents a less solid cultural building block, so to speak, when compared with the role that the experience of war has traditionally played in the shaping of national strategic cultures. In other words, the EU founding myth, regardless of the unprecedented role that it had played in the transformation of a Europe never 'so prosperous, secure or free', represented an inevitably weak cultural platform on which to base the use of force, which is what a security strategy – or at least the more controversial parts of it – is mainly about. Nevertheless, the European option clearly has its appeal, as reflected, for example, in the re-education of the German public and Europe at large over the course of the 1990s, leading to the general acceptance and even encouragement of German armed forces being used for purposes other than territorial defence, even as it challenges supposedly deep-rooted national strategic cultures built on the experience of suffering two world wars (Howorth 2004). However, the success and prominence granted to the European integration project in the shaping of the status quo inevitably leaves an obligation, whether moral or instrumental, upon the EU to continue the enlargement process, thus 'making a reality of the vision of a united and peaceful continent' (ESS: 1). This has made it progressively harder to identify an 'other' that may serve as a reference point for the European 'we', a concern that has been raised at every juncture in the integration process.

Despite the obvious tacit awareness of a set of common values that constitute a European epistemic community, the ESS also lacks references to core European values or beliefs (i.e. Christianity or liberal democracy), as well as the more moral tone that the NSS tends to display. While 2002 NSS, underpinned by the unique position of the United States, described a global responsibility for spreading moral principles revolving around the central ideas of freedom and liberalism (see e.g. NSS: 3), the ESS, in contrast, restricts the EU's primary role to the maintenance of regional stability, while recognising that the EU 'should be ready to share in the responsibility for global security' (ESS: 1).[10] Only in its own neighbourhood does the ESS explicitly identify a responsibility for promoting certain values, since 'it is in the European interest that countries on our borders are well governed' (see ESS: 7; and Berenskoetter 2004: 6). In terms of tone then, the ESS offers a comparatively modest strategic outlook, which is inevitably carried down through the rest of the document.

The reluctant military actor: acting comprehensively as an end

Since it is, after all, called a security strategy, it is notable how few pointers the ESS offers on the use of military force, at least when judging from the amount of comment that the EU's move into the military realm has attracted. The absence of military references in the document can, of course, be attributed to the lack of agreement amongst the Member States on this particular issue (see e.g. Toje 2005: 121). Yet the apparent preference given to non-military instruments in the ESS is also, as indicated above, rooted in distinctive features of a European strategic culture, and represents thus at least partly a conscious or path dependent European choice. If we start with what the ESS actually does say about the use of force, the only place where this is explicitly mentioned is in connection with failed states in which 'military instruments may be needed to restore order'

(ESS: 7). The use of the term 'restore' seems, in turn, to restrict military means to the post-conflict phase, and then only in concert with other reconstruction tools (Berenskoetter 2004: 13). At the same time, the ESS does recognise a need for a stronger focus on military instruments, and even proactive military engagement, as reflected in the call for a strategic culture that fosters 'early and robust intervention', and the recognition of the need for 'the full spectrum of instruments' to be available for the EU (ESS: 11). In fact, the somewhat ambiguous treatment of the issue of military force and the apparent cautious downplaying of any references to such, seem to counteract previous and subsequent steps towards a stronger military role for the EU.

This perceived disparity is best explained with recourse to the peaceful rationale from which the ESS started out, which from the outset resonates badly with a strong military focus.[11] On the one hand, most Member States do seem to appreciate that military power is necessary for lifting the EU's weight on the world stage, and that engaging in military operations is a rational way to boost its hard power. Yet, on the other hand, they are well aware of the fact that the move into the military realm in certain respects does conflict with the very image of the EU and the ideas, values and norms that uphold it. In that sense, acting militarily, but well within the overarching conflict preventive (read: more benign) parameters, has become an end in itself and a way to legitimise military force as an inherent and natural part of a European strategic culture.

When read as a traditional security strategy, the ESS does not immediately or principally lend itself to the usual ends/means teleology.[12] In looking at how the military dimension has been incorporated into the EU, therefore, it is arguably better understood as the product of a logic of *appropriateness* rather than of a logic of *consequences* (see discussion of security governance in Chapter 1). The CSDP is, indeed, a pertinent example of how culture binds rationality. We could thus add a notion to the 30-year-old strategic culture dichotomy of *rational* man vs. *national* man, namely that of *supranational* man: i.e. when acting – and we should here include both individual, state and institutional actors (see Chapter 3) – within the auspices of the CSDP, all actors are induced or compelled to do so in a way that falls within certain premeditated conceptions of how the EU as a collective should behave. That is, the way in which to act has become a source of a European 'self'. The 'other', as the omnipresent contrast against which an identity needs to be shaped (see Campbell 1992; van Ham 2001, 2005) is in this logic to be found in the United States.

Despite the reconciliatory motive of the ESS, which predominantly came to the fore in a general convergence on the interpretation of threats (terrorism, proliferation of weapons of mass destruction [WMDs] and 'rogue' or 'failed' states),[13] a gap was evident in the particular approaches to counter or manage the threats. A central point of the subsequent debate was the real and perceived difference between the *preventive engagement* of the ESS and the *pre-emptive action* of the NSS. The latter, referred to as the Bush doctrine, signalled that the United States would be willing not only to prevent but also forestall an adversary from attacking vital US interests by way of a pre-emptive military attack (NSS: 19). However, Solana, speaking on behalf of the EU, made it clear that preventive engagement (ESS: 9–11) stopped at the 'mainstreaming of conflict prevention without implying any obligation to undertake pre-emptive military strikes either by the EU or by individual member states' (Solana quoted in Toje 2005: 128). The message was further underlined by the change of wording, reportedly due to German insistence, away from 'pre-emptive engagement' after the first version of the ESS was presented in Thessaloniki in June 2003. However, some of the more striking differences were gradually toned down after the initial shock of the 9/11 attacks eventually came to pass. The 2006 version of the NSS gave, for example, a more sobering account of the terrorist threat and the 'protracted struggle' (as opposed to 'war') against it.

Yet, beyond the more obvious differences the ESS was at its core a confirmation of a broad, multidimensional or *comprehensive* notion of security that had emerged over the years (Barcelona Report 2004; Biscop 2004, 2007). At the heart of this approach is the integration of all dimensions of foreign policy, from aid and trade to diplomacy and the military, and a preference for conflict prevention through dialogue, cooperation and partnership rather than armed intervention. However, the idea of a holistic approach was, as Sven Biscop (2008: 13) points out, certainly not new. Organisations such as the UN and the OSCE had been promoting comprehensive security already during the Cold War, while the EU mostly played the part of the follower, at least when it came to actively promoting the idea – although peace through cooperation had, of course, been the central rationale for the European integration project from the start. However, in the mid 1990s the EU also started to reform its structures for conflict prevention and crisis management, joining the 'comprehensive trend' that gained momentum in the first decade after the Cold War (see Biscop 2008; Schneckener 2002). Eventually a comprehensive security logic received something of an omnipresence in EU documents, as reflected, for example, in the *Stability Pact for Central and Eastern Europe* (European Council 1995), as well as in actual policies, such as the Stability and Association Process(es) (SAP) in the Balkans and the Euro-Mediterranean Partnership programme (EMP). The acknowledgement of the *need* for comprehensive approaches was, in turn, gradually translated into a potential *asset* for the EU – i.e. something that the Union was 'particularly well equipped' to do (ESS: 7).

This created a strong almost teleological drive to highlight integrated civil–military concepts as a way to legitimise and take the CSDP forward. This was also duly reflected in the ESS, which stated that, 'none of the new threats is purely military; nor can be tackled by purely military means [but] each requires a mixture of instruments' (ESS: 7). Incidentally the lack of preparedness of the US-led coalition in Iraq for dealing with the massive challenges that emerged in the wake of the war, and the dawning of the fact that a 'war' on terror could not be won militarily, placed the EU firmly in the driver's seat of the ongoing comprehensive trend. Or as Sven Biscop remarks (2008: 16):

From being absent in the Iraq debate, the European Union thus became a trend-setter, or perhaps more accurately, helped to clear the obstacles for the already existing trend towards a holistic approach to continue after the low point of the Iraq crisis.

Eventually, the EU also warmly endorsed (or perhaps *hijacked* is a better word) the *Comprehensive Approach* – a term that in its abbreviated, conceptual form was initially associated with NATO civil–military operations (NATO 2004) – and started to refer to it as a success factor for its policies and operations.[14] In that sense, it was successfully 'written into' the EU's strategic narrative and accepted as an inherent part of its strategic culture.

Concluding remarks

Today, the Comprehensive Approach has grown to become something of a *raison d'état* for the Union's overall security policy, and a focal point for the incorporation of the military dimension into the EU domain. It represents a powerful idea around which to build a European strategic culture for several reasons. First, it fits well into the conventional narrative of the European integration process as a project for peace by underlining the military dimension's secondary nature – i.e. the EU prefers to act using its traditional strengths as a non-military power, and has successfully done so in the past 'making a reality of the vision of a united and peaceful continent' (ESS: 1), but must also be able to use force to tackle emerging crises in its neighbourhood and beyond. It has a stated non-aggressive purpose and has allowed the EU, at least until recently, to portray itself as a 'benign interventionist' (see e.g. Gowan 2009) perhaps not devoid of, but somewhere above the national interest. This is covered in depth in Chapter 6.

Secondly, the Comprehensive Approach represents a source of a strategic 'self' for a peaceful Europe without enemies. As such, a contrasting 'other' is typically found in the United States, but without having to resort to the kind of negative stereotype imaging of an adversary that has often dominated national strategic cultures in the past. As such, an idea of a European 'us' could also be reconciled with the idea of enlargement, which represents still the quintessential foreign and security policy tool for the EU.

Thirdly, the Comprehensive Approach underlines that the CSDP represents something different and that it does not duplicate NATO. This was a precondition for the CSDP in the first place, as reflected perhaps most explicitly in US Secretary of State, Madeleine Albright's famous three Ds – no decoupling of NATO, no discrimination and no duplication – formulated in her speech to the 1998 NATO summit. That the term Comprehensive Approach, as a concept albeit not an idea, originated in NATO was then perhaps somewhat ironic, but the way in which the EU has taken ownership of the term underlines that the EU is inherently and intuitively better equipped to carry it through. As such, the Comprehensive Approach also represents a potential comparative advantage for the EU, or a European *way of warfare* that has suddenly come into fashion with the need for post-conflict stabilisation and reconstruction in places such as the Balkans, Central Africa, Iraq and Afghanistan.

Finally, the Comprehensive Approach was also duly reflected in the Lisbon Treaty, which holds that CSDP 'shall be an integral part of the common foreign and security policy' and 'shall provide the Union with an operational capacity drawing on civilian *and* military assets' (TEU art. 42.1, emphasis added). Further, the Lisbon Treaty embraced the revised Petersberg tasks, which are, in a sense, the mission statement of the CSDP.[15] The new formulation includes 'joint disarmament operations, humanitarian and rescue tasks, military advice and assistance tasks, conflict prevention and peace-keeping tasks, tasks of combat forces in crisis management, including peace-making and post-conflict stabilisation' (TEU, art. 43.1). Significantly, the treaties now place a responsibility for ensuring 'coordination of the civilian and military aspects of such tasks' upon the High Representative of the Union for Foreign Affairs and Security Policy (TEU art. 43.2). As such, the Comprehensive Approach – although the term as such is not used – has also received greater prominence in the treaties.

As a strategic narrative, therefore, the ESS has proved to be a good 'corporate strategy' for selling the idea of the CSDP, but also for anchoring subsequent steps towards giving it a clearer purpose and direction. However, as the CSDP matures, the question is whether this strategic narrative will be challenged by competing, less appealing narratives if the EU should fail to produce ways, means and results that fall within the inevitable constraints and expectations that come with it (see Gilbert 2008). Strategic culture is, after all, not a one-way street, but the product of the *dynamic interplay* between discourses or narratives, on the one hand, and practices, on the other.

A strategic narrative relates to and codifies ideas and values that exist 'out there' already as the cultural boundaries inside which the strategic actor operates. The narrative can be constructive, in the sense that these boundaries can be incrementally and cautiously shifted. Yet a complex multi-level actor such as the EU in particular – as, indeed, any actor – has limited control over how the narrative plays out when confronted with other actors and real-world events. A strategic decision, Clausewitz reminds us, will always have both intended and unintended consequences that reflect back on the strategic actor in ways over which it has limited control. A decision to intervene in one situation at one point may create expectations or precedents for similar situations in the future. Likewise, a repeated focus on the EU's unique credentials and potentials as a comprehensive actor creates expectations that it will also act decidedly comprehensively, and invite criticism if it fails to produce ways, means and results that reflect this. The next chapters of this book show that, despite consistent steps towards integrating civilian and military aspects of the CSDP, these expectations have only partly been met.

3 | In pursuit of the EU interest: state, individual and institutional agency in the CSDP

It is hard for anyone to argue after receiving one of Solana's bear hugs.

Council Secretariat official (May 2006)

The previous chapter showed that the Comprehensive Approach has become an expression of, or an omnipresent reference point for, the EU's approach to security; *how* to act has become an end in itself when it comes to the CSDP. Still, if we revisit the three criteria for strategic actorness, the first criterion requires that the EU also has a capacity to translate common security interests into actual political decisions. If we recall the discussion of security governance in Chapter 1, this is a process that for the EU involves multiple actors at different levels within and beyond the state. In his discussion of the *Forgotten Dimensions of Strategy*, Michael Howard reminds us of the fundamental importance of the social dimension of strategy, or the social forces and attitudes of those on whose commitment all the other dimensions ultimately depend (Howard 1983b). Having traditionally been the business of state leaders and generals, decisions on the use of force are no longer exclusively prepared, discussed and taken by a small elite of strategic decision-makers. They are, as argued in Chapter 1, rarely the product of actors' fixed preferences, but result rather from social interactions where preferences are likely to change through mechanisms of learning, bargaining, persuasion, etc.

As a main rule, all decisions on the CFSP/CSDP have to be taken by consensus. This has often been seen to hamper the efficiency of the EU as a strategic actor, which is also why the EU has repeatedly sought to modify its consensus rule. However, as the first part of this chapter shows, these attempts have had little impact on the way that security interests are formulated, or the procedures by which political decisions are formally taken. Instead, we must look to other developments to explain why the EU in several areas has been able to conduct a fairly efficient foreign, security and defence policy. In accordance with the security governance approach, the chapter, therefore, widens the scope of actors to include state, institutional and individual actors. In addition, the mechanisms through which each category may influence policy-making are diversified, in order to reach a better understanding of the various informal practices that have facilitated the EU's capacity to formulate efficient security policies without losing the legitimacy that the consensus principle has ensured.[1] As a general hypothesis, the relationship between state, individual and institutional agency in CSDP can be seen as a triangular one, where each type of actor has a rather specific role to play. That is, a collective actor such as the EU relies essentially on a combination of a minimum level of consensus among 27 Member States, all of whom need to feel a sense of ownership of the CSDP; an institutional framework that ensures the maximum level of consistency and coherence possible in the absence of any clearly identified and accepted leadership; and the political entrepreneurship of individuals at all levels, who may fill policy with content, grasp opportunities and push the policy-making process on.

By looking at the *interplay* between the state and institutional and individual agency in EU foreign policy-making, we are able to test the so-called Brusselsization thesis (see Chapter 1; Allen 2004; Nuttall 2000). In particular, by combining institutional accounts of socialisation in the Council Secretariat, which is generally well covered in the EU literature (Duke 2005; Duke and Vanhoonhacker 2006; Juncos and Reynolds 2007; Meyer 2006), with mechanisms derived from network analysis, we may gain a better understanding of how and to what degree there has been a shift from national to EU institutions. As indicated in Chapter 1, network approaches offer convincing explanations of how power within organisations often comes from the degree to which an actor is at the centre of many relationships or processes other than formal placement. To this end, a number of mechanisms that facilitate or restrict actors' influence within a governance structure can be identified, such as relative placement in the structure, direct or indirect access to decision-making, access to and control of information, control of and ability to set the agenda, independence, and trust received from other actors in the network. These mechanisms also help explain how some actors may carve an independent role for themselves inside an EU security governance structure, as seen in the 'individualisation' of responsibility for various aspects of the EU's security and defence policy that emerged during the 'Solana era' (see e.g. Allen 2008).

Since the foreign policies of individual Member States are generally well covered in the EU literature (see e.g. Hill 1996; Manners and Whitman 2000), the findings presented in this chapter add mainly to existing data relating to the institutional level – i.e. where collective interest formation is expected to be strongest, or collective policies most efficiently formulated, but where the distance to the constituent parts that lend legitimacy to these policies is the furthest. It is this general dynamic between efficiency and legitimacy, and the way in which it is affected by shifting patterns of influence amongst a growing number of actors involved in the CSDP that this chapter seeks to address. Individual policies or decisions are, therefore, not mapped in a systematic fashion, but rather used to illustrate general shifts in patterns of influence.[2] In terms of structure, the chapter first goes through the attempts to modify the consensus rule, arguing that they have had little impact on CSDP policy-making. It then moves on to analyse the formal and informal roles and influence of institutional, individual and state actors in that order.

The evolution of EU foreign policy-making: a search for efficiency

As part of what prior to the Lisbon Treaty was referred to as the second pillar of the EU, the CSDP has been and remains subject to decisions by the Council. As a main rule, all decisions in the Council have to be made by consensus (TEU art. 15.4). This effectively grants every Member State a right of veto over all decisions. This has often proved to be the bottleneck of the CSDP, especially noticeable in times of crises. A series of attempts have, therefore, been made to modify the consensus rule to create more efficient decision-making procedures.

The most significant revision of voting procedures was the 1997 Amsterdam Treaty, which opened up for Qualified Majority Voting (QMV) once a 'common strategy' was adopted. QMV was also made possible following a decision on a 'common position', setting out the Union's policy on particular geographical or topical issues vis-à-vis third countries, or a 'joint action' when operational action is needed. The Lisbon Treaty opened a fourth option for QMV to be used after the Council has adopted a proposal by the High Representative of the Union for Foreign Affairs and Security Policy (TEU art. 31.2). The inclusion of QMV by the Amsterdam Treaty was an attempt to increase efficiency by way of tools that the EU had used with great success in other policy areas, which have now become 'communitarianised'. However, the scope of QMV was and remains restricted by the fact that no vote may be taken if opposed by a Member State for reasons of 'fundamental national policy' or if a decision has 'military or defence implications' (TEU art. 31.4). In addition, common strategies as a policy instrument have rarely been used. If they are, they tend, as described by Solana, 'to be too broadly defined, lacking clear priorities and vague because they are written for public consumption' (quoted in ICG 2001: 34). Others have been less diplomatic in their regard for them as 'virtually useless as strategic documents' (interview with Council Secretariat official, May 2003). To reduce the rigidity of the consensus rule, therefore, other measures have been introduced in subsequent Treaty revisions, seeking instead to bypass eventual vetoes by more flexible means, such as 'opt-outs', 'constructive abstention', 'enhanced cooperation' and, most recently, 'permanent structured cooperation'.[3] We shall briefly go through each of them.

The first option has only been used once, as Denmark was granted the only explicit opt-out from the prospective CSDP after the initial rejection of the Maastricht Treaty in a 1992 referendum, allowing the rest of the Member States to include the CSDP in the Treaty and eventually move on with the plans for a 'progressive framing of a common defence policy' (TEU art. 42.2). Denmark also obtained three other opt-outs (from the European Monetary Union (EMU), Justice and Home Affairs (JHA), and the notion of EU citizenship, which is no longer valid). However, polls indicate that the Danish people are ready to drop the defence opt-out (46 per cent for and 38 per cent against, see *AngusReid Global Monitor* 2007). Full exclusion from the CSDP has not been an issue for other accession states, although Ireland demanded assurances that its neutrality be respected when it agreed to sign the Lisbon Treaty after a second referendum on 3 October 2009.

The second option of 'constructive abstention' was introduced by the Amsterdam Treaty (TEU art. 31), opening up the possibility that a Member State can abstain from a vote in the Council under the CFSP without blocking a unanimous decision. By making a formal declaration of abstention, it will not have to apply that particular decision, but accepts that the Union is bound by it, and must refrain from any unilateral action that might conflict with it.

The third option of 'enhanced cooperation', originally established by the Amsterdam Treaty (TEU art. 20), was extended in the 2001 Nice Treaty also to cover the CFSP. The clause allows a minimum of eight Member States to move on with enhanced cooperation, but the veto option, which was lifted in the first and third pillars, was retained. In addition, matters having military or defence implications were again excluded, which severely limited its scope.

The fourth option of 'permanent structured cooperation' was introduced by the Lisbon Treaty. The idea, keenly promoted by France and Germany, is that a handful of countries 'whose military capabilities fulfil higher criteria and which have made more binding commitments to one another in this area with a view to the most demanding missions shall establish permanent structured cooperation within the Union framework' (TEU art. 42.6) – creating a sort of 'defence Eurozone'. It is a significant step forward, in the sense that the clause does not include the 'enhanced cooperation' threshold of eight Member States, and it directly applies to the CSDP, opening up to QMV also here, although decisions on military operations still require a unanimous vote in the Council.

As it turned out, Permanent Structured Cooperation was made possible by a trade-off that allowed the British, on the one hand, to pursue their 'no progress without capabilities' line by including a rigorous 'capability criteria' for joining the core group. The French and the Germans, on the other hand, could pursue their 'more autonomous CSDP' line, which has been obvious ever since the so-called Brussels 'Chocolate Mini-Summit' in April 2003.[4] At present, it is the capability aspect of Permanent Structured Cooperation that has received the most attention. However, in the long run, the Lisbon Treaty does signal a turn towards a more integrationist approach, whereby some Member States will be able to move on with cooperation and the others will have to 'catch up' if they want to join the club later. Some of the new Member States in particular have not been too happy with this development, since it might increase the danger of a 'two-speed' Europe.

In addition, despite the persistent search for more efficient procedures, it should be pointed out that even within the constraints of the present decision rules, the EU has displayed a consistent and efficient policy towards, for example, the Western Balkans (without the initial adoption of a common strategy). This is not due to enforcement mechanisms such as QMV, but rather the existence of alternative practices for coordinating Member State policies, which can ease the formal constraints exerted on EU foreign and security policy-making by voting procedures, at least in areas where the Member States want the EU to have an impact. In fact, though the number of Member States has increased, there is little to suggest that the EU has found it significantly harder to produce decisions on the CFSP/CSDP. Rather than looking at changes in the way that decisions are formally taken, we must look to other developments to determine why the EU has been able to conduct its foreign, security and defence policy in the fairly effective manner that it has. One of the most significant developments in this regard has been the expansion of the Council Secretariat since the late 1990s.

The expanding role of the Council Secretariat in the CSDP

The various institutions and bodies that, directly and indirectly, are involved in the CSDP add up to a rather complex structure in the sense that, below the different configurations of the Council, the hierarchy starts to get fuzzy, competencies overlap and responsibilities are not always clear-cut. However, in terms of role and function, one can roughly divide between those bodies whose main purpose is (to support) policy-making, and those whose tasks are more related to implementation. This chapter covers the former, while Chapter 4 covers the latter. Some institutional structures are still in the making, following the entry into force of the Lisbon Treaty, notably the European External Action Service (EEAS). Others have so far only started to define their role and functions, which reflects the fact that the Lisbon Treaty 'often does little more than sketch the broad outlines, leaving the details to be filled in at a later date' (Duke 2008). This will be 'work in progress' for several years to come. In the following, the new structures are discussed when appropriate, and to the extent that the potentials and challenges facing them can be discerned for the time being.

The massive institutionalisation of the CSFP/CSDP may be seen to reflect the high level of ambition that the Member States have had for this policy area. Yet some would say that the focus has been misplaced and, indeed, that this is typical of the EU. However, relatively speaking, all of the institutional apparatus involved in the CSDP, including those parts which are found within the Commission, remains small when compared with other parts of the EU. Moreover, the desire and willingness to create new structures cannot only be attributed to the Union's supposed bureaucratic tendencies, but also need to be seen as practical attempts to alleviate the problems and shortcomings associated with the decision-making procedures and the largely dysfunctional pillar structure. This is reflected in the fact that where competencies appear to overlap between units, as we shall see below, they tend to diversify tasks and develop different areas of expertise between them. Yet part of the reason for the lack of rationalisation of the institutional structures has also been that a major revision of voting rules and institutions to accommodate enlargement has been awaited, so that the focus has rather been on how adding new institutions could solve more immediate problems of policy overload and lack of leadership (Howorth 2007: 67). That said most of the institutional apparatus did survive the Lisbon Treaty.

However, at least for the area of foreign policy, one element that did not survive was the system of leadership by rotating national Presidencies, an arrangement widely recognised as inefficient and overtly susceptible to national politicisation. It has been argued that the rotating Presidency has been an important mechanism for bringing different issues to the fore (van Staden *et al.* 2000: 12). Yet it effectively left the EU with three foreign ministers, insofar as the Member State holding the Presidency of the Council for six months at a time shared responsibility for external representation with the Commissioner for External Relations and the High Representative for the CFSP (HR-CFSP).

The Lisbon Treaty changed this in two important respects. First, the establishment of the post of High Representative of the Union for Foreign Affairs and Security Policy replaces the role of the national Presidency as the official driver for and voice of the CFSP/CSDP. The powers of the new permanent President of the European Council, to be elected for a term of two and a half years, renewable once, are to be exercised *without prejudice* to the extended powers of the High Representative, who is essentially in charge of carrying out the CFSP/CSDP (TEU art. 15.6). After Lisbon, the permanent President prepares and chairs the European Council, the High Representative presides over the new Foreign Affairs Council (FAC), while the rotating national Presidency chairs the General Affairs Council (GAC). There is, as such, a point to be made about the rotating Presidency, which is, in fact, not abolished at all, as some have been led to think. Despite the Lisbon Treaty's rather clear division of labour between the Presidency and the High Representative, subsequent holders of the Presidency have also appeared reluctant to leave the CSDP alone. The Belgian Presidency (second half of 2010) kicked off by organising a seminar on Permanent Structured Cooperation in July 2010, in which a joint Position paper by Belgium, Hungary and Poland was presented, while Poland had the CSDP high on the agenda when it took on the Presidency in July 2011. The small to medium Member States do not, in other words, appear ready to give up the agenda-setting role that the rotating Presidency ensured, although the right to speak on behalf of the Union in foreign policy has been taken away.

The second key innovation of the Lisbon Treaty with regards to foreign policy leadership was the merging of the posts of Commissioner for External Relations and the old HR-CFSP. By merging the two posts – the new High Representative of the Union for Foreign Affairs and Security Policy is now also the First-Vice-President of the Commission – the intention was to improve coordination and ensure consistency between the external policies of the Council and the Commission. However, this formula does not really amount to a merger of two positions, but attributes instead to one and the same person the exercise of two functions – i.e. a *personal union* (see Grevi *et al.* 2004: 4; Norheim-Martinsen 2008). It is questionable how much impact a double-hatting will have on practical coordination, since responsibilities and institutional structures, for the most part, remain separate. While formally expanding the powers of the High Representative, it mercilessly subjects this person to an inevitable conflict of interests and loyalty. This is readily observed in Lady Catherine Ashton's frantic shuttle diplomacy between the Commission, the Parliament and the Council in her first years as High Representative, and may partly explain her relative absence on the global scene during this time. It may simply be too big a job to be handled by one person. I shall return to this in the next section.

In the end, the Lisbon Treaty does not really clarify the blurring of lines of responsibility between the Commission and the Council, which has been a consistent source of tension since the establishment of the CFSP/CSDP. Some of the grudges on the Commission side may also be partly justified insofar as the CFSP/CSDP has led to a gradual 'second pillarization' of parts of the Union's external relations portfolio.

Treaty-given responsibilities have shifted from the Commission to the Council, for example in the area of civil protection. This also has an accountability side to it. The removal of responsibilities away from the Commission means removing policies further away from the scrutiny of the European Parliament. The build-up of the new European External Action Service (EEAS) has left the Parliament with more influence over what is bound to become an influential part of the EU's external relations portfolio, since it controls the EEAS budget. However, in general the Parliament's role in CFSP/CSDP matters remains weak.

Further to the accountability issue, some findings suggest that national parliaments have been given little room to scrutinise government decisions pertaining to the CSDP in particular. When looking into the EU's first military missions, operations *Concordia* in Macedonia and *Artemis* in the Democratic Republic of Congo (DRC), Giovanna Bono found that some governments had informed national parliaments only after the decision to launch an operation had been made in the European Council. She also found that some governments used the pretext of lack of time and different forms of urgency procedures to bypass national parliaments (Bono 2005).[5] Such practices may have improved the efficiency of the CSDP, but arguably at the cost of legitimacy. Still, the most pressing concern has been to *reach* decisions, as reflected in the establishment of several bodies and posts whose principal task has been to facilitate a consensual environment amongst the Member States.

The most influential in this respect has been the Political and Security Committee (PSC), which was permanently set up in 2001. As described in the Treaty of Nice (art. 25), the PSC is tasked with monitoring international developments in the area of the CFSP, contributing towards defining EU policies by delivering opinions to the Council, monitoring implementation of policies, and exercising full political and strategic control of crisis management operations. The potential overlap with the Committee of Permanent Representatives (COREPER), which was previously tasked with preparing all Council meetings, was solved after the renaming of the GAC to GAERC (FAC after Lisbon) by the 2002 Seville Council and the separation into the 'internal' and 'external' agendas of the Council, the preparation for which is now roughly divided between the COREPER and the PSC respectively. The significant influence of the PSC is rooted both in the fact that it received wide treaty-given rights and authorities, and that it consists of high-level permanent representatives from each of the Member States. This has provided considerable room for a collective work-form amongst senior diplomats with due access to all the information, proposals, views and initiatives relating to a given issue, to emerge, which, in turn, has earned the PSC such labels as the 'linchpin' and 'workhorse' of the CFSP/CSDP (see Duke 2005; Meyer 2006). As such, the PSC and the individuals who inhabit it score high on key network indicators, such as central placement in the structure, direct access to decision-making, access to and control of information, and trust received from other key actors in the network (i.e. their own governments and their fellow equally connected PSC colleagues).

There was, as described by Jolyon Howorth, some initial disagreement on the level of seniority of the national representatives, but in later years the PSC has been made up of mostly senior officials who are well connected in their home capitals (Howorth 2007: 68–71). Being national ambassadors, this is where their loyalties are. Yet as permanent residents in the Justus Lipsius building, meeting at least twice a week, the PSC ambassadors have, according to Christoph Meyer, developed into 'an unusually cohesive committee with a club atmosphere, high levels of personal trust and a shared "esprit de corps"' (Meyer 2006: 124). The findings of Duke (2005), Howorth (2007), Meyer (2006) and Juncos and Reynolds (2007), which are based on interviews with PSC ambassadors going back to the first and second generation of envoys, all point towards the formation of a collective interest in and a commitment to finding common grounds for consensus.[6] This follows in a tradition that, as Simon Nuttall documented already in 1992, goes back to the European Political Cooperation (EPC) period:

> The consensus rule does not, as some claim, reduce the policy of the Twelve to the lowest common denominator; rather it tends to encourage a median line. The reason for this is the dynamism of the discussion in the Political Committee and to a lesser extent in the Ministerial Meetings ... This is not surprising, given the club atmosphere and the predisposition of the diplomats to regard the failure to agree as the worst of outcomes. (Nuttall 1992: 314)

The PSC and its forerunner have, therefore, had a rather practical consensus-*shaping* role at the heart of a growing policy network. Despite the more proactive policy-*making* role that was envisioned for it (especially by the French), Howorth's findings also suggest that 'it works best in what is considered its "core business" – the planning, preparation and oversight of operations, whether civilian or military' (Howorth 2007: 71). In so doing, it receives advice from the European Union Military Committee (EUMC), which was created alongside the PSC in 1999 and is composed of the Member States' Chiefs of Defence Staff (CHOD), usually attended by their Military Representatives (MILREP).[7] There is also the Committee for Civilian Aspects of Crisis Management (CIVCOM), which deals with exactly what its name suggests, but this body reports formally to the COREPER, which places it somewhat on the side of the CFSP/CSDP. However, it does also receive instructions from and share information with the PSC when necessary for coordinating civilian and military aspects of crisis management operations. The EUMC's chief task is to offer to the Council, via the PSC, its *unanimous* advice on all military matters, including recommendations for action. As such, it has a function and collective work-form, especially amongst the MILREPs, similar to the PSC, ultimately enabling the Member States to commit forces to and carry out military operations (Howorth 2007: 74). The EUMC is, in turn, supported by a permanent European Union Military Staff (EUMS) of some 200 officers from the Member States who work under the political and military direction of the PSC and the EUMC. Amongst other tasks, which are dealt with more thoroughly in Chapter 3, it supports the PSC in carrying out its key function, which is the largely practical and collective effort made by the ambassadors towards coordinating the Member States on issues pertaining to all phases of an operation.

Another Council body with strong connections to Member State governments is the Policy Planning and Early Warning Unit (Policy Unit), which was established together with the post of High Representative for CFSP (HR-CFSP) in 1999. Despite being placed within the Secretariat, which is supposed to be neutral, the Policy Unit has been described as the most politically connected part of the CFSP institutions (interview with Council Secretariat official, May 2003). It is staffed by one diplomat from each Member State and was, as former Policy Unit representative and current head of the joint EU Situation Centre (SITCEN), William Shapcott, described it:

intended as a nucleus of support for Solana, of policy-oriented officials with links to their national diplomatic services who could supply him with information, with advice – both inputs from those countries but also independent advice as they developed their own contacts working on his behalf. (Shapcott 2004)

Both when it comes to tasks and work-form, the Policy Unit appears to have a similar role to the PSC. They both coordinate national preferences and offer advice to the Council either directly or via the High Representative, and they have developed tight personal relationships amongst themselves and a collective work-form.[8] Yet, whereas the PSC's tasks are mostly practical and related to the conduct of civilian and military operations, the Policy Unit engages more in monitoring, analysis and long-term planning. As such, it can be seen as sort of a laboratory for the future of the CFSP/CSDP, albeit with the essential precondition of being tightly connected with national capitals. As one official put it: 'We have all got lists with right phone numbers on them' (interview with Council Secretariat official, May 2003). In addition, the Policy Unit used to play an important role in ensuring that the Presidency stuck to the agenda and maintaining continuity, or as remarked: 'Should long-term planning be left to the Presidency, which may follow its own national agenda? Is that the way to harmonise views? No!' (interview with Council Secretariat official, May 2003). Further to this last point, interviewees report in general that they do feel that the Member States welcome and trust their advice and that the Policy Unit has a real impact on the Council's agenda. As such, the Policy Unit scores high on many of the same network indicators as the PSC, but lacks the latter's formal role as a gatekeeper for the political decisions that go to the Council. In return, the Policy Unit controls the day-to-day working agenda of the Council Secretariat, and is also allowed to play a more proactive, entrepreneurial role.

However, one concern that has been raised is that some of the new Member States have tended to send diplomats without the seniority needed to ensure the direct contact with and trust in the Member States that are required for information to run freely between Brussels and the national capitals (interview with Council Secretariat official, May 2006). Another concern is the increase in workload due to enlargement, and the expansion of issues that are dealt with by the Policy Unit. During the debates leading up to the Constitutional Treaty, some envisioned that an expanded Policy Unit should form the core of a service reminiscent of a national Foreign Office, but at the time it was decided to keep the unit small despite the increase in workload, so that it could retain what had been its most important role and asset, which was to work as the hub of a network with direct and deep contacts within the Member States.

In addition, during the formative first ten years of the CSDP, the unit performed an important service for the HR-CFSP, to whom it reported directly, and helped consolidate Solana's role as 'Mr CFSP'. This particular role for the Policy Unit has already changed with the establishment of the new post of High Representative and the new European External Action Service (EEAS), into which the unit has now merged. In any case, the Policy Unit would only represent half a personal cabinet for the High Representative, whereas the other half would have to come from the Commission. How this is to be solved – and, indeed, how powerful a personal tool for Lady Ashton the EEAS will eventually become – still remains to be seen.

The Solana legacy: the changing power of individuals in the CSDP

In the Convention leading up to the Constitutional Treaty the idea – strangely familiar after five years of Solana in office – was that having a dedicated individual lead in foreign policy would help ensure greater visibility, efficiency, coherence and consistency in the Union's external relations. The original title of Union Minister for Foreign Affairs was scrapped together with the Constitutional Treaty. But the Lisbon Treaty, nevertheless, added the role of First-Vice-President of the Commission, a right of initiative, a right of representation and a responsibility for implementation to the role that Javier Solana had carved for himself during his ten years in office (TEU art. 27).

At first, the decision to establish the position of a HR-CFSP back in 1996/1997 followed a French proposal for the creation of a ministerial level figure that would ensure continuity, table policies and represent the Union to the outside world (Grevi *et al.* 2004: 2). Yet in the end, largely because of British opposition, the role of the HR was restricted to: assisting the presidency 'in matters coming within the scope of the common foreign and security policy'; contributing towards the 'formulation, preparation and implementation of policy decisions'; and engaging in political dialogue 'when appropriate and acting on behalf of the Council at the request of the Presidency' (was TEU arts. 18 & 26). The HR was to act also as Secretary General of the Council, with emphasis on the latter function. He/she was intended to fill the role of an administrator, while the role of policy initiator was initially played down. However, when the time came for choosing an individual to fill the post in 1999, some of the Member States, amongst them Britain who had come to reconsider its stance on the CSDP at Saint-Malo in December 1998, now recognised the need for a high-profile politician rather than a diplomatic or ambassadorial figure to push the process on. The choice fell on Javier Solana, a former NATO Secretary General and Spanish Foreign Minister (Crowe 2003: 538).

The HR was given few resources to begin with, but the rather loose job description left considerable wriggle room for Solana, who was also appointed Secretary General of the Western European Union (WEU). He gradually carved a stronger role for the HR, leaving the daily business of the Council to his Deputy, while devoting his own attention to the CFSP. Through institutional reforms he also placed himself at the centre of an expanding policy network. He had the Policy Unit, SITCEN and the EUMS report directly to him; he was appointed Head of the European Defence Agency (EDA); and he was, as former NATO Secretary General, trusted and respected in most European capitals and, therefore, gradually given more leeway to act on behalf of the Union. A first showcase of the added role that Solana could play came with the crisis in Macedonia in 2001, which was defused with the help of the shuttle diplomacy by Solana and NATO Secretary General at the time, George Robertson, which led to the signing of the Ohrid peace agreement on 13 August 2001. Solana also played a central role, together with Chris Patten, at the time EU External Relations Commissioner, in encouraging democratic opposition against Slobodan Milosevic in Serbia, and he later repeated the feat by extending early EU support for the peaceful revolutions in Georgia and the Ukraine.

However, in other areas Solana's impact was dwarfed by one-upmanship and the search for short-term prestige by successive holders of the rotating Presidency, most recently in the crisis in Georgia in September 2008, which turned out to be a one-man show with a hyperactive French President Sarkozy at the reigns. As Brian Crowe also points out with regard to the EU's role in the Middle East, for example, it was neither the Presidency nor the Member States that pushed Solana forward, but rather a personal invitation from the Egyptian president to attend the breakthrough Sharm el Sheikh summit in 1999.[9] It seems a fair judgement, therefore, that 'Solana's role, while increasing, [was] somewhat chequered, expanding incrementally and against rather than with Brussels' (Crowe 2003: 542).

On the other hand, Solana did get a lot of publicity, seemingly answering a need in the media for a recognisable EU face and voice. The way that journalists routinely referred to him as the EU foreign policy *chief* was an exaggeration by any standards, but it nonetheless contributed towards consolidating his presence and weight in the political landscape. Solana also played a key role as a political entrepreneur, and by giving the EU a voice in world affairs by helping to reinvent and reproduce an EU strategic narrative.

As discussed in Chapter 2, Solana and his team were instrumental in the process that eventually led to the adoption of the 2003 European Security Strategy (ESS). This was far from a minor accomplishment. The ESS was produced and agreed upon surprisingly quickly, as well as being clearer, shorter and refreshingly free from the bureaucratic jargon that one would perhaps have expected. This would arguably not have been possible without the individual and institutional capacities that had been built over the latter years. By 2003, the Member States had gradually grown accustomed to receiving strategic advice from Solana and his Policy Unit in the form of Policy Option Papers (POPs). Hence, as Alyson Bailes sums up, by 2003 they were 'familiar with the idea of "strategies", and they were looking (more and more exclusively) to Solana and his team to produce them' (Bailes 2005: 8). The drafting was kept under close control by a small team of Solana's associates, headed by one of his most trusted advisors, Robert Cooper, Director General for Politico-Military Affairs in the Council Secretariat. After a run-up, in which the Member States and the Commission were heavily involved, the final document was then adopted without difficulty at the Council meeting in Brussels on 12 December 2003. What stands out from the way that the ESS came about is the novelty and, indeed, efficiency of the process, which represented a 'working style' that went far beyond the traditional intergovernmental procedures of the Council.

A central element of this working style has been to personalise responsibility for specific regions or policy areas. This resulted, in turn, in a steadily growing team of specialist diplomats who answered directly to Solana. Indeed, Solana was reported to favour personal relations over institutions, while his working style was described as refreshingly hands-on – as in non-bureaucratic (interview with Council

Secretariat Official, May 2006). During his time in office, the European Council appointed nine EU Special Representatives (EUSRs), in addition to three Personal Representatives for Solana and a coordinator for anti-terrorist activities.

The impact and role of some of the EUSRs in particular is interesting when it comes to the role of individual agency in the CFSP/CSDP. The purpose of the EUSRs has been to provide the EU with permanent representation in troubled regions and countries, to channel information, and 'to play an active part in promoting the interests and the policies of the EU' (European Council 2005b). However, their mandates have differed in accordance with the political context for each deployment. The EUSR in Bosnia-Herzegovina, for example, was tasked with coordinating civilian and military CSDP operations with Commission activities – a rather unforgiving task, but typical of EU ad hocery, whereby one hoped that the personal skills of the charismatic Lord Ashdown, the first EUSR in Bosnia, could help bridge the institutional divide between the Union's respective activities on the ground.[10] In this particular instance, Ashdown as holder also of the Office of the High Representative (OHR), established by the Dayton Peace Agreement, carried forward the authority to impose legislation and sack elected officials, which he did, prompting the resignation of the Bosnian Serb Prime Minister in 2004 (see *Financial Times* 2004). Interestingly, Ashdown had sacked officials before in his capacity as High Representative, but it was not until he was appointed EUSR that the mix of roles was criticised. Despite the fact that Ashdown, through his proactive style, managed to push through much-needed reforms in Bosnia, the way he exercised his powers was pointed out as being problematic for an organisation such as the EU, which prides itself on exporting values such as democracy, human rights and rule of law (David Chandler and Misha Glenny quoted in House of Commons 2005: 63–64). As High Representative and later EUSR, Ashdown carried out his authority much like a traditional Colonial Governor General, whereas other EUSRs have resembled more UN special envoys than policy initiators.[11]

With the establishment of the European External Action Service (EEAS), half of the 11 EUSRs have or will eventually disappear, as their functions are taken on by EU Ambassadors in the country delegations. The remaining EUSRs are still under review. Overall, the EEAS is expected 'to give the EU a stronger voice around the world, and greater impact on the ground' (*Wall Street Journal* 2010). However, a number of questions remain as to role (policy initiator or implementer), composition, accountability (to the Council, or to the Commission and the Parliament), financing, appointments, rotation schemes, etc. As the EU develops its own diplomatic service – and with it the inherent career paths, bureaucracy, norms, rules and procedures of the traditional national diplomatic services – there is a danger of losing some of the inherent dynamism and flexibility that often characterised CFSP diplomacy in the Solana era. Consistency in EU external representation is bound to improve with one EU diplomatic service, but potentially at the cost of individual entrepreneurship and political initiative.

Personalisation of responsibility has to some extent left room for individual characteristics to define the way that the CFSP/CSDP has been carried out. This may at times pose a problem for continuity. Yet dedicated individuals may also be the ones to infuse the organisation with proactiveness by sticking their neck out, tabling proposals, creating trust and grasping opportunities when they appear (see Hermann *et al.* 2001). In his analysis of bargaining power in the European Council, Jonas Tallberg argues that individual characteristics of state leaders do play a considerable role when it comes to decision-making in the Council (Tallberg 2008). Prime Minister of Luxembourg Jean-Claude Juncker, for example, is frequently described as one who commands great respect and authority, 'because of his long time in the European Council, his extreme experience and competence, his capacity to put European interests before national (of which there are few) and his networking abilities and close relationship with especially German and French leaders' (Tallberg 2008: 700). As such, state leaders and centrally placed people within the organisation may punch above their weight, often setting the agenda by wielding their personal authority and expertise.

Political weight, in other words, sometimes rests more with the person who wields it than with the formal powers of office, which begs the question what kind of political authority Lady Ashton brings to the table as Solana's successor as High Representative. The position of HR-CFSP/Secretary-General of the Council Secretariat, when established in 1997, was an administrative one on paper, but one to be filled by a political heavyweight in the end. In contrast, the expansion of authorities and powers of the new post has not, most commentators agree, been met by an equally powerful political figure to match it.

Solana was trusted and well known to the Member States as former NATO Secretary General, and displayed a particular interest in developing the military dimension of the CSFP. In contrast, Lady Ashton's background as EU Commissioner and her lack of experience from security and defence politics come across as more 'inward' looking. She has appeared more intent on laying the groundwork for internal EU consistency and coherence than on pushing the CSDP agenda, although it should be pointed out that until she gets the EEAS fully up and running, Lady Ashton is virtually filling two jobs without a staff to help her. However, she did receive due criticism for failing to attend the first meeting of European defence ministers, in Palma de Mallorca in February 2010, after she took office in November 2009. French Defence Minister Hervé Morin was quoted as saying: 'Isn't it rich that this morning, to display the ties between NATO and the EU, we have the NATO Secretary-General here but not the High Representative for the first meeting since the Lisbon Treaty came into effect' (quoted in *The Times* 2010). Instead she attended the inauguration of Ukrainian President Viktor Yanukovych, which again illustrated the inevitable overstretch of having one person fill two jobs.

However, it also illustrated the blurred division of competencies between the High Representative and the new permanent President of the European Council. It was pointed out that either the latter or the President of the Commission could have gone to the Ukraine, leaving Lady Ashton to chair the symbolically important first defence summit after her taking office. Some form of division of labour in external representation seems almost inevitable in the future, although the Lisbon Treaty is not very clear on this point. As such, it will constitute a latent source of tension over leadership in the years to come, although the choice of former Belgian Prime Minister Herman Van Rompuy as the first permanent President of the European Council seems to confirm a desire for a predominantly administrative role for the post – at least for the time being. Having established his reputation as a 'builder of impossible compromises' in Belgian politics (Mevel 2009), Mr Van Rompuy has a distinctively low-key profile when compared to some of the other candidates that were mentioned for the job, such as Tony Blair, Felipe Gonzáles and Jean-Claude Juncker.

In the end, it is probably safe to say that despite the enhanced powers of the new posts created by the Lisbon Treaty, the Member States opted for two political figures – some would call them 'lightweights' – with reputations as consensus builders rather than as grand visionaries to fill them. This may also reflect the general mood towards the CSDP amongst some of the Member States after a period of heavy activity. That said, even if he was a more visible leader, Solana several times during his ten years in office expressed a keen awareness of the limits of his office vis-à-vis the Member States. In his own words: 'Sometimes you have to know the limits of what you have, and sometimes that means disappearing at the right time' (*International Herald Tribune* 2006). For a while, it was even suggested that the frequency of Solana's media appearances more than anything else reflected the level of agreement amongst the big EU-3 – France, Britain and Germany.

The impact of big and small Member States on the CSDP

Investing in strong international institutions is often seen as a way for small states to control the actions of bigger states (see e.g. Keohane and Martin 1995). However, it is a balancing act, since if institutional constraints are too narrow it may lead to a situation where the big states decide that their interests are better served by way of bilateral relations or concert-like cooperation with other big states (Wiwel 2005: 405). As such, a strengthening of institutions is no guarantee against great power dominance. The solution may be for the smaller states to grant the big states additional weight, as in the UN Security Council, but aiming to leave as much power as possible in the hands of a body in which they, in principal, have equal opportunities to affect decisions, as in the UN General Assembly. However, in the CSDP most decisions still have to be made by consensus, and there is no equal to the Security Council, at least not formally.

The persistent attempts to modify the consensus rule covered at the start of the chapter are all meant to increase the efficiency of the decision-making process, but also to serve as a guarantee against big state directorates inside the Union, since a coalition of big Member States alone cannot reach the threshold of eight required for 'enhanced cooperation'. In reality, especially when it comes to the CSDP, big countries have a much better chance of influencing a decision than the smaller states, since only they have the capabilities to see that they are implemented (Wiwel 2005: 402). This should hardly come as a surprise to anyone. Most of the major steps in the history of the CFSP (and EPC before that) have relied, to a large extent, on the initiative and collective efforts of the big EU-3. However, in the past, great power cooperation was arguably more covert, whereas in later years a more formalised role for the EU-3 seems to have become more commonplace as well as accepted by the smaller Member States, to the extent that some talk about the consolidation of a *directoire* model (Hill 2004; Gegout 2002). Some of the following examples may serve to illustrate these developments.

Looking back, the 11 September 2001 terrorist attacks may have represented a turning point in relations between the EU-3 and the rest of the Member States. In the first months of the Afghan campaign, leaders of the EU-3 met on at least two occasions (on 19 October and 4 November) to coordinate military support to the United States, deliberately and openly keeping the other EU Member States at arm's length (see Wiwel 2005: 403). The leaders of Italy, Spain and the Netherlands, and the Belgian Presidency and Solana, were eventually invited to join the meeting in November, but only after considerable political pressure. The deliberate omission of the EU also prompted eight Member States to launch a complaint to Commission President Romano Prodi, who supported them, but in the end no action was taken. When the Belgian Presidency tried to restore unity by announcing on 14 December that the EU would send a multinational force to Afghanistan, the UK and Germany were quick to stress that it was an international force with contributions from some EU Member States, but that it did not involve a formal role for the EU.

Only a year later, the controversy over Iraq was to momentarily shatter the image of the EU-3 (see Chapter 2). Again the debates were kept outside EU structures. Ambassadors in the PSC, which would normally engage with this kind of crisis, received 'very strict instructions' from their home capitals to keep Iraq off the agenda (see Howorth 2007: 68), to the visible annoyance of many of the smaller Member States.

As a third case in the wake of 9/11, Iran spurred a renewed initiative by the EU-3, but one that did not stir the same degree of resistance from the other Member States. Desperate to avoid another war in the region, the British, French and German foreign ministers visited Tehran on 21 October 2003, ten days before the UN Security Council was to discuss further sanctions. During their visit, the EU-3 upheld the EU's offer of a Trade and Cooperation Agreement (TCA) if Iran complied with the demands of the International Atomic Energy Agency (IAEA). So, even if the EU-3 acted independently of the EU, thus avoiding normal

CFSP procedures, they did act within the parameters of the Union's long-standing policy of 'constructive engagement' towards Iran, and with the implicit support of the rest of the EU Member States. Solana was also brought onboard, and, following his first visit to Tehran in January 2004, he soon filled the role as a mediator in the dialogue between the EU and Iran (see e.g. Carbonell 2004). In the end, a '3+1' model, avoiding the cumbersome procedures of the Council, yet keeping it informed through Solana, seemed to work fine at least as long as the rest of Europe were happy with the way things were handled (Allen and Smith 2005).[12] However, it was remarked with regard to the EU's offer of trade concessions that it is normally not up to the EU-3 to give away what belongs to 27 (interview with Council Secretariat official, May 2006).

In the long run, the smaller Member States are unlikely to approve of being reduced to passive bystanders, even if the bigger Member States de facto are seen to control the CFSP/CSDP. Member States such as Italy and Spain, and perhaps an aspiring power like Poland, would be loath to see a formal *directoire* established without them, especially after they became part of the informal group of six (G6) on internal security matters (see e.g. *Deutsche Welle* 2006). Indeed, as events unravelled in Lebanon during the summer of 2006, Italy was quick to assume a leading role when President Chirac failed to deliver on his initial promise of 2,000 troops to the UN peacekeeping force (UNIFIL II). Moreover, when faced with this new peak in the conflict, the unity of the EU-3 seemed to crumble again. France, with the support of most of the other EU Member States, was critical of Israel's military offensive and demanded an immediate ceasefire. Britain and Germany, the latter traditionally cautious over criticising Israel and eager to mend its ties with the United States, sided with Washington, DC and refused to condemn the attack. Moreover, Solana, who reportedly entered into a flurry of phone diplomacy with Middle East leaders before flying to Lebanon at the height of the crisis, found his hands tied by the Finnish Presidency, which refused to let him negotiate on behalf of the Union (see e.g. *The Economist* 2006; *United Press International* 2006).

After several delays, the EU Member States did manage to act as one bloc on this issue. In an emergency meeting of European foreign ministers on 25 August 2006, the Member States acknowledged the need for a strong European presence in Lebanon and promised 6,900 soldiers to the 15,000 strong UNIFIL II force, with substantial contributions from

Italy (3,000 troops), Spain (1,000 to 1,200) and Poland, adding 500 to its existing troops, with promises of more to come if needed. France managed to save face by adding 2,000 troops to its already existing 400, but handed over command of the force to Italy in February 2007. Hence, three aspiring EU powers, Italy, Spain and Poland, suddenly found themselves in the driver's seat in the Middle East, saving the day after the EU-3 failed to assume leadership when a crisis mounted in a region referred to as one of the topmost priority areas for the Union (see European Council 2003d).

On the one hand, this showed again that Europe cannot always trust the EU-3 to provide it with efficient external leadership, even in a situation where the Member States for the most part see eye to eye. On the other, it showed that other Member States may be able and willing to step up if and when the EU-3 fails to do so. This ability to appear in different configurations, sometimes referred to as *variable geometry*, has been seen by some as a central asset of the EU.[13] More variable geometry can also create an intra-European dynamic where different states are induced to take the lead within the stronger EU bloc rather than going it alone – and get their reward in receiving ownership of EU foreign policy.

Still, when military action is required, capabilities will often be decisive for the kind of influence a Member State wields over a policy decision. The smaller states have the most to offer when it comes to trade, aid and diplomacy, but will rarely be able to mount, let alone sustain, a military operation without the involvement of the EU-3, even if they should get the go-ahead to do so (see Chapter 6). A heavier focus on military capabilities will necessarily tip the scales in favour of the bigger states. We see, therefore, that despite the relative strengthening of the CSDP institutions, the relative influence of the smaller states on security and defence policy appears to have diminished over time.

As far as the other option – variable geometry – is concerned, opportunities are quite limited for some. Small states, or institutional actors such as the High Representative and the EUSRs, are allowed to play the game only when it does not conflict with the national interests of the EU-3, who in turn expect loyalty when they take the initiative, or else they take their business outside the institution.[14] In addition, several studies suggest that the small states will lose an important source of influence on Council decisions with the weakening of the rotating Presidency, due to their loss of various privileges of the chair, such as control of the agenda, access to information and procedural control (Bunse 2006; Elgström 2003; Tallberg 2003a, 2004, 2006, 2008; Thompson 2008). In other words, the loss of the formal role and prestige that holding the Presidency offers is probably less dramatic than the loss of the informal source of influence that being at the 'hub' of a network structure ensures, even if only temporarily. Despite the short terms, the rotating Presidency has offered a chance for the smaller states to learn the ropes of the Council, which may increase their chances of informally wielding their influence in the longer run, because they know who the influential (hubs of) actors are.

This is partly why many of the smaller Member States were against capping the powers of the rotating Presidency in the first place (Bunse *et al.* 2005). This is also why, as mentioned above, Member States who have held the rotating Presidency after the entry into force of the Lisbon Treaty have continued to try to set the CSDP agenda. This may not pose a problem, insofar as initiatives are coordinated with the High Representative, but it adds to the general confusion over foreign policy leadership in the EU, which was one of the key things that the Lisbon Treaty was, indeed, meant to clarify.

Concluding remarks

The aim of this chapter has been to assess if the EU has developed a capacity for collective interest formation that may sustain efficient and legitimate security policy-making. It has shown that the image of an intergovernmental decision-making polity, in which all decisions at some point need to pass a unanimous vote in the Council, should be modified to incorporate the role of institutional and even individual actors. The final decisions are mostly intergovernmental, but the processes that enable them are better described as those of an informal governance structure. That is why the EU has proved itself as a far more potent decision-maker, even in the area of security and defence, than having 27 veto-wielding Member States might suggest. Bearing in mind the inherent constraints of being a collective of independent states, the EU, therefore, fulfils our first criterion for a strategic actor, insofar as informal structures and procedures allow it to strike a balance between efficiency and legitimacy.

Beyond the formal intergovernmental procedures, the centralised institutions play a key role in facilitating consensus, creating trust and tabling proposals. The recipe has been to establish tight working relations amongst permanent national representatives in the PSC and the Policy Unit (and COREPER). Findings suggest that these representatives, when interacting and socialising over time, cease to be mere agents of national interests and develop a collective stake in reaching common grounds for agreement. Their influence has been secured through central placement, direct access to decision-makers in the Council and other key players such as the Council Presidency and the High Representative, privileged access to information, control of the agenda, the ability to suggest policy options on their own initiative, and a high level of trust in their home capitals. As a result of their privileged position and their interaction with other like-minded individuals in a highly institutionalised environment, they come to represent actors in their own right. That they are not merely socialised into a collective that sees the defence of European interests as its *raison d'état*, but also has considerable informal influence over policy-making, strengthens the 'Brusselsization' thesis.

The gradual move away from a purely intergovernmental system towards more of a governance structure has also given more room for individual agency. Solana especially played a key role as a political entrepreneur and as an EU voice *whenever* he was given room to act. Indeed, personalisation of responsibility in the hands of often high profile diplomats or political figures has become a rather successful way for the EU to deal with problems of coordination and leadership, and to create awareness for specific regions or policy areas. The High Representative, the special coordinators and the EUSRs have until now given the EU considerable flexibility in terms of external representation and presence, while easing problems of coordination between Commission and Council initiatives by letting personal relations make up for the formal lack of coordination.

Nonetheless, the role of Solana was somewhat chequered, expanding against rather than with Brussels. The institutional expansion, of which he was a part, and which he arguably helped engineer and make acceptable, may also be seen to have backfired in the sense that the more the formal powers of institutions are strengthened, the more the real influence of institutions over great power policy is undermined. Whereas until recently, the EU has been careful to avoid the formation of big power directorates, the possibility of taking cooperation outside, together with the strains of enlargement, seem to have re-invoked the idea of a two-speed Europe, as reflected in the inclusion of Permanent Structured Cooperation in the Lisbon Treaty. Various ways of acting on behalf of the EU, either at the formal request of the Council or through concert-like coordination between big EU Member States acting on their own but backed by the other Member States, have proved quite efficient. The smaller states have also been happy with it as long as the EU-3 has stayed within the boundaries of an agreed EU policy, as in the Iran question.

Finally, the gradual expansion of CSDP activities has highlighted the importance of institutional routines in the implementation of policy, which suggests that institutions have an equally important role to play as enablers. This will be addressed in the next chapter.

4 | The institutional link: creating a civil–military organisation fit for purpose

The only thing harder than getting a new idea into the military mind is to get an old one out.

Sir Basil Liddel-Hart

If we recall the third feature of security governance, discussed in Chapter 1, the CSDP has become a highly institutionalised policy area. This makes the exploration of the institutional and administrative capabilities that sustain it a central task in assessing the EU's ability to act in accordance with its strategic interests, however elusive they may be. While there has been considerable focus on the shortcomings in European military capabilities in analyses of the CSDP, few seem to fully appreciate the importance of the institutional capabilities that are essential for its implementation. In strategic terms, institutions can be seen to belong in what Michael Howard (1983b) refers to as the often overlooked logistical dimension of strategy, in the sense that effective institutions enable strategic action. Of course, the trucks, aircraft and helicopters often associated with military logistics are important for the transformation of strategic objectives into actual operations, and will, therefore, be thoroughly covered in the next chapter. But first we need to look into the institutional 'movers' that provide the bridge between interests (ends) and capabilities (means). To a strategist like Colin Gray (1999a), this bridge or link represents the very essence of strategy.

The point of departure for this chapter is that the institutionalised character of the CSDP opens up to the application of more traditional models and approaches found in strategic studies. This may cast a fresh light on the impact of the institutionalisation process on the EU as a strategic actor. Central to this process has been the ambitions towards a Comprehensive Approach, which was discussed in Chapter 2. A Comprehensive Approach is fundamentally dependent on an institutional capacity for integrated civil–military planning.

Looking at the level of integration between civilian and military elements in the CSDP institutional set-up will, therefore, serve as a timely test of the degree to which the EU has developed an organisation that reflects the Comprehensive Approach.

Organising civil–military relations is an area that has occupied strategists and military historians for some time already. The concern has traditionally been how or when political leaders should interfere in the military sphere once a decision to use force has been taken. However, in view of recent conflicts a more pressing concern has been how and when to integrate civilian and military instruments to gain success in contemporary peace operations. This has resulted in an extensive scholarship – and an ongoing debate – within the strategic studies community on how traditional models of organising civil–military relations affect and are adapted to current thinking on how to deal with the complex challenges of today's security environment. However, this perspective is often overlooked by many EU scholars, who, by typically focusing on the novelty and uniqueness of the EU's understanding of a Comprehensive Approach, tend to treat institutional change as a good in itself, even though frequent institutional changes are, as it often turns out, not necessarily to be taken as signs of a healthy civil–military organisation 'fit for purpose' (see Forster 2006: 43).

To situate institutional developments in support of the CSDP in the broader strategic literature on civil–military relations, this chapter discusses two classical models for organising the civil–military interface: Samuel Huntington's so-called 'normal' or stovepipe model (Huntington 1957), and Morris Janowitz's 'constabulary' or integrated model (Janowitz 1960). By tapping into the current debate, it shows that, despite the different original purpose of and context for these models, they are still highly relevant for many of the issues that states – and international institutions like the EU and the UN – are battling with today. The models are then used to assess the numerous attempts to improve civil–military relations at all EU levels. The chapter argues that, for several reasons, the many institutional innovations over the last ten years have largely sustained a 'Huntingtonian' separation of the civil–military interface, despite the stated objective of and efforts made towards developing a more 'Janowitzian' EU 'culture of coordination'. It then moves on briefly to revisit the development of an institutionalised intelligence analysis capacity in the Joint Situation Centre (SITCEN) to see whether this unit can serve as a better 'pathfinder' than, for example, the Civil–Military Planning Cell (CivMilCell) for reconciling the civil–military interface.

Two models for organising the civil–military interface

The traditional point of concern for the management of civil–military relations has been how to create effective military forces under proper civilian control. It has been observed that it is 'extremely difficult [for democracies] to escalate the level of brutality and violence to that which can secure [military] victory' (Merom 2003: 15). This was also Samuel Huntington's concern in his seminal study *The Soldier and the State* (1957), which is still referred to as the 'normal theory' of civil–military relations. Indeed, for almost five decades, Huntington's model represented a blueprint for organising civil–military relations. As such, it has sustained a particular structure and culture underpinning how civil–military relations are approached and organised in most democratic states, while it is only recently that people in the strategic community have started to question the legacy and appropriateness of Huntington's model for the security challenges of today.

If we go back to the roots, the central premise in Huntington's model (1957) is his conception of the military profession as a vocation not dissimilar to, for example, medicine or law, which are all recognised by expertise in a particular area of human affairs, and a sense of belonging and commitment to other members of one's group.[1] As with other vocations, military professionalism is definable, universal and capable of being isolated. In Huntington's view, it is possible to separate military means from political ends. The officers and soldiers ought to represent apolitical servants of the state. Their sole purpose is to fight and win the nation's wars, which is the 'functional imperative' or criterion by which the quality of the armed forces ought to be measured, not the political end for which it fights. Huntington's answer to the question how to create effective armed forces under proper civilian control is, therefore, a strict division of labour between political decision-making and military implementation. He calls this 'objective control', which relies on extensive military professional autonomy over a clear jurisdiction of professional practice, namely the conduct of war. A necessary precondition for effective armed forces under civilian control is, therefore, an ideological as well as physical separation of the military and civilian spheres.

In his book *The Professional Soldier: A Social and Political Portrait* (1960), Morris Janowitz warned against the consequences of this separation. Taking issue with Huntington's view of military professionalism, Janowitz claimed – somewhat ahead of his time – that 'the use of force in international relations has been so altered that it seems appropriate to speak of constabulary forces, rather than of military forces' (Janowitz 1960: 418).[2] This change of role, he argued, added a new set of requirements to the military profession. Proper civilian control and effective use of the armed forces can only be achieved by political integration and education of the officer corps. This cannot be achieved by separation, because of the inevitable political and social impact of the military establishment on civil society. In Janowitz's view, the professional military officer:

is sensitive to the political and social impact of the military establishment on international security affairs. He is subject to civilian control, not only because of the 'rule of law' and tradition, but also because of self-imposed professional standards and meaningful integration with civilian values. (Janowitz 1960: 420)

In place of Huntington's 'objective control' through separation, Janowitz advocated 'subjective control' through integration with civil society. However, his concern was the same as Huntington's – how to create effective armed forces under civilian control. It was not the need for coordination between armed forces, NGOs and a host of different actors on the ground in places like Afghanistan, Iraq or the Democratic Republic of Congo (DRC), a point which could be raised with regard to the appropriateness of using the two models to discuss more current concerns. However, as an ideal type of organising the civil–military interface, Janowitz's model of tight integration to break down cultural barriers between the military profession and the rest of society represents an obvious contrast to Huntington's model. It represents also a wholly different way of thinking about civil–military relations, which has again become relevant in the context of peace and stability operations and the need for comprehensive strategies, planning and command arrangements that incorporate all instruments of power.

In a recent edited volume that discusses Huntington's impact on civil–military thinking in the United States, two of the authors claim:

'Nowhere are the deficiencies of such an approach [i.e. Huntington's] more evident than with respect to stability operations' (Schadlow and Lacquement Jr. 2009: 114). Recent operational experience shows that effective crisis management requires a quick response from flexible teams of people with various professional backgrounds who can address different types of challenges, i.e. filling immediate security gaps, while, at the same time, starting to build local capacity. Civilian instruments cannot simply be 'bolted on' once peace is restored, but need to be involved already in the early phases of planning for an operation. A strict separation of planning and command structures – although Huntington's arguments for such a model were perfectly reasonable in the Cold War context in which they were conceived – has today become an obstacle for the kind of tasks that the military is expected to carry out.

However, while Huntington, and the way in which his arguments have 'colored the military's self-perception for an entire generation' (quotation in Schadlow and Lacquement Jr. 2009), have become a source of considerable debate inside the US strategic community (Barnett 2004; Feaver and Kohn 2001; Nielsen and Snider 2009), these are issues that have received less attention in Europe. In the EU debate, they have been largely absent (however, see Gordon 2006). Still most European states draw on a Huntingtonian model, and retain what Rupert Smith refers to as heavily 'stovepiped' civil–military organisations (Smith 2007; see also Forster 2006). One notable exception is Britain, which is probably the state that most closely resembles the 'Janowitzian' model (Egnell 2006, 2009). This means that even if the EU's origins as a peace project and long history of being a strong civilian power seem to suggest that it is in one way historically predisposed to becoming a comprehensive civil–military actor, the EU idea of developing a 'culture of coordination' is up against a very different type of culture that has dominated civil–military thinking in most of the EU Member States for a generation.

This tension between a traditional civil–military culture with deep roots in the Member States, on the one hand, and an evolving 'in-house' civil–military culture within the Council Secretariat, on the other, explains well the shape and direction that the EU's civil–military organisation has taken. The cultural inclination to think in terms of separation represents a particularly strong path dependency, insofar as 'cultures' are notoriously hard to change (Pierson 2004; see also

Chapter 2 of this book). Developing a particular culture requires, on the other hand, targeted measures that essentially facilitate extensive human interaction over time. However, as this chapter shows, in the EU, certain Member States have used institutional reform rather as a way to push through national agendas, producing frequent but often ineffective institutional change. At the same time, there has been a lack of attention inside the Council Secretariat paid to effective measures for breaking down professional and cultural barriers between civilian and officers, such as co-location and joint exercises.

Flawed by design

One factor needs to be appreciated when looking at the organisation of the civil–military interface in the EU: while the relationship between civil society and the military has traditionally been a central element in the shaping of states, for the EU, military force is, ten years after Saint-Malo, still the odd element out (van Ham 2005). As discussed in Chapter 2, the infusion of a military component into an organisation, whose identity and rationale is nested in the accomplishment of bringing peace to the European continent, presented the Union with a very real clash of organisational cultures. But despite the obvious challenges, adding a military element in itself presented the EU and its Member States with the opportunity of moulding and pursuing a specific type of approach – a *comprehensive* one that did not favour certain policy instruments over others, that was not burdened by out-dated doctrines and ingrained military thinking, and that could start afresh in the build-up of duly integrated planning and command structures (Gordon 2006: 351). The question is whether this has, in fact, been the case.

When military officers started moving about in the Justus Lipsius building in 2000, it marked the introduction of a military culture in the EU, which not only meant that civil servants had to get used to the sight of uniformed personnel on their way to work, but had to start actually interacting with them at different levels. To be able to integrate this new element into the EU machinery, Solana, soon after his appointment as HR-CFSP, stated on several occasions the need to build a 'strong in-house strategic culture'.[3] One of the early steps was to co-locate all crisis management bodies in the Kortenberg building in order to establish a secure environment for them, while providing the physical preconditions for increased interaction between different branches. Part of this co-location exercise included splitting up the Council Secretariat, moving the Directorates dealing with CFSP/CSDP matters in the larger DG-E out of the Justus Lipsius building.

Incidentally, and perhaps symbolically significant, the move separated these units from the 'ordinary' business of the Council Secretariat. It also meant moving them further away from the Commission's premises. The physical separation reflected a very real conceptual and institutional separation of the long-term conflict preventive considerations of the Commission, and the Council's responsibility for short-term crisis management as part of the CFSP. Such a division of labour would, at the outset, appear to be practical, and perhaps unavoidable because of the pillar structure, but drawing such a sharp line has sustained a somewhat artificial separation of areas of responsibility. This has proved a significant challenge for the coordination of conflict preventive and crisis management tools, especially when it comes to areas where competencies are disputed, such as in the area of civil protection (see e.g. Ehrhart and Quille 2007; Gourlay 2006). Although fully appreciating the gravity of the significant challenges posed by this situation, this chapter concentrates on the organisation of the civil–military interface in support of CSDP activities, more specifically the planning for and carrying out of military and civilian operations.

As described in Chapter 3, civilian and military elements are coordinated in the Political and Security Committee (PSC), which provides the overall strategic assessment in a crisis situation, and exercises full political control over CSDP operations. It receives advice from and instructs the European Union Military Committee (EUMC) and the Committee for Civilian Aspects of Crisis Management (CIVCOM), and provides thus a minimum level of coordination by merging the organisational outputs of the two branches. Below the politico-strategic level, the civilian and military 'arms' are divided. Until recently, it has also been a striking feature of the EU's crisis management framework that there has been no clear hierarchy of civilian and military sub-units that correspond to each other and interact – at least not in a formalised manner – at the lower levels. There has been no direct civilian equivalent to the European Union Military Staff (EUMS), which operates under the direction of and reports to the EUMC.

On the civilian side, tasks have been loosely divided on a functional and geographical basis between the Policy Unit and the DG-E, whereas the CIVCOM is formally attached to the COREPER. However, it has started to report more substantially to the PSC in step with the gradual increase in operational activities in the CSDP. In addition to these organisational differences, and perhaps partly due to them, the EUMS has in practice been somewhat on the side of the traditional DG structure, although it is formally an integral part of the Council Secretariat.

Although most people are keen to point out that working relations have improved, interview data indicate that military personnel to a lesser degree than civilian personnel engage in interaction with other units, unless it has occurred within the space of those parts that have targeted civil–military coordination specifically, i.e. the CivMilCell, or when practical operational needs has demanded it (see also Khol 2006: 127). Integration of the civil–military interface in a 'Janowitzian' sense has, therefore, been largely absent below the politico-strategic level in the EU. Part of the reason for this is arguably that:

Whilst Council statements frequently reiterate the requirements for coordinated planning ... it initially failed to create a genuinely 'coherent' structure. Rather it facilitated periodic comings together of what remained essentially separate and parallel planning processes which enjoyed only occasional convergence, particularly during the routine and initial phases of a crisis. (Gordon 2006: 352)

It was not until late 2003 that the Council started taking concrete institutional steps towards more coordination between its civilian and military branches. By then, successive European Councils since 1999, and the Swedish (2001) and Danish (2002) Presidencies in particular, had highlighted the need to do more in this area (see Khol 2006). In November 2003, the Council put forward the concept of Civil–Military Coordination (CMCO) in a paper addressing 'the need for effective co-ordination of the actions of all relevant EU actors involved in the planning and subsequent implementation of the EU's response to the crisis' (European Council 2003b). CMCO must not be confused with CIMIC, which is a militarily derived concept concerned with force protection by way of cooperation with civilian and local authorities on the tactical level, as part of a complex military operation (see Khol 2006: 124–125). The EUMC adopted its own version of CIMIC, heavily influenced by NATO's concept, for EU crisis management operations in 2002 (European Council 2002). CMCO, on the other hand, was envisaged as an internal mechanism and a process for creating a 'culture of coordination' rather than putting 'too much emphasis on detailed structures and procedures' (Khol 2006: 127).

Nevertheless, the period since 2003 has been marked by a number of institutional add-ons to make up for an original structure that is perhaps best described as being 'flawed by design' (or perhaps 'devoid of design'), to borrow a phrase from Amy Zegart (1999). As Radek Khol points out: 'The framework for crisis management efforts was created by the military, while civilian input came later on and did not change the strategic planning approach fundamentally' (Khol 2006: 127). In addition, institutional developments have often resulted from struggles and compromises between the Member States, and have, therefore, reflected other considerations than the desire to create an effective civil–military organisation. This is illustrated in the next section, which gives a brief recapitulation of developments since 2003, while highlighting some of the problems and challenges that the EU has imported to its civil–military organisation along the way.

Reforming the civil–military structures

To be able to plan and conduct its first military operation in Macedonia in 2003, the EU, both for political and structural reasons, had to rely on NATO assets, access to which was secured by the long overdue Berlin Plus agreement in March 2003. In practical terms, operation *Concordia* was carried out with NATO-SHAPE as operational headquarters.[4] An EU Staff Group (EUSG) of nine officers was established, and D-SACEUR was designated EU Operation Commander. Berlin Plus did not provide for a permanent EU presence in NATO-SHAPE, but the EUSG was kept on for lessons learned when *Concordia* was terminated in December 2003, since an EU takeover of NATO's operation SFOR in Bosnia was anticipated. As part of the larger defence package, endorsed by the December 2003 Council and entitled 'European Defence: NATO/EU Consultation, Planning, and Operations', a permanent EU Cell at NATO-SHAPE was also established, while NATO was invited to set up liaison arrangements with the EUMS (European Council 2003c). The EU Cell has grown to some 20 EU officers, while since December 2004, the EU's military operation *EUFOR Althea* in Bosnia has been conducted from NATO-SHAPE.

For mainly political reasons, Berlin Plus was a precondition for the EU to get off its feet militarily in 2003, after the CSDP was declared operational at Laeken in 2001, but it has in many ways hampered the development of an integrated civil–military organisation in support of the CSDP. Due to the physical and conceptual separation below the politico-strategic level, it inevitably pushed the level of coordination upwards to meetings between the Political and Security Committee (PSC) and the North Atlantic Council (NAC). Work in the PSC–NAC channel has, however, been blocked by the conflict between Turkey and Greece over the Cyprus question. Meetings were originally scheduled once a month, but have in reality been less frequent. When they do meet, discussions tend to be limited, while attempts to discuss closer practical collaboration between NATO and the EU are effectively put down by a handful of states. A NATO official reported that the political climate has gradually deteriorated to a stage at which one refrains from entering into debates in the first place rather waiting for a formal objection (interview with NATO official, NATO-SHAPE, May 2006).

On the practical side of things, a situation where a CSDP operation is carried out from within NATO naturally leaves the EU with a limited opportunity to learn from or make adjustments to the operation as it proceeds. Moreover, *EUFOR Althea* has arguably not produced the kind of mutual reinforcement and practical development of EU–NATO relations that were first envisioned. A case in point is that while EU officers have become well integrated at NATO-SHAPE, carrying out their duties as any NATO officer would, contact with the EUMS is limited. According to one EU officer, there is an inherent scepticism in Brussels of anything linked to NATO, while 'there has neither been any evaluation of what the EU has got out of Berlin plus, nor of how relations can be further utilised' (interview with EU officer, NATO-SHAPE, May 2006). NATO has also, on the initiative of D-SACEUR, attempted to set up informal staff-to-staff contact points with the Council Secretariat, but these have been met with scepticism on the part of EU officials (interview with NATO official, NATO-SHAPE, May 2006).

NATO's practical influence upon the EU's approach to the civil–military interface has naturally been significant by virtue of the fact that most EU military officers have considerable experience from the Alliance (Bono 2004). But its legacy has waned in step with the growing emphasis on internal EU civil–military coordination through the

CMCO process since 2003, as further steps were introduced in a second document titled 'Civil-Military Co-ordination: Framework Paper of Possible Solutions for the Management of EU Crisis Management Operations', adopted in May 2006 (European Council 2006a; see also Ojanen 2006).

Albeit having Berlin Plus as framework for *EUFOR Althea* was a political necessity at the time, it has arguably remained a heavy constraint on effective coordination with other EU activities in the region. Reliance on the PSC–NAC channel has been problematic, but it is also clear that the potential for developing closer relations on the working level has been forfeited, and that there has been considerable resistance at the EU institutional level towards cooperation beyond the strictly necessary. There is, as such, both political and bureaucratic forces at play, but the lack of cooperation may also reflect a perceived gap between the strategic concepts of NATO and the EU respectively.

Having initially drawn heavily on NATO's CIMIC approach, the EU's civil–military thinking was first centred on the operational and tactical levels, while lacking a 'strategic' component (Gordon 2006: 351). CMCO raised the awareness of the need to connect civil and military resources along the whole spectrum from strategic planning to actual implementation in response to a crisis, while integrating CIMIC conceptually in the overall CMCO approach (Ehrhart and Quille 2007: 13). Implicitly it also highlighted the paradox of branching out the responsibility for military operational planning and command to another organisation, which operates on a different understanding of civil–military relations altogether. NATO does not have civilian capabilities with which to coordinate, while its approach to CIMIC 'has tended to "instrumentalise" the civil sector in support of a military mission and creates perceived obstacles to more genuinely "holistic" strategy' (Gordon 2006: 348; see also Smith 2007: 396). In this context, developing an autonomous institutional capacity for planning and running CSDP operations made practical sense, although it was political rather than functional imperatives that pushed for institutional change.

The political controversy surrounding the establishment of the EU Civil–Military Planning Cell (CivMilCell) goes back to the informal 'Chocolate Mini-Summit' between France, Germany, Belgium and Luxembourg in April 2003, which was described in Chapter 2, and particularly the French initiative to set up an autonomous EU military operational HQ (OHQ) outside Brussels. The so-called Tervuren-initiative was heavily criticised by Britain, which deemed it an unnecessary duplication of existing structures. As a compromise, the establishment of the CivMilCell was agreed as a part of the above-mentioned defence package endorsed by the December 2003 Council (European Council 2003c).

Although the document made it quite clear that 'NATO is the forum for discussion and the natural choice for an operation involving the European and American allies', it sanctioned the conduct of EU *autonomous* military operations. In such cases, the main option would be 'national HQs, which can be multi-nationalised for the purpose of conducting an EU-led operation' (European Council 2003c: 1–2). This formalised a lead nation principle, which had already been used for the military operation *Artemis* in Congo, which was launched in June 2003 and led from Paris, whereas five national HQs (Britain, France, Germany, Italy and Greece) were identified for use in future operations. The other option was, somewhat defensively worded, the possibility that:

In certain circumstances, the Council may decide, upon the advice of the Military Committee, to draw on the collective capacity of the EUMS, in particular where a joint civil/military response is required and where no national HQ is identified. Once such a decision is taken, the civilian/military cell in the EUMS would have responsibility for generating the capacity to plan and run the operation.

And the document went on to make it perfectly clear: 'This would not be a standing HQ' (European Council 2003c: 2).

To navigate clear of all duplication charges, the document also high-lighted the added value in being able to run joint civil–military opera-tions (Quille *et al.* 2006: 14) However, since the establishment of the CivMilCell and the OpCen were a result of a compromise including France – who really wanted an autonomous military OHQ – the new unit naturally received a heavy military bias, placed as it was inside the EUMS (Gordon 2006: 354). The CivMilCell was developed by mili-tary officers, and by 2006, one year after it was formally established, people on the civilian side regarded it as a definitive military unit, and had yet to be significantly involved in or even informed about its tasks and functions (interviews, Council Secretariat, May 2006).

The military bias was augmented by the fact that in case of a situation where the OpCen was to be actually manned, 'the centre would operate separately from the strategic role of the EUMS, under a designated Operation Commander', but still 'a core staff, essentially "double hatted" from the EUMS, would be required to maintain the necessary level of readiness' (European Council 2003c).[5] As such, the OpCen and the CivMilCell, despite its fairly balanced composition in the end of military and civilian personnel,[6] largely reflected traditional civil–military thinking, in which the civilian side was invited to take part in the military planning process, but de facto given a military support role (Smith 2007: 396–397).

Although there is still uncertainty as to if and when the OpCen will be activated, there is an expectation that it will only be used 'in case of a predominantly military operation' (European Council 2008a). The military component will then be organised, as any military OHQ, in five divisions, including a CIMIC division, and the civilian component will remain under the control of the new Crisis Management and Planning Directorate (CMPD, used to be under the control of DG-E, see below). This means that the agreement on OpCen does not really provide for *integrated* operational planning, merely co-location and prospects for working 'hand in hand', as stated in the Council document (European Council 2008a), while there appears to be a high threshold for invoking the capacity. Of course, civilian and military operations have different operational needs, which need to be reflected in mandates and in planning and command options (Quille *et al.* 2006: 16). There is certainly no need to set up a full military OHQ to run most civilian operations, but one would expect that the OpCen would benefit from having also a permanent civilian 'core staff' to plan for this. This would presumably improve connectivity across the whole spectrum of strategic and operational planning.

The use of the CivMilCell in connection with the planning for the operations in Aceh and Sudan, which involved military observers and advisors, underlined its potential for linking work across the civil–military interface (Hansen 2006: 27). But the operations themselves were not classified as integrated operations, but as civilian missions to be carried out from DG-E, which had after all developed considerable experience over the course of planning and conducting more than 15 highly diverse missions since 2002. But due to lack of established procedures and constant understaffing on the civilian side, there has been limited capacity for turning these experiences into lessons learned (interview, Council Secretariat DG-E, May 2006).

Lowering the threshold for invoking the OpCen capacity could have been a suitable way of pooling resources. As preparations for the OpCen were underway in 2006, people on the civilian side also anticipated that future civilian operations would be able to draw upon the new capacity (interview, Council Secretariat DG-E, May 2006). That proved not to be the case. Instead the Council decided on 18 June 2007 to set up the somewhat ambiguously titled Civilian Planning and Conduct Capability (CPCC). The name of the unit reflected British opposition against giving it formal status as a civilian OHQ, although it has been routinely referred to as such (interview with CPCC official, Council Secretariat, April 2009). Accordingly, it does not have an ordinary planning unit, but it does have a Planning Methodology Unit (consisting of eight people), which assists in the drafting of civilian strategic options and operation plans. Apart from that, it resembles an ordinary OHQ, organised in a Mission Support Unit (13 people) and a Conduct of Operations Unit (39 people), totalling 64 persons.

The CPCC drew on the staff and expertise of DG-E IX (Civilian Crisis Management Directorate), which remained intact for a while, retaining responsibility for political and strategic guidance, but which has now been merged into the Crisis Management and Planning Directorate (CMPD). We shall return to the CMPD below. However, in terms of strengthening the civilian crisis management arm in the CSDP, the CPCC was clearly a step forward. It increased manpower, and established procedures and a suitable physical environment (premises, secure lines of communication, etc.) for planning and conducting civilian operations, which until 2007 had been conducted more or less ad hoc from inside DG-E. It also established a parallel structure to the military chain of command by identifying a Civilian Operation Commander to lead the CPCC, who answers directly to the PSC and the High Representative (Grevi 2007: 38). As such, it went some way towards evening out the initial military bias that had characterised the EU's civil–military organisation from the start.

But at the same time, it confirmed a 'Huntingtonian' separation of the civil–military interface by formalising a system of two chains of command, and by identifying specifically where they were to be bridged, namely at the politico-strategic level in the PSC, and at the level of strategic planning in the CivMilCell (now moved to the CMPD). As such, the Council Secretariat resembled still what Rupert Smith calls a traditional stovepipe structure from the tactical to the strategic, in which, except in particular cases, there is little interaction between the 'pipes' (Smith 2007). The danger is that such a rigid system lacks flexibility and to some degree weakens the incentive for nurturing contacts between the civilians and the military officers.

It is also worth noting that such a strict formalisation of civil–military relations resonates badly with a British 'Janowitzian' approach, which may partly explain its principled stance against many of the institutional add-ons in support of the CSDP. British scepticism is often viewed in context of its 'privileged relationship' with the United States and dismissed as typical Euroscepticism. However, since the change of course in the lead up to Saint-Malo in 1998, Britain has consistently supported the strengthening of the CSDP (see Howorth 2000, 2005). But its focus has been on capabilities rather than on institutions, as reflected in its insistence on strict capability criteria for Permanent Structured Cooperation in the Lisbon Treaty (see Chapter 5). France, on the other hand, has been eager to set up permanent institutions as a means to strengthen the military side of the CSDP. This French drive is often viewed against the background of its ingrained scepticism towards NATO ever since its decision to leave NATO's integrated military structure in 1966. However, France has now reintegrated fully into NATO's military structure, a move initiated in 2009. How this will reflect upon the CSDP still remains to be seen, but it is perhaps worth noting that, whether incidentally of intentionally, the EU's civil–military organisation has come to resemble a French 'Huntingtonian' system of strict separation, and a fairly conservative French approach to civil–military coordination in general (see Ehrhart and Quille 2007; Forster 2006).

As a result, the overall EU civil–military coordination process has been dominated by two parallel objectives or strategies, which are not necessarily mutually exclusive, but may get in the way of each other: one has been the set-up of strong, balanced civilian and military institutions, which are bridged by units with a specified, formal responsibility for civil–military relations, while the other has been the nurturing of a 'culture of coordination' that shall ideally transcend and reduce those formal institutional barriers.

Building a culture of coordination

Being able to work together requires a common perception of challenges and concepts amongst the people involved, a shared situational awareness, and a mutual understanding of and respect for the other side's qualities and responsibilities. In short, things need to make sense, common sense, to everyone involved. Yet the problem is that people with different professional backgrounds are used to different organisational structures (hierarchy vs. network), different ways of solving problems (intuitive vs. analytical), different views on good leadership (authoritarian vs. inclusive), different ways of communicating (accepting orders vs. encouraging discussion), etc. This is why not only civilians and soldiers, but also humanitarian workers and police officers or lawyers may seem to find themselves at odds with each other in crisis management operations. Building a 'culture of coordination' at the EU level, therefore, inevitably means attempting to reconcile inherently different professional cultures. This can hardly be achieved without extensive human interaction.

This point finds support in the fact that once an operation is up and running, people who are engaged in the same theatre of operations tend to work out practical ways of working together.[7] To coordinate the activities of the EU Police Mission (EUPM) and EUFOR *Althea* in Bosnia, for example, people in DG-E VIII and IX and EUMS soon set up weekly informal Core Team Meetings (CTMs), which were supplemented by expanded CTMs including the EU Special Representative (EUSR) and representatives from the Commission. Within these Core Teams, which have since then been routinely set up for other CSDP operations, civil–military coordination has reportedly become a matter of routine, and there are no major difficulties in sharing information and views across institutional boundaries (interviews with Council Secretariat officials, May 2006). As one commentator, quoting an EUMS official working in the CivMilCell, also remarked: 'During a crisis "when people are dying on us", it becomes easier to reach practical arrangements on the ground and in Brussels on how to tackle the situation' (Knutsen 2008: 37). In the event of major challenges, the incentive for working together is stronger and cooperation will often follow naturally. That is not necessarily the case in the early phases of strategic and pre-operational planning, with the result that civil–military coordination often is insufficient.

To counter this, the EU, on Solana's initiative, drafted the concept of *Comprehensive Planning*, inspired by the UN's Integrated Mission Planning Process (IMPP) (Ehrhart and Quille 2007: 11; see also Eide *et al.* 2005; European Council 2005a). The overall purpose was to improve CMCO by engaging all relevant EU actors at the earliest stage of the planning process. It is supposed to be valid for all phases of EU engagement, and to cover transitions from one operation or mission to another, including between the Council and the Commission. However, it remains a non-binding concept, which is, therefore, dependent on the goodwill of the parties involved.

No permanent structures for Comprehensive Planning have been put in place, but so-called Crisis Response Coordinating Teams (CRCT) have been established on an ad hoc basis for crisis management operations since 2003 (see European Council 2003e). A CRCT is envisaged as a flexible grouping of senior officials at director level from the Council Secretariat and the Commission, who will convene to help prepare the overall Crisis Management Concept (CMC), which elaborates the EU's political objectives and proposes to the PSC a broad set of options (Gordon 2006: 352). To this end, it performs an early joint situation assessment, and seeks coherence between the range of civilian and military Strategic Options proposed via CIVCOM and the EUMC. The Crisis Management Concept, in turn, lays the framework for the Concept of Operations (CONOPS) and the Operation Plan (OPLAN).[8]

As a result of the Comprehensive Planning Initiative (CPI) and subsequent elaboration of the concept, the EU has taken a few potentially significant steps towards creating a shared situational awareness at the Director level, which is designed to trickle down to lower levels as they develop their concepts and plans. It has also brought about some clarification of concepts and procedures. However, at the same time it has been accompanied by institutional developments that have placed the responsibility for developing corresponding military and civilian Strategic Options, CONOPS and OPLANs firmly within the civilian and military chains of command respectively. In addition, as Stuart Gordon points out: 'There is already some evidence to suggest that the CRCT concept has not yet functioned optimally in the planning of current EU operations and exercises and that other, more *ad hoc* liaison processes have tended to emerge as a reaction to specific problems' (Gordon 2006: 352). Often, more immediate and practical problems encountered in the daily running of other operations tend to take the focus off the overall picture. Moreover, Comprehensive Planning has not created incentives for closer human interaction at lower levels beyond the eventual implicit requirements that more integrated Crisis

Management Concepts will have for the elaboration of subsequent concepts and plans. This will have to be stimulated by other means.

One way is stimulation through simulation of real-world scenarios in joint exercises. By 2009, the EU had carried out three crisis management exercises: CME 02 in May 2002, CME/CMX 03 together with NATO in November 2003, and CME 04 in May 2004. Between 2004 and 2009, it also carried out three military exercises: MILEX 05 in November 2005, MILEX 07 (testing the OpCen) in June 2007, and MILEX 08 in June 2008. Information on these exercises is not available to the public, but judging from frequency alone, they come across as too rare and isolated events to have any significant impact on working relations, or to even involve the same people more than once or twice, due to length of rotation periods at least on the military side. It is also a case in point that the EU Battlegroup training system makes no provisions for EU-led exercises involving the strategic level or civilian crisis management elements (Lindström 2007: 28). Moreover, to the extent that we may infer some conclusions from experiences with other multinational crisis management exercises, they are often not designed to specifically test human interaction. Crisis management exercises often follow a military agenda, in which the aim is to test concepts against skills in a close-to-real setting. To be able to do this in a way that allows evaluation of operational status, the concepts and skills need to be specified as objectively as possible. Players are, therefore, told not to 'fight the setting', which is a phrase well known to military officers, but one that often comes across as problematic for people with other professional backgrounds. This is a source of considerable tension both in simulated and real crisis management operations.

Summing up, neither the few exercises that have been carried out, nor the institutional developments or ad hoc arrangements that have been put in place seem to have produced sufficient incentives for a 'culture of coordination' to take root at the level of strategic and operational planning. Solana characterised the CivMilCell as a 'pathfinder, leading the way to a more complete integration of civilian and military expertise within the Council's structures' (European Council 2005a: 9; cited in Ehrhart and Quille 2007: 7). Yet, as shown above, the political controversy surrounding the establishment of the CivMilCell severely hampered its potential scope of action, and even to some degree served as a substitute for a 'culture of coordination' to evolve. In fact, another unit may come across as a better 'pathfinder' for civil–military integration, considering how it was established, its staff composition and its role with regard to the strategic planning process.

The joint SITCEN: a pathfinder for EU civil–military integration?

SITCEN has received only occasional coverage in the CSDP literature, and is usually only briefly mentioned in presentations of EU crisis management structures. Part of the reason for this is probably that the unit has been hard to place in the institutional hierarchy, while the secrecy surrounding it has made it notoriously difficult to study. Nevertheless, its apparently free role is exactly why it presents itself as an interesting case. Also, despite the methodological challenges of studying intelligence issues, there is potential for synthesising the findings of a growing body of literature on the emergence of a European *Intelligence Community* with the institutional focus of this chapter. Note that while the former's focus tends to be on the EU's performance along the whole intelligence cycle (collection, processing, analysis, dissemination, tasking and control) (see e.g. Müller-Wille 2002: 61–62), and covers also other institutions (e.g. Europol, the EU Satellite Centre and the EUMS Intelligence Directorate), the focus here is solely on the joint analysis function of SITCEN as part of the strategic and operational planning process in support of the CSDP.

The establishment of SITCEN was a far less politicised, and publicised, event than those described above. As William Shapcott, head of SITCEN, in a rare official appearance, has described:

Indeed, he [Solana] was shown a paper fairly soon after he arrived that suggested setting up some sort of mechanism, and he said, 'No, we really need to wait for the Member States to come forward with ideas in this area.' … By 2001, around the time of 9/11, a number of Member States approached Solana to say, 'We would like to go one step further. We would like to start sharing more sensitive information. We would like to see an attempt made to undertake common assessments of particularly critical issues in terms of the Union's foreign policy'. Several Member States made this approach. Solana thought that the time had come and he decided to give the Situation Centre, which had existed as a sort of empty shell until then, a particular intelligence assessment function, and we set about establishing which Member States would like to participate and were prepared to send information. (Shapcott 2004)

SITCEN was separated out from the Policy Unit in 2001, and has since developed largely away from the public eye. In terms of placement in the institutional hierarchy, it has officially been 'a department attached to the High Representative, situated within the Private Office of the Council Secretariat of the Council' (Müller-Wille 2008: 61). In fact, the Council has not adopted any legal act or similar publicly available document that formally establishes SITCEN as an EU agency or outlines its tasks and responsibilities (Müller-Wille 2006: 111). Its free role grew out of its initial function, which was to support the High Representative personally in his work by keeping him supplied with fresh news updates and analyses of current events. However, it has gradually gained the 'character of an intelligence agency' (Müller-Wille 2006: 111), whose main task is 'the production of intelligence analyses with a view to support EU policy making' (Solana quoted in Duke 2006: 617). The post-Lisbon reshuffling of institutions in Brussels, including the merging of parts of the Council Secretariat into the European External Action Service (EEAS), did not fundamentally change SITCEN's roles and functions. It retains its informal status and remains, for all means and purposes, still directly attached to the High Representative.

After the March 2004 Madrid bombings, SITCEN was given a specific responsibility for counter-terrorism assessments. Since 2002, it also has cooperated with the Club of Berne, a network consisting of mainly the Heads of the internal intelligence services of the old EU-15 plus Norway and Switzerland.[9] In a meeting of the Club of Berne on 21 April 2004, it was decided that the Counter-Terrorism Group (CTG), established by the Club of Berne in September 2001, should act as the interface between the EU and the internal security services on terrorist matters.[10] The idea, originating in a paper prepared by Solana on how to implement the European Council Declaration on Combating Terrorism, was that 'the group [CTG] should have a small presence in Brussels imbedded within the Situation Centre, and that we would therefore be able to fuse inputs from internal and external services' (Shapcott 2004). Although the scope of its work has inevitably shifted towards anti-terrorist activities, SITCEN reports shall cover 'the broad range of internal security and survey the fields of activity of services in the areas of intelligence, security, investigation, border surveillance and crisis management' (Dutch Presidency Note to the Informal Meeting of the JHA Council, October 2004, unpublished doc no: 12685/04; quoted in Statewatch Bulletin 2004).

The way SITCEN has evolved has been remarkably sheltered from the political disturbances and national agendas that have left their marks on other institutional developments described above. It apparently received strong support from the larger Member States from the very start, but Britain played a key role by making senior British officials available for its staff, including its Director, William Shapcott (Crowe 2005: 22; Duke 2006: 619; see also Grant 2000). SITCEN staff are meant to incorporate both civilian and military expertise, and were initially drawn from the Policy Unit and the EUMS Intelligence Directorate (INTDIR). Its expansion since then has been incremental, following the principle of 'positive selection' of national officials from selected Member States. In other words, not all the Member States are represented, which reflects the issue of *trust* in SITCEN's ability to handle sensitive information (Müller-Wille 2008: 62; Walsh 2006). In 2002, SITCEN comprised seven seconded national officials (one each from France, Germany, Italy, the Netherlands, Spain, Sweden and the UK), in addition to two diplomats from the Policy Unit, three military officers from the EUMS (two from the INTDIR and one from the Operations Directorate), and one police officer from the DG-E (Police Planning Team) (see Müller-Wille 2008: 62).[11]

SITCEN's character as an 'insiders' club' has been possible due to its still unspecified role inside the Council Secretariat; it never was intended as a representational body, such as the PSC, COREPER, EUMC or the Policy Unit. However, what, according to Müller-Wille, makes the whole arrangement acceptable to the 'outsiders' is the fact that all the Member States receive SITCEN products without exception, even if they do not have access to the background material. All Member States can also submit intelligence to SITCEN directly with a view to being incorporated in its products. And since SITCEN does not produce raw intelligence itself, the information shared by one Member State on a specific issue is accessible through other channels if another Member State so desires (Müller-Wille 2008: 63). One should also note that the Commission routinely shares information emanating from its secure 'crisis room' and its External Service with SITCEN. It also receives SITCEN products via the PSC on the basis of parity with the Member States (Duke 2006: 618).

Finally, whereas the added value of the CivMilCell and the OpCen could be questioned, at least as the principal argument behind their establishment, most commentators, although pointing out that the

EU's intelligence capabilities should not be exaggerated, agree that SITCEN has performed an important analysis function, producing 'intelligence that no national agency is willing to produce' (Müller-Wille 2008: 60), and that 'no national agency could easily substitute for the Centre' (Duke 2006: 620). Indeed, the high quality of its analyses can, according to former Head of British Secret Intelligence Service (MI6), Sir Richard Dearlove, be singled out as a key source of its influence (interview, 2008). It has also been pointed out that although it does not generate raw intelligence of its own, it still makes an original contribution by producing intelligence that is customised for the Council and the High Representative (Müller-Wille 2008: 60). As such, SITCEN has represented an important institutional capability in its capacity to obtain and analyse information, both secret and open, to support sound decisions at all levels of the organisation. Indeed, being a (strategic) actor depends, as argued by Andras Szigeti, to a large extent on some capacity to absorb and process information (Szigeti 2006: 21–22). Or, as summed up by Müller-Wille:

> The efficiency of the ESDP will depend not only on what operative military capabilities and civil means are available. Its success will heavily rely on both what military intelligence and civil information is fed into the system, and on how it is processed and combined before being presented to the decision-makers … In the long term, synthesized military and civil analysis is imperative in order to assure the credibility of the CFSP, and above all, the only way to prevent and deal efficiently with crisis. In addition, the ESDP would not appear as a mere substitute for the Alliance, duplicating its functions, but rather as a unique complement to it. (Müller-Wille 2002: 61)

SITCEN has, in and by itself, made significant progress towards reconciling the actors of the civil–military interface. Since January 2007, the so-called Single Intelligence Analysis Capacity (SIAC) has also provided a formal link to the Intelligence Directorate (INTDIR) of the EUMS (see Fägersten 2008: 56–57). The SIAC does not provide for a fully integrated structure, but ensures that when there is a need for information on a certain issue, for example, an emerging conflict SITCEN and INTDIR coordinate requests for information, upon which they then base their joint assessment of the situation. In addition to the civil–military role, however, SITCEN has also worked towards bridging the divide between external and internal security. Although it is directly tied to the High Representative, it routinely reports to and advises on possible actions to be taken by a range of actors, including the Justice and Home Affairs Council, the Commission, Europol, Eurojust, the European Border Agency (EBA), the Police Chief's Task Force, etc. Anecdotal evidence suggests that this *joint* capacity, combined with increasing access to valuable information and trust in confidentiality, has allowed SITCEN to achieve a good reputation particularly with those Member States without the national capacity to produce high quality intelligence assessments themselves. However, as pointed out by Shapcott, SITCEN is 'caught in a situation of doing a lot of really concrete work, not being able for operational reasons to make a big issue out of it, and, therefore, being exposed a little bit to people who assume, because they cannot see it, that there is nothing happening' (Shapcott 2004).

Concluding remarks

This chapter has revisited the EU's institutional capabilities for implementing the CSDP. As a comprehensive strategic actor, the EU is fundamentally dependent on an institutional capacity for integrated civil–military planning. Looking at the level of integration between civilian and military elements in the CSDP institutional set-up it is, therefore, necessary to be able to assess whether the EU has developed an organisation that reflects a Comprehensive Approach.

On the one hand, the EU has sought a 'Janowitzian' approach to the civil–military interface, perhaps best captured in its aim of developing a 'culture of coordination' as part of the CMCO process since November 2003. But on the other hand, it has, through the institutionalisation of its crisis management structures, confirmed a 'Huntingtonian' separation of its civilian and military arms. From the very start, the military arm was simply 'added to the civil structure as a separate limb', as noted by Björn Müller-Wille (2002: 61). And since civilian crisis management was also new to the EU, it had to start building institutional structures from scratch. In this context, 'the military were first to seek to restructure the operational civil-military interface and harvest any potential synergies' (Gordon 2006: 340). The military side simply had structures in place that could be adapted to the new strategic environment. This was not the case with the civilian side, which initially came out on its heels.

This tendency has been reinforced by the highly politicised process of institutionalising the CSDP, behind which looms the ever present struggle between those wanting an autonomous EU military capability and those wanting to avoid duplication. This led to a military bias throughout the strategic and operational planning process, which only recently has been 'evened out' by a strengthening of the civilian arm through the establishment of CPCC and the post of a Civilian Force Commander. The result has, nevertheless, been a classical stovepipe structure, which has not appeared to create the necessary incentives for a 'culture of coordination' to take root.

This does not necessarily mean that the institutionalisation of the CSDP has failed the EU's stated ambitions, or that the current institutional separation of the civil–military interface is set in stone. Developments merely confirm the complex nature of an evolving governance structure, as captured by the 'collective purpose' feature described in Chapter 1, in which compromises amongst a variety of actors (military and civilian, state and non-state) will often result in suboptimal solutions, which nevertheless sustain a broader collective purpose in the long run. Today, the EU is more capable of planning for and carrying out CSDP operations along the whole civilian–military spectrum than only a few years ago – and the tendency has been to do it alone (see Chapter 6).

The growing autonomy from NATO is a telling point in more than one respect. Clearly, strained political relations have been one reason why Berlin Plus has not become the platform for a more fruitful EU–NATO relationship that was intended. But, also on the practical working level, it appears that resistance within EU institutions has been a major obstacle for more cooperation between the two. Continuing to rely on the physically and doctrinally separate operational planning capacities at NATO-SHAPE, in any case, comes across as counterproductive to the effective integration of the EU's civilian and military instruments. This is also a problem with the primacy given to national OHQs as the preferred option for military operational planning for autonomous CSDP operations. This, according to former Director of the European Defence Agency (EDA), Nick Witney, 'inevitably means loss of continuity and momentum while the choice of OHQ for each operation is made, and the chosen headquarters gears itself up' (Witney 2008: 48).

The creation of the OpCen as part of the CivMilCell was potentially a step forward towards a fully integrated EU OHQ, but it was endowed with a high threshold for activation. The creation of the CivMilCell in itself gave rise to high expectations, but it received an unfortunate military bias due to the political controversy that preceded it. Solana's Comprehensive Planning Initiative (CPI) may have facilitated integration throughout the strategic and operational planning process, but it has remained a non-binding concept. It did, nonetheless, make some headway towards clarifying concepts and procedures, which may, in turn, lead to a greater degree of shared situation awareness throughout the planning cycle.

The establishment of a new Crisis Management and Planning Directorate (CMPD), which became operational in 2010, was intended to lift civil–military planning activities *out* of the EUMS, *up* to Deputy Director level, and *back* to the Crisis Management Concept (CMC) stage. It was staffed with people from the old DG-E VIII and IX, the CivMilCell and other EUMS units, and the Commission. However, since there has been no money to hire people, it has not been reinforced with more civilians. There is, therefore, an inherent danger that the military bias has been carried on into the new Directorate, since the some 60 civilians involved in the CPCC remain meshed in the daily running of multiple operations, trying to 'shoot the wolf that is closest to the sledge' (interview with Council Secretariat official, May 2009). For the time being, it is still too early to judge the effects of the CMPD upon civil–military relations in the EU.

What is more certain is that, in the end, people tend to stick with their own, and cater to more immediate practical issues if not in some way induced to break with their usual habits. Simulating real challenges in joint exercises is one way to create incentives for human interaction, which may be built upon in subsequent crisis situations. But at present, CSDP crisis management exercises are too rare, while, judging from experience from similar multinational crisis management exercises, they are not likely to be designed to properly test and improve human interaction.

Given the need to think anew, SITCEN comes across as a perhaps more appropriate pathfinder than the CivMilCell (and perhaps also the new CMPD), given the qualities that seem to be the exact opposite of those that identify other CSDP institutional creations over later years: it had a pragmatic rather than a politicised starting point; it was given a free role in between the civilian and military chains of command; its very function is to provide integrated civil–military analysis at an early stage of the planning process; staff composition is balanced between military officers and civilian analysts; and its added value is clear. The very fact that not all EU Member States participate, and that those who want in need to prove themselves as trustworthy and competent, bears also some resemblance to the *pioneer approach* envisioned in the Permanent Structured Cooperation clause of the Lisbon Treaty, which perhaps makes SITCEN an appropriate pathfinder for improving other capabilities too.

5 | Building European capabilities: beyond the transatlantic gap

You cannot send a wiring diagram to a crisis.

Lord George Robertson, former Secretary General of NATO[1]

Having looked at institutions as policy framers and enablers, this chapter moves on to address the means or the capabilities at the EU's disposal. This is an area that, in accordance with the fourth feature of security governance, has been subject to important changes in the ideational or normative relations that regulate European defence acquisitions and planning. On the other hand, it is an area that for many years has been subject to a dominant 'gap'-thinking. In 1993, Christopher Hill introduced the concept of a 'capability–expectations gap', arguing that the EU had been talked *up* to do more than it could actually deliver with the capabilities at hand (Hill 1993: 47). Today, it is the notion of another 'gap', a transatlantic one in which Europe's armed forces are being talked *down*, that dominates the debate (Gompert *et al.* 1999; Kagan 2003; Schake 2002; see e.g. Coletta 2005; James 2006; Yost 2000). While not denying that gaps exist in several areas, this chapter argues that the analysis of Europe's force developments in recent years has been hampered by a one-sided focus on a military transatlantic capability gap. Instead, the chapter takes a more *Eurocentric* perspective in its analysis of the extent to which the EU fulfils our second criterion for a strategic actor – the capacity to generate relevant capabilities for declared aims. The focus here is on the capability *generation* part, whereas the actual use of capabilities in operations is covered in Chapter 6.

The notion of a transatlantic capability gap is fundamentally rooted in the strategic lesson that technological superiority leads to a comparative advantage that often has a decisive effect on the outcome of war (Howard 1983b: 104). This lesson was the driving force behind the development of the concept of Network Centric Warfare (NCW), which epitomised US force transformations in the post-Cold War period, and which has (re-)raised the issue of interoperability between US and European military forces. However, recalling Howard's four dimensions of strategy, when faced with the US preoccupation with technology it is important to note that in singling out the *techno-logical* to be one key dimension of strategy, Howard is equally clear on its limitations if it is not coupled with the other three dimensions. His key message when highlighting the technological dimension is the unquestionable *comparative advantage* that technological innovation had produced in the major wars fought between the second half of the nineteenth century and the late 1970s, when his essay was first published. Yet recent experiences in Iraq and Afghanistan, as in most operations where European and US forces have been involved in the last 10 to 15 years, have shown that technological superiority cannot secure victory. Comparative advantage cannot be obtained exclusively by way of technological superiority, but is a matter of commanding a broad range of capabilities, including non-military capabilities, to deal with a multitude of challenges, of which actual fighting is but one.

A 'capability' must, therefore, be seen as a much broader and con-textually dependent category than quantitative approaches often employed in analysis of capabilities suggest. Or as K.J. Holsti holds: 'One reason that gross quantities of resources cannot be equated with effective influence relates to the distinction between the state's overall capabilities and the relevance of resources to a particular diplomatic situation' (Holsti 1995: 122). That is why in this chapter we are not primarily concerned with counting military hardware or comparing defence budgets, which are only of limited value to our understand-ing of the EU as a strategic actor. This is not to say that quantitative measures of capability should be discarded. However, given the par-ticular focus of this book, we are more interested in knowing how the EU has influenced both the military and the civilian force gen-eration process(es) in Europe, and connected this process to a set of interests particular to the EU. Again, the security governance approach offers other lines of inquiry than the more traditional, quantitative approaches to these issues.

A central question is whether the EU has taken steps also in this area beyond a purely intergovernmental, bottom-up approach of pledging nationally owned capabilities to force pools, and moved towards more collective or integrated arrangements for force generation. One such trend would be the gradual recognition of the different roles that EU

Member States may take on along a spectrum of niche and lead nation capabilities. This, in turn, suggests a move towards a more heterarchical structure, in which different Member States may be granted influence within the structure based on the *relative* value of the resources they put on the table (see first feature of security governance in Chapter 1). A second trend would be the introduction of new actors that may in different ways influence the force generation process, such as the European Defence Agency (EDA) (see second feature of security governance). However, the most significant trend would arguably be a change in ideational relations between the actors, as reflected in the identification of new norms of reference, or benchmarks, from those which have marked the force generation process before (see fourth feature).

The chapter proceeds by first establishing what a capability is, before briefly discussing the notion of a transatlantic gap to determine what its consequences are for the CSDP in particular and for capability thinking in Europe in general. It then moves on to analyse the military and civilian capabilities enhancement initiatives under the CSDP in that order, before briefly looking into issues of broad interoperability within the CSDP.

The capability gap and the concept of interoperability

Taking strategy as a point of reference, capabilities can broadly be equated with means, which, in turn, relate to ends or interests.[2] Capabilities as such are, therefore, hardly relevant without an understanding of the interests they serve. In addition, capabilities draw their relevance from the context in which they are employed, or as David Yost points out, 'scenarios differ, and the employment of capabilities is scenario-dependent' (Yost 2000: 97). Yesterday's capabilities will not necessarily be relevant for today's scenarios, as reflected in the paradigmatic consequences that the end of the Cold War had on Europe's large standing armies when the territorial threat from the Soviet Union disappeared. Capabilities are, as such, in need of constant adaptation to remain relevant to the interests they are meant to serve and the scenarios in which they are employed.

However, capabilities will also often define interests, or as remarked by one commentator: 'The existence of certain capabilities and fields of expertise is converted into an inclination to discover goals these abilities might serve' (Schroeder 2006: 10). Moreover, the way in which to act, and the capabilities with which to engage, may sometimes even become the end, as explained in Chapter 2. Acting European, or within the parameters of a European strategic narrative or culture, has become a source of legitimacy for the military component of the CSDP, while opening up to the idea that the EU has other capabilities to draw upon. One of the reasons why the notion of a transatlantic gap still persists is rooted in a situation where one party is in a position to decide what a relevant capability is, whereas the other is forced to follow suit in order to remain *interoperable*.

The traditional understanding of *interoperability* concerns 'the ability of systems, units and forces to provide services to and accept services from other systems, units and forces and to use these services so exchanged to enable them to operate effectively together' (NATO Standardization Agreement, AAP-6 quoted in Boyer and Lindley-French 2007: 7). Interoperability is, on the one hand, a practical concept that must encompass 'technical and cognitive, as well as organisational and doctrinal, dimensions' (Boyer and Lindley-French 2007: 7). But it is also a concept with clear political connotations, insofar as the efforts made at remaining interoperable, especially if one country is seen to do more in this respect, may and will be seen to reflect the other countries' willingness to share the burden of alliance.

As Andrew James points out, the issue of burden-sharing has been a source of tension within NATO since its earliest years (James 2006: 223–224). But the debate resurfaced with particular force during the 1999 Kosovo bombing campaign, which highlighted a technological gap that had become ever more apparent between Europe and the United States in the post-Cold War period (see Yost 2000: 103–107). This gap had by then been accentuated by another rapidly growing gap in spending since around 1990. While Europe chose to cash in on the peace dividend, the United States instead sought to extend and exploit its unrivalled military superiority by eventually placing the concept of Network Centric Warfare (NCW) at the heart of a far-reaching military transformation process, often seen to aspire to a Revolution in Military Affairs (RMA).[3] The result has been a situation where today most European states are not able to fully operate militarily together with the United States, at least not in complex expeditionary operations. This may be worrisome in itself, but such consequences need to be set in the right context.

Comparisons of military capabilities make sense only insofar as European states want to use force *in the same way* as the United States, or if they want to develop similar military capabilities *to influence* US policy. For NATO, the loss of interoperability is a problem for the continued viability of the Alliance. Having to operate alongside rather than together with each other may be seen to harm unity within and raise into question US willingness to defend European interests on its own, as more Alliance partners forego the ability to operate together with it, not only in out-of-area operations but also in a situation where the collective defence clause (Article five of the North Atlantic Treaty) is invoked again.[4] But in practical terms interoperability has become more of a national concern for European states that wish to take part in coalitions led by the United States. When it comes to whether Europe will lose influence on US policy-making if disparities in military strength continue to grow, one commentator has questioned 'whether Europe should try to simply produce smaller versions of what the US possesses just to keep the US happy' (Lindley-French 2002a).

A report commissioned by the European Parliament has advised that 'interoperability in an EU context must afford its member-states an opportunity to think strategically based on a long-term security perspective' (Boyer and Lindley-French 2007: 6). As the authors go on to argue, although the EU has hitherto largely avoided separate interoperability standards that would replace those of NATO, due to constraints amongst several Member States, there are two compelling reasons that could see the need to re-evaluate this approach: the perceived impossibility of ever being able to keep up with the United States; and the fact that the EU's Comprehensive Approach is different from the United States' Full Spectrum Operations (FSO). The point is that the combination of growing defence expenditure to cover ever more costly equipment and continuing defence budget cuts will only widen the gap, while other parts of Europe's military (and non-military) capabilities are being neglected. Also, differences in strategic outlook between Europe and the United States render other interoperability standards than the traditional NATO understanding necessary (James 2006).

A *broad interoperability* concept was, indeed, introduced in the EU *Headline Goal 2010*, which defines it as 'the ability of armed forces to operate together and act in conjunction with other civilian instruments' (European Council 2004c: note 1). On the one hand, broad interoperability adds to the complexity of military interoperability. But, on the other, by including civilian aspects of interoperability, the spectrum of relevant instruments that can be 'counted' towards narrowing the transatlantic gap can be seen to have widened, insofar as Europe is able to offer capabilities that the United States does not possess (see e.g. Biscop 2006). This is in itself not a key point. Broad interoperability does not free the EU of its responsibilities for military interoperability. However, it does open up new ways of thinking about capabilities in Europe. Although the NATO and EU generated capability initiatives had similar starting points and remain interlinked, NATO's Allied Command Transformation (ACT) process, initiated at the 2002 Prague Summit, is committed to a US transformation model that indiscriminately imposes the same set of (too) high standards on every Member State (see Boyer and Lindley-French 2007: 10; Yost 2000). The EU, on the other hand, has been more open to, for example, diversifying tasks between Member States, and looking into ways to reform systems and procedures for defence acquisitions and production. As the process has moved along, a clearer understanding of the kind of tasks that the EU Member States are expected to carry out under the CSDP has also emerged, although this remains subject to continuous political controversy.

The Headline Goal 2003: (re-)counting old capabilities

The tasks that were to be carried out under the CSDP were not the main concern back in 1999. Or in the words of a Commission official: 'The capability gap was so obvious that no one wanted a real assessment' (interview with Commission official, May 2003). Instead, it was the overwhelming concern for the shortcomings in Europe's military capabilities, which had become all too apparent during the Kosovo campaign, that spurred the parallel NATO Defence Capabilities Initiative (DCI) at the Washington NATO Summit in April, and the EU Headline Goal (HLG) initiative at the Helsinki Council in December the same year. The objective and methodology of both initiatives were to have Member States commit to out-of-area operations by pledging national capabilities to shared force catalogues, largely irrespective of whether it happened inside NATO or the CSDP. There was considerable overlap between the HLG and the DCI, and roughly 70 per cent of the DCI initiatives were considered relevant to the CSDP (King's College 2001:

13–15). As Admiral Moreno Barberá, Head of the first EU Headline Task Force, also remarked:

it is important to get over the idea that what has been done up to now will necessarily be the same after 2003. Normally, solutions adopted to create something new, as is the case with the Helsinki Headline Goal, require many *ad hoc* steps which may not apply once the goal is attained. (Quoted in Ulriksen 2003: 130)

The benchmarks identified by the HLG were loosely derived from the Petersberg tasks, adopted from the Western European Union (WEU) and incorporated into the Treaty on European Union (TEU) by the 1997 Amsterdam Treaty (entered into force in 1999). The Petersberg tasks were originally defined as 'humanitarian and rescue tasks, peace-keeping tasks, and tasks of combat forces in crisis management, including peacemaking' (old TEU article 17). As such, they would be seen to cover almost all types of military operations up to collective defence, which still remains outside the scope of the CSDP. Moreover, the Petersberg tasks were and still are described in terms of function and not distinguished by the level or type of force required for each of the tasks, which has, in turn, complicated analysis of what is implied by operations on the 'low' and 'high' end of the scale (van Staden *et al.* 2000: 8).[5] Some operations at the low end, i.e. 'humanitarian and res-cue tasks', may require more sophisticated military resources, more manpower and a longer-term commitment than 'peacemaking' at the high end. It does not make immediate sense, therefore, to state that the EU is ready to take on tasks at the low end but not the high end, nor is it particularly useful to set specific force levels for each of the tasks.

The identification of the Headline Goal was, therefore, of only lim-ited value in terms of defining the EU's 'level of operationality'. The first set of goals, agreed at the 1999 Helsinki Council, set 2003 as the target date for establishing a Rapid Reaction Force (RRF) of 60,000 troops, with appropriate naval and air support, to be deployed within 60 days and sustained in theatre for up to 12 months.[6] At the 2001 Capabilities Improvement Conference (CIC) in Brussels, the Member States identified a substantial range of forces available to meet the HLG, including 100,000 troops, 400 combat aircraft and 100 naval elements. However, most of these forces were already pledged to NATO under the parallel DCI, or to the UN (Schake 2002). No additional capabilities were created, and crucial shortfalls remained in strategic lift, tactical transport and C4ISR (command, control, communications, computers, intelligence, surveillance and reconnaissance).

As a step towards remedying these shortfalls, the EU launched a European Capability Action Plan (ECAP) at the Laeken Council in December 2001, which established a set of guiding principles to increase the effectiveness of capability efforts, including better coordination between Member States and with NATO. Still, the shortfalls took some of the zest out of the Laeken Declaration, which announced the CSDP operational for *some* Petersberg tasks only. It, nonetheless, signalled a not insignificant change of focus away from the negative and paralysing preoccupation with Europe's perceived military inferiority. Despite the little real progress made in terms of increasing defence budgets or filling crucial gaps in the force catalogue, the mere notion that the CSDP was now operational, that a first goal had been reached, seemed to give the EU and its Member States the confidence to set their own qualitative benchmarks as the HLG process entered a second phase.

The Headline Goal 2010: from quantity to quality (I)?

The new Headline Goal, endorsed by the Council in June 2004, and which set 2010 as the new target date, was considerably more to the point. The document put great emphasis on 'qualitative requirements', such as deployability, sustainability and interoperability of forces. It focused on improving the capability enhancement process, including the development of scenarios to facilitate better classification of capabilities to tasks. The subsequent development of five scenario families that describe the kinds of operations that the EU wants to be able to conduct was a clear improvement from the more generic description of operations contained in the Petersberg tasks. In terms of process, the document also called for the development of new Headline Goal Catalogues as required by the Capability Development Mechanism (CDM), introduced in 2003 (European Council 2003a). The CDM consists of a requirement catalogue, a force catalogue and a progress catalogue. Finally, the Headline Goal 2010 gave the impression of greater trust in distinct *European* resources, including an emphasis on civilian crisis management instruments 'that can be employed together with military instruments' (European Council 2004c). We shall return to these below.

However, the most significant element of the HLG 2010 was the further strengthening of the EU's rapid reaction capacity through the 'ability to deploy force packages at high readiness as a response to a crisis either as a stand-alone force or as part of a larger operation enabling follow-on phases' (European Council 2004c: 2). The idea of having smaller sized rapid reaction force packages grew out of the experience gained in the EU's military operation *Artemis* in the DR Congo in 2003 (see Chapter 6). The possibility of using this operation as a template for an EU force concept had already been raised at the Franco-British Summit in London on 24 November 2003.[7] Specifications for a 'Battlegroup Concept' were then identified in a 'food for thought' paper released by France, Germany and the UK on 10 February 2004 (France/Germany/UK 2004). Based on this concept, the envisioned force packages were required to be 'militarily effective, credible and coherent'. This was translated into 'a combined arms battalion sized force package with Combat Support and Combat Service Support', i.e. some 1,500 troops with appropriate logistical, naval and air support (European Council 2004c: 2). It was envisioned that the EU should be able to deploy a battlegroup no later than ten days after a decision to launch an operation.

At the November 2004 Military Capabilities Commitment Conference, the Member States made initial pledges towards establishing 13 self-sustained multinational battlegroups. Some were to be formed by a nation alone, while others were to be made up by a framework nation with other nations contributing niche, or specialist, enabling capabilities (France/Germany/UK 2004). The first EU Battlegroup (EUBG) was declared operational in January 2005, and Full Operational Capability (FOC) was reached in 2007. From that point on, the EU was to have two battlegroups on standby at all times, ideally enabling the EU to conduct two concurrent crisis response operations simultaneously (see Lindström 2007: ch. 1). By the end of 2008, some 20 EU Member States had done their 'tour of duty' in one or several of the first eight EUBGs.

However, none of the initial EUBGs saw any action, nor have any of the subsequent EUBGs, for that matter. This raises questions of the practical – and political (see Chapter 6) – feasibility of the Battlegroup Concept in the first place. Also, the individual contributions have varied in how they have responded to criteria for military effectiveness. This has been a particular challenge for those EUBGs that have been made up by contributions from multiple Member States. The Nordic Battlegroup (NBG), on standby for the first half of 2008, is a particularly telling case, since it was the most multinational of the EUBGs in this first period, involving four EU Member States plus Norway. Still it was considered to be one of the more successful ones, or as noted by *The Economist*:

> Some contingents, such as the Nordic Battlegroup, are a model of integration. They may be small, but many experts think the battle-groups are a more useful tool for crises management than NATO's hard-punching response force. (*The Economist* 2008)

But insofar as the NBG was not actually deployed anywhere, its relative success must be seen in relation to other criteria. We shall, therefore, take a closer look at the NBG experience to illustrate the role that the EUBGs have played in the capability process, and to illustrate some of the particular challenges that they have had to face up to.

The case of the Nordic Battlegroup

In 2004, Sweden, as the first of the smaller EU Member States, took upon itself the responsibility to act as framework nation for a group of contributing states that would eventually comprise Finland, Norway, Estonia and Ireland. Sweden used this opportunity as a catalyst for transforming its military forces, and between 2004 and 2008 considerable effort and money was invested in creating a small but effective Swedish expeditionary force (Granholm and Jonson 2006: 19–21). For Sweden, the NBG was also seen as a way to rid itself of its legacy of *alleingang* as a neutral power (interview with Norwegian MoD official, December 2008). Unlike the previous development of the EU Rapid Reaction Force (RRF), it was reported that there was little domestic debate around Swedish participation in the EUBGs, and that it was relatively easy to build a consensus around the NBG initiative (Granholm and Jonson 2006: 14). Ireland, which joined the NBG in 2007, was in a similar position, since full participation in the NBG implied a change of national law that prohibited Irish armed forces from participating in multinational exercises outside the homeland (Kristiansen 2008). As such, the NBG was a window of opportunity for two traditionally neutral states to make their first binding commitments to an international force. The traditional pattern for states like Sweden and Ireland has been to arrive in theatre with peace forces three to six months after a UN mandate has been given (see Granholm and Jonson 2006: 21). Entering into a battlegroup, on the other hand, commits the participating states to have standing forces that may be first on the scene presumably under a UN mandate, but this is not stated as a formal requirement (Lindström 2007: 52).

Although the Swedish Armed Forces favoured a national battlegroup, multinationality for several reasons became an explicit objective of the NBG – policy-makers wanted to share the risks and costs of putting up a battlegroup, while making it easier to swallow politically (Granholm and Jonson 2006: 14; interview with Norwegian MoD official, December 2008). Eventually multinationality became a political objective of the Battlegroup Concept itself.[8] It has been seen as a way to foster integration, and to grant those Member States that cannot provide a battlegroup on their own an opportunity to participate in the CSDP (Mölling 2007: 7). For the NBG, the multinational character resulted in a somewhat larger battlegroup than stipulated, or perhaps strictly needed (Kristiansen 2008: 30–31). Although the actual fighting force, which was supplied in full by Sweden, comprised 1,500 troops, the NBG in the end totalled some 2,800 personnel. This is, by the way, not unusual for EUBGs, which often end up larger than the stipulated 1,500 troops. Some of the individual contributions were clearly more helpful than others, such as for example the Irish IED (Improvised Explosive Device) team, and, if the NBG had been deployed, some parts of the force would almost certainly have stayed behind or been transported in later (Kristiansen 2008: 31). On the other hand, the multinational composition of the NBG was also a practical way for a small state like Sweden to take on responsibility for a battlegroup. Sweden did not have sufficient field medical capacities, for example, for which it turned to Norway to supply, and it had to rely on outside partners to supply key logistics.

Although from a military effectiveness point of view, such 'more the merrier' thinking is clearly not an asset for an expeditionary force, the NBG did receive praise for the way it managed to mould a surprisingly integrated and effective force out of contributions from five nations with limited logistical resources (Kristiansen 2008: 32). From its Force Headquarters (FHQ) located in Enköping, the NBG carried out the full planning process in preparation for the standby period together with the dedicated Operations Headquarters (OHQ) in London, and was, as the first EUBG, actually able to deploy and train the full force in an exercise in Luleaa in Northern Sweden in November 2007. However, some crucial capability shortfalls, which have continued to hamper subsequent EUBGs, were never properly addressed or put to the test.

First, the framework nation is responsible for pre-identified operational and strategic enablers. Sweden had to make arrangements for deploying and sustaining the NBG within ten days of an eventual decision to launch an operation. Drawing on the *Artemis* experience, the only really viable solution for any EUBG would be deployment by air.[9] Sweden itself only had a small fleet of eight medium-sized C-130 Hercules aircraft, which meant that it would have to rely on others to supply strategic airlift capacity for the NBG. This was also partly the case for tactical airlift.[10] The problem, which is covered extensively in the CSDP literature, is that European states are still severely short of the kind of aircraft needed for deploying large quantities of troops and personnel over great distances simultaneously (see e.g. Andersson 2006: 29–31; Lindström 2007: 31–40; Vlachos Dengler 2002b). The combined EU transport fleet consists of some 600 small to medium-sized military aircraft. Most of them are really tactical transport aircraft, which fall short of the kind of tonnage and range required for effective strategic airlift in operations outside Europe (Lindström 2007: 32).[11]

The Swedish solution was to join the 2005 NATO Strategic Airlift Interim Solution (SALIS), which was, as the name indicates, an interim arrangement through which 15 European states chartered six civilian Antonov An-124–100 aircraft from Ukraine. The arrangement was meant to cover the period pending the delivery of the Airbus A-400-M aircraft, which has been purchased by seven European states. However, this project has suffered several delays.[12] During the NBG standby period, Sweden together with 11 NATO Member States also signed a Memorandum of Understanding confirming participation in the NATO Strategic Airlift Capability (SAC) initiative for the collective acquisition and operation of three Boeing C-17s. These are based at Papa Airbase in Hungary and operated by multinational crews. In addition, Britain has leased five C-17 aircraft from Boeing since 2009. This means that the EU is for the moment formally covered through the SAC and the British aircraft. It will also within the coming years, pending budgetary cuts and delays in delivery, take some significant steps towards filling the strategic airlift shortfalls through a mix of national and collective aquisitions.[13]

On the personnel side, the framework nation is, in addition to putting up the actual battlegroup, responsible for making arrangements for a pre-identified strategic reserve force. The Swedish Armed Forces were not able to put up such an additional reserve. A request was forwarded to the UK, but arrangements were never formalised, which meant that it would have had to be improvised in case of need.[14] Pre-identified reserves have been a consistent problem for all of the multinational EUBGs, and several (non-optimal) solutions have been proposed (Lindström 2007: 53–56; Mölling 2007: 8). The problem is ultimately rooted in the general lack of European forces available for deployment in international operations. The IISS' *Military Balance* shows that only 2.69 per cent of Europe's 2.65 million men and women under arms were deployed in 2007. This is well below the NATO target of 8 per cent of ground forces on operations and 40 per cent being deployable (Giegerich and Nicoll 2008: 13). It should be noted that the percentage of deployed and deployable troops, in relative and absolute terms, has been growing steadily together with a reduction in Europe's large standing armies from 4.51 million in 1995 to 2.65 million in 2007. Then again, there are large variations between the states (see below). However, the point is that there is a mismatch between available troops and competing demands for forces to active deployments in Afghanistan and elsewhere, in addition to parallel demands for troops to the NATO Rapid Reaction Force (RRF) (Kaitera and Ben-Ari 2008: 7). In this highly competitive environment, suitable troops are hard to find.

Whereas the 2010 HLG represented a qualitative improvement from the 2003 HLG, it seems that the EU put all its eggs in one basket with the prominence and prestige given to the Battlegroup Concept. This raises a central question: is the Battlegroup Concept a relevant force model for the EU? It is a well-known fact that armies prepare to fight the last war. The initial EU RRF concept, conceived in 1999, was based on the experiences in the Balkans during the 1990s. Likewise, the Battlegroup Concept built, as described above, directly on operation *Artemis* in DR Congo in 2003. During the three months EUFOR was deployed, a small but effective EU force of some 1,800 soldiers managed to establish secure conditions in an area limited to the immediate surroundings of Bunia, capital of the Ituri province, to allow

MONUC to regroup and move to a Chapter VII mandate. However, as it often turns out, the chances are slim that the same conditions will apply to the next scenario. Pre-identified force packages such as the EUBGs have to strike a balance between being flexible enough, while also tailored to fit the most likely contingencies. Although the political reasons for not deploying the EUBGs should not be underestimated, none of the contingencies in which the EU has intervened have been 'perfect fits' for the Battlegroup Concept (see Lindström 2007: 58–59).[15]

In fact, Sweden wanted to send the NBG to Chad in 2008, but never got the go-ahead to do so, partly due to a narrow interpretation of what constituted a 'battlegroup situation' (see discussion in Chapter 6). This experience prompted the Swedes to initiate a discussion among the Member States during their Council Presidency (first half of 2009) on how to take the Battlegroup Concept forward (Sundberg and Nilsson 2009; Swedish EU Presidency 2009). Aiming to strengthen *usability* as one of their three priorities for the CSDP, the other two being capabilities and operations, the Swedes organised a seminar on the use of EUBGs in July 2009, in which questions such as whether the EUBGs could be made available for other than rapid reaction operations, and how to improve coordination between the two EUBGs on standby, were raised. However, no official agreements or decisions came out of the discussions. Nor did they touch upon the utility of the Battlegroup Concept as such.

Aside from the political controversy of using the EUBGs, part of the problem has to do with their limited size. It has been remarked that 'if the EUBGs were deployed as stand-alone force in a high-intensity operation in a hostile environment, the risk of failure would be extremely high' (Kaitera and Ben-Ari 2008: 3). Of course, this is not the kind of environment in which the EUBGs are likely to be used anyway, but given the ever present uncertainty about the potential scale of a crisis, a more robust force model would certainly reduce the risk, and thus make it more relevant for political decision-makers to use them.

In comparison, the parallel NATO Response Force (NRF), conceived at the 2002 NATO Prague summit, called for a joint force package consisting of a brigade-size land component of approximately 10,000 troops, in addition to maritime and air components, totalling roughly 25,000 troops.[16] The NRF was declared fully operational at the 2006 NATO Riga summit, but this was no longer the case six months after, mainly due to diminished US contributions (Kaitera and Ben-Ari 2008: 5). The rather ambitious NRF concept has, thus, proved to be unsustainable at a time when the bulk of NATO's deployable forces are still tied to the ongoing ISAF (International Security Assistance Force) operation in Afghanistan. At the unofficial NATO meeting in Noordwijk, Netherlands, in 2007, the NRF concept was adjusted to so-called *graduated readiness*, which implied a considerably smaller NRF force after 2008 when the initial rotation scheme ended (Kaitera and Ben-Ari 2008: 5). Then again, the main objective of the NRF has arguably been to provide an incentive for force transformation amongst the European NATO Member States in order to remain interoperable with US forces. This renders the fact that the NRF has not been deployed nor continued to fulfil the identified force targets less important, insofar as ISAF has been the real catalyst for transformation (see Binnendijk and Kugler 2003; Kaitera and Ben-Ari 2008: 6).[17] The Battlegroup Concept, on the other hand, has not been associated explicitly with transformation goals (Granholm and Jonson 2006: 12).

The question is, therefore, whether the EUBGs will continue to receive much patronage if their relevance or likelihood of ever being used is put into doubt, regardless of whether the obstacles are political or practical. Having forces on standby is neither significantly less expensive nor resource-consuming than having them deployed, while the political leverage gained by putting the forces in harm's way is undoubtedly higher. The point is simple – not using the EUBGs has and will continue to undermine the credibility of the concept. But in addition, this has muddled the role that the EUBGs have played in transforming and integrating armed forces, in particular the forces of small and medium-sized states.

Sweden actively used the NBG as a catalyst for transforming its armed forces towards expeditionary capabilities. A similar effect has been noted amongst some of the Central European states, although in many cases it is hard to discern whether transformation has been spurred by participation in NRF or the EUBGs (Mölling 2007: 6). However, this is of little practical consequence, since the use of NRF benchmarks has been encouraged in EUBG training and standardisation to ensure interoperability between NATO and EU forces (Boyer and Lindley-French 2007; for an example, see Swedish Armed Forces 2008). In most cases, the same forces will also rotate between being on standby for either organisation. However, beyond the streamlining of standards for training and equipment, and the popular notion that NRF means roughly the same as the EUBGs, only bigger and more robust, there are some differences between the concepts when it comes to flexibility and the incentives they offer to different categories of Member States.

Lead and niche nations: the CSDP as arena for role specialisation

The Battlegroup Concept offers a good deal of flexibility in terms of formation, ranging from single nation to multinational EUBGs, and the capabilities to be included beyond the minimum requirements outlined above. Different Member States may and do have different reasons for and means of participating in an EUBG. Large states such as Britain and France have no trouble setting up a single nation EUBG with support of their own OHQ, and appear to prefer to do so with only symbolic contributions from other states. As such, participation in EUBGs for these states has, at the outset, little impact on the internal transformation or integration with other states. Smaller Member States, on the other hand, are given strong incentives to transform and integrate their armed forces with partner states and the pre-identified OHQ structure. The NBG, for example, gave a significant boost to long-dormant plans for tighter Nordic Defence Cooperation (NDC), which continued to evolve in the period after the battlegroup was dissolved (Granholm and Jonson 2006: 14; see also O'Dwyer 2008; Stoltenberg 2009).

In fact, the flexibility of the Battlegroup Concept, and the simultaneous identification of six EU Member States that were to develop the capacity to lead CSDP operations from national OHQs (Britain, France, Germany, Italy, Spain and Greece) (see Chapter 4) (this was also a consequence of operation *Artemis*) can be seen to have accentuated and formalised ongoing trends towards some role specialisation and tighter cooperation between armed forces in Europe. These trends have been evident for some time, and can be attributed partly to the increased demand for expeditionary forces in international operations, and the need to spend smarter in view of shrinking national defence budgets (Missiroli 2002). However, they are ultimately dependent on some form of shared normative framework or arena in which these new capability practices may evolve. Both NATO and the EU have been instrumental in creating this arena, but whereas NATO, through its ACT and NRF initiatives, has put the same rigorous demands on all its Member States based on a US expeditionary warfare model, the EU has arguably been more open to diversifying the incentive structure in a way that appeals to states along the whole force spectrum.

Today, Europe's armed forces can be arranged into three main categories (Forster 2006; see also Giegerich and Nicoll 2008: ch. 3). In the first category, the British and French armed forces have as their main function an *Expeditionary Warfare* role, focusing principally on deployment outside national borders. This transformation represents, according to Anthony Forster, 'the most striking characteristic of trends in Europe since the late 1990s', and most states' armed forces have taken steps in roughly the same direction, although it is far from given that they will end up with the same structure (Forster 2006: 47). The largest category is still made up of states such as Finland, Greece, Norway and the post-communist states, which remain committed to a *Territorial Defence* model, and have retained conscription and relatively heavy armoured formations (Forster 2006: 53–57). However, most of them struggle to combine large standing armies with the qualitative (and financial) demands on forces to NRF and ongoing NATO operations, and have in reality moved towards semi-professional forces for international operations, while their territorial defence capacity is being bled. Finland remains a notable exception. A third category consists of states that have adopted what Forster refers to as a *Late Modern* model, including Denmark, Germany, Belgium, Italy, the Netherlands, Portugal and Spain. These states retain a dual mission for their armed forces, 'providing what might be termed a "residual Territorial Defence function", but in parallel a commitment to provide a significant contribution as a proportion of overall force size to international peacekeeping' (Forster 2006: 62). Some states in this category, such as Belgium, have gradually shifted more of their weight towards the latter role, tailoring their forces to cater specifically to international operations, but forgoing the ambition of being able to defend national territory (Ulriksen 2003: 157).

Individual states have, in other words, adopted different ways of transforming their forces to cater to an expeditionary warfare model, and have, as such, moved in roughly the same direction, albeit not consolidated around an ideal form. Many of the smaller European states in particular have come to view NATO standards as something of a straightjacket, while it has been pointed out that 'the [ACT] certification process has proved so complex that it is either unaffordable and/or unattainable for many EU members that are also members of NATO' (Boyer and Lindley-French 2007: 10). Contemporary trends may, therefore, rather point in the direction of some intra-European division of labour, in which the small states develop niche capabilities that can be plugged into the force structures of a handful of lead nations. France in particular appears to regard the development of an expeditionary warfare model, as well as taking the lead in two CSDP operations (*Artemis* in 2003 and EUFOR Chad/CAR in 2007, see Chapter 6), as important means of increasing the amount of influence it has within the EU (Forster 2006: 47; Rieker 2005). Other states have aspired to become lead nations by developing framework capabilities, such as OHQs, or seeking to integrate the capabilities they lack through permanent or ad hoc arrangements with partner states. Yet others have gone for sought-after niche capabilities, such as the Irish IED capacity or Luxembourg's purchase of *one* A-400-M transport aircraft. The appeal of such a system, the contours of which have become more apparent as the CSDP has progressed, is that it offers incentives for some states to change in order to *lead*, while also rewarding states for developing capabilities that increase their *influence* within the system.

A similar line of argument is offered by Janne Haaland Matlary, who has adopted Robert Putnam's classical 'two-level game' approach to show how the EU invariably offers incentives for states to 'pool' sovereignty in the security and defence field (Matlary 2006; Putnam 1988). She claims that since states want to share the risk of intervention, and contemporary Peace Support Operations (PSOs) demand integration and the involvement of international organisations to an increasing extent, the EU has become a useful arena for its Member States: 'EU governments now use military force for general foreign policy aims related to gaining international influence, and view EU membership also in this perspective' (Matlary 2006: 110). In this context, the main concern is no longer 'the defence of national independence but the quest for influence' (Aggestam 2005: 16; quoted in Matlary 2006: 110). As such, 'sensitive questions about national sovereignty' have become an inherent part of the 'incremental capacity-building process' (Matlary 2006: 111). That is, all of the EU's capability initiatives and programmes so far have been created from the bottom up, and none of them has *formally* impeded on national sovereignty. But the de facto incentive structure that has emerged has, nonetheless, modified the priority that all of the EU Member States, not only the small ones, seem to put on the national sovereignty norm, while incrementally replacing it with more collective norms. Nonetheless, the reluctance of individual Member States to enter into collective capability arrangements shows that this process is, indeed, a slow train coming.

A remaining problem is also that there may be few incentives at the national level for initiating capabilities, such as typically strategic airlift carriers, may have few incentives for being initiated at the national level, whereas there are difficulties in filling certain 'holes' in the capability catalogue without some 'top-down' management. There also appear to be limited incentives for changing to more collective practices on the capability *acquisition* side (procurements + production), which inevitably leads to continued inefficient spending and unnecessary duplication of national assets. To deal with these problems, the 2010 HLG also identified the creation of a common European Defence Agency (EDA) as one of its central objectives.

The European Defence Agency: managing the system top-down?

At the June 2003 Thessaloniki Council, agreement was reached on the establishment of a defence agency, following a Franco-British proposal earlier that year. The EDA was formally launched on 12 July 2004. It was set up as an EU Agency acting under the authority of the Council, with Javier Solana as Head of Agency and chairman of the Steering Board. It was endowed with four principal tasks: harmonising defence capabilities development and identifying capability needs for the CSDP; consolidating the European defence technological and industrial base; promoting research and technology; and facilitating armaments cooperation. Since 2006, a strategy for each of these areas has been elaborated.

The idea of creating a defence agency grew out of several more or less failed attempts at increasing coordination of arms procurement and production in Europe during the 1990s. The EDA formally replaced the West European Armaments Group (WEAG), which had been established in 1992 in the framework of the Western European

Union (WEU). It also adopted a much broader agenda than the Organisation for Joint Armaments Cooperation (OCCAR), which had been established in 1996 (acquiring legal status in 2001) by Germany, France, Italy and the UK, and which remains engaged in downstream management of a few key defence equipment programmes, most notably the A-400-M transport aircraft. Other initiatives include the 2000 Framework Agreement, signed by the UK, France, Germany, Italy, Spain and Sweden, based on the 1998 Letter of Intent, and designed to ease export regimes and harmonise national rules related to defence procurement (see Eliassen and Sitter 2006). These initiatives represent pragmatic attempts to overcome some of the more technical and procedural obstacles to a more effective European defence industry, but they remain limited in terms of membership and fall well short of a defence *agency*. What was it, then, that prompted the much more ambitious EDA initiative in 2003?

First, as argued by Eliassen and Sitter (2006: 10), the increased role of the EU in security and defence matters around the turn of the century added to the pressure for a common approach to armaments that had increased steadily since the end of the Cold War, which had left Europe (and the world) with a large surplus of armaments producers (see also Bitzinger 2003). Secondly, the Commission assumed a more active role against the defence sector's position as a 'bastion of interventionist and protectionist policy in an increasingly free-market and integrationist European Union' (Eliassen and Sitter 2006: 3, 10). This took the form of increased pressure for opening up to competition in the defence market, especially in the area of 'dual use' products, i.e. products that are designed for military use but have significant civilian applications (e.g. radios) and vice versa (e.g. doors for frigates). This meant that more products, which used to be subject to national exemptions under article 296 of the TEU, were included in the internal market, which, in turn, increased the Commission's leeway to comment also on defence market issues (see Eliassen and Sitter 2006: 11; European Commission 2003, 2007; Mörth 2003a). Thirdly, the defence industry itself started to put pressure on governments to ease up on protectionist practices, as the European defence industry started to consolidate through a series of national mergers (e.g. the merger of British Aerospace and GEC Marconi to create BAE Systems) and transnational mergers (such as the merger between the German DaimlerChrysler Aerospace AG (DASA), the French Aérospace-Matra,

and the Spanish Construcciones Aeronáuticas SA (CASA) to create
the European Aeronautic Defence and Space Company (EADS)) (see
Vlachos Dengler 2002a). These companies still have to deal with a
very nationally oriented mindset, but the close identification of interests between national defence industries and governments has grown
significantly weaker, thus removing some of the principal obstacles on
the national level to a more consolidated European defence market.

Once the weight of the 'national factor' softened, the idea of creating a European Defence Agency quickly matured in step with what
André Barrinha has deemed a 'move from a military sector dynamic to
a clear economic one reinvented as the main existential logic related
to defence industry' (Barrinha 2008: 10, see also Barrinha 2010). Put
rather crudely, the defence industry is no longer primarily or exclusively subject to the logic of national survival but of economies of scale,
although much remains before a truly competitive European defence
market is a fact. The change of tone since around 2000 is, nevertheless,
significant. The very legitimacy of the once strong norm of retaining
a strong national defence technological and industrial base has gradually been losing out to what can be referred to as the 'existential condition' argument – that Europe must unite for its own survival, or face
a gradual corrosion of its military clout (Barrinha 2008: 23). Within
this new normative context, the EDA's 'name and shame' tactic has
become a rather effective instrument for compliance, despite the lack
of *binding* commitments made by the participating states (Norway
plus all EU Member States except Denmark).

Since 2006, the EDA has operated an intergovernmental *voluntary*
regime aimed at encouraging cross-border competition and transparency in the European defence equipment market. It is based on a
voluntary Code of Conduct (CoC), adopted on 1 July 2006, which currently includes 25 of the 27 EU Member States (except Romania and
Denmark) plus Norway. The regime covers contracts exempted from
the internal market by article 346 of the Treaty on the Functioning of
the Union (TFEU, was article 296 of the TEU), and thus complements
the Commission's initiatives in the area of 'dual use' products.[18] In
principle, and increasingly so in practice, the bulk of European defence
procurements are, in other words, covered by some form of EU regime.
However, in place of the strict enforcement mechanisms employed in
the internal market, the voluntary regime is based on a monitoring
and reporting system to help ensure compliance with the Code and

increase the transparency of the regime, such that 'peer pressure' can be exercised in cases of non-compliance. To this end, all defence contracts over one million euros are to be posted on a European Bulletin Board (one for Government Contracts, EBB1, and one for Industry Contracts, EBB2). Data on the extent to which governments do, in fact, comply with the CoC are not available. However, the periodical EDA reports suggest that there has been a steady increase in contract opportunities posted on EBB1, and sub-contract opportunities posted on EBB2, while exemptions from the CoC reflect 'a reasonable and relatively restrictive use of the follow-on exceptions' (EDA 2008).

Still, although the regime may bring about more efficient spending, it is certainly not a given that all of Europe's capability shortfalls will be filled by relying on market mechanisms, since some collective needs do not necessarily correspond with national priorities. It has been suggested that the EU, through a common EU fund, should organise joint procurements along the line of NATO's AWACS fleet (see e.g. Naumann 2000). Although it is unlikely that such a fund would receive much patronage, given the current state of European defence budgets, we do see some willingness on the part of EU Member States to enter into collective procurement schemes in the NATO Strategic Airlift Capability (SAC) initiative mentioned above. However, insofar as the idea is gaining some practical salience, the EDA could become an important catalyst for similar projects in the future. Also, by promoting collaborative defence research, the EDA has taken steps to avoid the massive duplication that still exists in research and development (R&D). EDA projects have been initiated to address, for example, Command, Control and Communications (C3) shortfalls. These are capabilities that have typically hampered interoperability, as armies often operate different radio systems that do not communicate with each other. With joint R&D, such problems can be avoided in the future, whilst linking R&D to concerted procurement may create economies of scale (Schake 2002: 32).

The EDA was also given a key role in the so-called 'Ghent framework' for pooling and sharing of military capabilities (Germany/Sweden 2010). Following a joint German–Swedish initiative, the Ministers of Defence of the EU Member States agreed on 9 December 2010 to take steps to counter the negative effects of the steady increase in both investment and operational costs in the defence sector, and the general (and steepening) decline in the Member States' defence budgets due to the financial crisis. First of all, the initiative is meant to ensure that the Member States coordinate their capability cuts in the future, so that not all cut in the same areas. In the longer term, the ambition is that increased defence cooperation could also lead to a broadening of military capabilities. The goal is to retain national control over key operational capabilities, while pooling and sharing less nationally sensitive resources, such as training, maintenance and some logistical capabilities. To meet these ambitions, the Ghent initiative identified three categories for intensified multilateral cooperation: category one includes capabilities and support structures that are deemed essential for individual nations and, therefore, maintained on a strictly national level. Future areas of cooperation could, however, be found in measures to increase interoperability in capabilities, such as combat, combat support, intelligence, fighter airplanes and war ships. Category two includes capabilities and support structures where closer cooperation is possible without creating too strong dependencies. This could include pooling of operational training facilities, non-deployable support structures and strategic and tactical airlift and logistics capabilities. Category three includes capabilities and support structures where mutual dependency and reliance upon partner states or international arrangements is acceptable. This could include support structures for education, training, exercises and long-term capability planning and development, such as military academies, test and evaluation facilities, or niche capabilities, such as aerial or maritime surveillance facilities.

As a first step, the Member States were requested to identify new areas for intensified multilateral cooperation within the three categories. Initial findings of the national analyses were then discussed by the Foreign Affairs Council (FAC) on 23 May 2011 (European Council 2011). At the meeting, the Member States recognised opportunities in a number of areas, but stressed the need for work at the EU level to support and push the process forward. This reflects the fact that, although being reliant upon national commitments to concrete pooling and sharing projects, the Ghent framework also needs some top-down management to counter national politicians' reluctance to enter into collaborative defence arrangements. As remarked by Tomas Valasek (2011): 'What makes obvious sense to experts and officials looks very different to national defence ministers' (see also Biscop and Coelmont 2011; Witney 2008). Collaboration takes years to yield rewards, and may initially cost more than it saves. Collaboration also carries real political risks, insofar as opposition politicians and journalists will often accuse the ministers of undermining national sovereignty. They will, therefore, need new incentives to move beyond the 'politically safer route of inaction' (Valasek 2011). This is where the EDA has a role to play. It has been tasked to produce a study on the financial benefits of military collaboration, which may help defence ministers to build a stronger case for closer collaboration amongst national audiences. The EDA has also formed a senior expert group, which has been touring European capitals sounding out governments on their plans to pool and share capabilities, and urging them to try harder.

In light of the current financial crisis in Europe, there seems to be a political momentum for more military collaboration at the moment, as reflected in the parallel NATO initiative on 'smart defence', which shares the basic goals and approach of pooling and sharing (see NATO 2010). This may open up a window of opportunity for the EDA to get more political traction from its work. The EDA has over the years become something of an independent agenda setter and a voice in the capability debate. It has produced a substantial number of policies and recommendations, and has been seen to have 'constituted itself as a privileged forum where national defence ministers and armaments directors, Commission, Council, and industry meet and harmonize views' (Barrinha 2008: 21; see also Oikonomou 2006).

In fact, the changing dynamics of the European defence industry have also spurred some analyses that draw attention to the alleged existence of a European 'defence-industrial simplex', or the way in which:

> both the military-armaments lobby and the technology-industrial lobby have worked at the EU level to create a simple but compelling relationship between the need for forces capable of 'robust intervention', the technological and industrial benefits of defence and aerospace research, and ... the creation of the European Defence Agency (EDA) in 2005. (Manners 2006: 193)

Although the phrase 'defence-industrial simplex' itself may come across as somewhat conspiratorial, the very idea that the gradual alignment of interests between the European defence industry and the proponents of the CSDP has strengthened the military element in EU policy, is probably uncontroversial (see e.g. Mawdsley *et al.* 2004;

Mörth 2003b). And as we shall see next, despite the EU's legacy as a civilian actor and the relative importance given to the Comprehensive Approach and the civilian dimension of the CSDP, the civilian capability process has received only marginal attention in the literature on the CSDP, almost to the point of neglect, when compared to the military side (see Howorth 2007: 124).

The civilian capability process: sending solicitors to war

As described above, Europe's main concern back in 1999 was its military shortcomings so painfully displayed by the Kosovo campaign. The subsequent military HLG, therefore, naturally received more attention than the parallel civilian process, also because the latter was an area in which it was more or less taken for granted that the EU was well covered. Both the EU and the Member States had considerable experience in sending police officers, observers and other personnel to various conflict zones, often in the aftermath of military intervention, and in the context of the presence of the UN, the OSCE and various NGOs. However, beyond the obvious military lessons, the Kosovo experience also revealed significant difficulties deploying a sufficient number of police personnel to UNMIK in the aftermath of the NATO-led military campaign (Nowak 2006: 18). Initially, therefore, the main motivation behind the development of the non-military crisis management dimension of the CSDP was limited to coordinating the various resources of the EU and the Member States to be able to respond more rapidly and effectively to crises.

The first significant step was made at the Helsinki Council in December 1999, which adopted an *Action Plan for Non-military Crisis Management of the EU* alongside the plan for strengthening the military component of the CSDP (European Council 1999).[19] Recognising the considerable collective and national civilian resources available to the EU, the plan underlined the need for: strengthening the synergy and responsiveness of national, collective and NGO resources in order to avoid duplication and improve performance; enhancing EU contributions to and performance within other organisations, such as the OSCE and the UN, and in EU autonomous operations; and ensuring inter-pillar coherence. Mirroring the military HLG, particular emphasis was put on developing a rapid reaction capacity, while urgent consideration was to be given to police capabilities. In accordance with the Action Plan, a second step was taken with the identification and approval of four priority areas of civilian crisis management by the Feira Council in June 2000. These were police, rule of law, civilian administration and civil protection. Targets were identified for each area, including: 5,000 police officers, 1,000 of which to be deployable within 30 days; 200 judges, prosecutors and penitentiary staff, 60 of which to be deployable in 30 days; a pool of experts for civil administration with concrete targets to be identified at a later stage (never happened); and 2–3 assessment or coordination teams to be dispatched within 3–7 hours for civil protection, as well as intervention teams of up to 2,000 persons to be dispatched within a week. By the time of the 2001 Laeken Council, at which the CSDP was declared operational, most targets had been met, and at the Civilian Capability Commitment Conference (CCC) in November 2002 it was confirmed that all targets had been exceeded through voluntary commitments by the Member States.

Initially, this appeared to confirm the image of the EU as a strong civilian actor, but, as on the military side, these first civilian targets were really an exercise in counting capabilities that were already there. Qualitative requirements, such as the actual availability, competence and sustainability of the personnel pledged, were still largely absent. Nevertheless, the fact of the matter was that before 1999 *Civilian Crisis Management* (CCM) had yet to enter EU security vocabulary. Rather, as Agnieszka Nowak points out, 'EU policy-makers used the expression "non-military crisis management" to describe any EU civilian involvement in crisis management' (Nowak 2006: 17). The identification of CCM as a specific element of the CSDP in the 1999 Action Plan initiated the gradual development of civilian-operational capabilities and mechanisms of coordination that 'is indeed particular to the EU and has no equivalent in other organisations' (Nowak 2006: 17). In particular, the 2001 Swedish Presidency put great emphasis on the civilian dimension of the CSDP, while for the first time exploring a more proactive role of civilian instruments in a CSDP report that resulted in the endorsement of the *EU Programme for the Prevention of Violent Conflicts* by the Gothenburg Council in June 2001 (Howorth 2007: 126; see also Jakobsen 2009).

Despite the meagre qualitative progress made in those early years, the EU identified and started filling an operational and conceptual vacuum, only partially occupied by the EU itself via first pillar activities and Member State involvement in UN and OSCE missions, by gradually building an institutional framework into which especially nationally generated civilian capabilities could be plugged, while moving beyond the ad hoc character of previous CCM practices (see also Chapter 4). This rather constructive role played by the EU in harvesting national experiences and creating a normative space in which civilian instruments have received a gradually and relatively more significant role compared to military instruments, a process which has been fuelled by the experiences in the Balkans as well as Iraq and Afghanistan, ought to be kept in mind when revisiting the many challenges that still remain.

The EU Police Mission in Bosnia-Herzegovina (EUPM), launched on 1 January 2003, was a first source of lessons learned for the EU in the area of CCM. First of all, it revealed the significant institutional challenges of coordinating the EUPM with other EU police-related activities, which were all subject to different approaches, time spans, decision-making structures, mandates, structures, etc. (interview with Commission official, May 2003; see Norheim-Martinsen 2005). The EUPM itself was given a small mentoring and advisory role, but no executive powers. Executive police work was generally left in the hands of the Bosnian police force, although EUFOR, the military CSDP operation *Althea* initiated in December 2004, was mandated to engage in gendarmerie type operations (see also Chapter 6). In addition, the Bosnian police force was already receiving advice and guidance from ten police and justice experts, employed by the Commission under the Stability and Association Process (SAP). Complicating the situation further, the EU was also engaged in activities under the external dimension of Justice and Home Affairs (JHA), addressing issues of corruption, organised crime and border control. Beyond the obvious operational challenges raised by this situation, it confirmed the key problem of inter-pillar coherence that had been anticipated in the 1999 Action Plan (see Marquina and Ruiz 2005).

On a general level, the EUPM experience revealed some problems of the methodology of increasing civilian capabilities. The 'boxing' of capabilities into the four priority areas identified in Feira (police, rule of law, civilian administration and civil protection), which were then negotiated and developed separately, effectively limited thinking on what was actually required in each particular case (Gourlay 2004: 12).

The quality of the personnel deployed relative to each situation, due to both poor external assessments and lack of training, also needed to be improved, whereas the actual recruitment of appropriate personnel was limited by a national 'force' generation process that was biased towards government employees, and effectively excluded people with (more) relevant experience, including independent consultants, academics and professionals engaged in NGO activities (Gourlay 2004: 7; Nowak 2006: 28).

These issues, in turn, reflected a more general problem of using the military model as a blueprint for civilian 'corps'. Eventually, EU policy-makers also realised that the initial subordination of CCM capabilities to military capabilities was simply not tenable, as it became clear that CCM as an instrument was not going to be used reactively and primarily after or alongside military forces, but preventively to avoid crises in faraway places such as Indonesia. As such, they needed to be self-standing, which requires a whole different administrative and logistical apparatus than that which was envisioned initially.

The Civilian Headline Goal 2008: from quantity to quality (II)?

Drawing on the initial lessons learned, a new Action Plan was endorsed by the Brussels Council on 17–18 June 2004 (European Council 2004a). The plan pointed to the need for more flexible, integrated 'packages' of CCM personnel, while broadening the range of expertise beyond the four priority areas identified above. Accordingly, the 2008 Civilian Headline Goal (CHG), also endorsed by the June 2004 Council, added monitoring missions and support for EU Special Representatives (EUSRs) to the original list, while noting that the EU should also be able to contribute to Security Sector Reform (SSR), and to support disarmament, demobilisation and reintegration processes (European Council 2004b). To this end, the EU was to be able to strengthen local institutions by means of advice, training and monitoring, and also to carry out executive functions in so-called 'substitution missions'. Mirroring the objective of the parallel military HLG 2010, the aim was set to deploy and sustain several civilian CSDP operations concurrently, including at least one large substitution mission, at short notice and in a non-benign environment.

Accordingly, priority was given to the development of rapidly deployable packages of experts in so-called Civilian Response Teams (CRTs), to be deployed within 30 days of a decision by the Council to launch a mission (European Council 2004b). At the same time, steps were taken towards a comprehensive EU concept for Security Sector Reform (SSR) (see Nowak 2006: 32–33; Spence and Fluri 2008), while the institutional and administrative capacity of the Council Secretariat to undertake civilian strategic and operational planning and mission support was strengthened (see Chapter 4). Regular stock-taking in Civilian Capability Commitment/Improvement Conferences show that the number of personnel has increased steadily across the 'six plus' priority areas, fulfilling thus the 2008 CHG, while routinely pointing to the need to do more, especially when it comes to creating synergies within and between the civilian and military areas of the CSDP. This was also the main theme in the 2010 Civilian Headline Goals, adopted in 2007, which took note of the growing demand for SSR, but included little new in terms of concepts or concrete targets (European Council 2007).

The civilian capability process shows that the EU has experienced a steep learning curve in its quest to develop an effective CCM capacity, a task that has proved perhaps more challenging than initially expected. The result has, nevertheless, been an emerging capacity that is, indeed, 'particular to the EU' and its Comprehensive Approach. The development of the CRTs in particular demonstrates that the EU has 'undertaken an important methodological step' away from the initial 'boxing' towards more flexible and integrated planning and deployment of civilian CSDP operations (Nowak 2006: 33). However, the question remains as to how it has affected the comparative advantage of the EU as a strategic actor. Or to rephrase: have civilian CCM capabilities substituted for or complemented military force in a way that renders the previously covered European military capability shortfalls less important?

Broad interoperability as comparative advantage

One problem is that, despite the relative strengthening of the civilian side and the growing emphasis on *broad interoperability*, civilian and military CSDP operations are still carried out separately. Several simultaneous and/or follow-up CSDP operations have been launched, but no 'integrated' civil–military operations, making use of the new civil–military planning and command structures in the Council Secretariat, have been carried out (see Chapter 6). Despite the apparent overlaps between the methodology, concepts and schedules between the military and civilian Headline Goals, the Huntingtonian separation of the EU civil–military interface (see Chapter 4) is, therefore, evident also when it comes to enhancing capabilities. As CCM has evolved to become a proactive instrument of the EU, to be used before a crisis erupts and the need for military crisis management supposedly becomes unavoidable, it has also become – and this might be good news in some respects – more separate from the military side. However, the problem is that it has become correspondingly harder to identify how CCM complements or substitutes for military force. As we shall see in the next chapter, the EU's operational pattern has become distinctively sequential, a point which may be seen to undermine the very idea of the Comprehensive Approach. It also reinforces the very plausibility of a division of labour between (NATO) war-fighting, on the one hand, and (EU) prevention and reconstruction, on the other. Inter alia, conceptually there is less added value to EU *military* crisis management as long as *civilian* crisis management instruments remain detached from it. The same point is formulated conversely in the Military Headline Goal 2010, which states that (broad) interoperability, or the ability of armed forces to interact with other civilian tools, 'is an instrument to *enhance the effective use of military capabilities* as a key enabler in achieving EU's ambitions in Crisis Management Operations' (European Council 2004c: note 1, emphasis added).

To raise the comparative advantage of civilian capabilities, it appears necessary, therefore, that a stronger link is forged between how civilian and military capabilities are being used in CSDP operations. Or in rather crude terms, to score burden-sharing points, the EU needs to start putting its civilian personnel in 'harm's way', i.e. early deployment into crisis areas, taking advantage of built-in military know-how concerning force protection, logistics, command and control (C2), etc. (Kaitera and Ben-Ari 2008: 11). This would almost inevitably lead to the subordination of civilian instruments to military structures and practices, and thus represent something of a relapse to the old conception of civilian capabilities – backing up military capabilities and helping to restore civil society after crises (Nowak 2006: 28). This need not imply that the EU cannot or should not continue to carry out the kind of CSDP stand-alone civilian operations that have been launched to date. However, to strengthen the EU's comparative advantage as a comprehensive strategic actor, it arguably needs to be able to – and, indeed, demonstrate clearly that it can – do both, by developing explicitly integrated concepts and engaging in explicitly integrated missions. This is addressed further in Chapter 6.

Concluding remarks

The purpose of this chapter was to assess how the EU has influenced both the military and the civilian capability development process(es) in Europe in order to sustain, and ideally increase, its capacity to generate relevant capabilities to promote common security interests, fulfilling thus our second criterion for a strategic actor. By employing a *Eurocentric* perspective on the capability issue, the aim has been to avoid the one-sided focus of the various 'gap' notions that have dominated the capability debates throughout the post-Cold War period. The continuous shortfalls in Europe's military capabilities have, indeed, been a trump card for CSDP sceptics who have resorted to 'hard numbers' to show why it is bound to fail. However, when disaggregating the capability question from its traditional transatlantic interoperability context, this chapter has showed that a variety of processes have emerged at the EU level that have started to change the normative frameworks within which both military and civilian capabilities are generated in Europe. This strengthens also the salience of the fourth feature of security governance, which concerns changes in ideational relations between actors involved in the CSDP.

From an initially quantitative focus, both the military and civilian capability generation processes have through the parallel Headline Goals moved towards more qualitative benchmarks centred on small, rapid reaction force concepts. Both the EUBGs and the CRTs have yet to prove their worth in operations, and it is likely that both concepts will have to be strengthened further to increase their relevance in future scenarios, which will almost inevitably require robust intervention by multiple teams of military and civilian personnel. Yet, even without being deployed, both concepts have contributed towards changing the normative framework for the ongoing transformation process(es) in Europe. On the military side, the Battlegroup Concept has, as illustrated with the NBG example, helped consolidate an intra-European division of labour by offering incentives for some states to change in order to *lead*, while rewarding other states for developing niche capabilities that increase their *influence* within the system. The European Defence Agency (EDA) has served as a catalyst for this process, by working towards more collaborative defence acquisitions procedures, and by becoming a key agent for a 'consolidate or perish' line of argument that has gradually weakened the legitimacy of the once so strong norm of the protection of a national defence technological and industrial base. However, national sovereignty concerns continue to block practical efforts to enter into collaborative capability arrangements. It remains to be seen whether the Ghent initiative on pooling and sharing will yield practical results. But the financial crisis seems to have opened a window of opportunity for the EDA to get more political traction from the conceptual work it has carried out over recent years.

On the civilian side, the EU has opened up the conceptual and operational area of civilian crisis management (CCM), eventually transcending the military support role that was first envisioned for it. As such, it has also escaped some of the methodological and conceptual problems associated with the initial subordination of CCM to military instruments, while creating a valuable additional set of tools for the EU. However, by turning towards a more conflict preventive role the CCM activities under the CSDP have not only accentuated challenges of civil–civil coordination between the Council and the Commission; the de facto conceptual and operational separation of civilian and military crisis management has also limited broad interoperability in the CSDP.

Insofar as the latter can be conceived as both a qualitative benchmark and a comparative asset, in the sense that it represents a different, sought-after way of warfare, creating integrated force packages as a preferred mode of deployment would perhaps better distinguish the comparative advantage of a *European way of war* (see Everts *et al.* 2004). A similar suggestion is offered by Boyer and Lindley-French, who ask whether Europeans, rather than following the US military lead, should 'invent their own "grammar" of warfare which better corresponds to European views on warfare but which nevertheless retains a high degree of co-operability with the US?' (Boyer and Lindley-French 2007: 5). This confirms Chapter 2's point that the way in which to act, and the capabilities with which to engage, may very well constitute an end itself.

For the EU, the Comprehensive Approach constitutes an alternative set of qualitative benchmarks for measuring capability developments and thus offers an alternative perspective on the 'gap' problem. Of course, overlapping memberships and alliance commitments through NATO will continue to put heavy transformation demands on Europe's military forces, since decision-makers on both sides of the Atlantic retain a key interest in being able to operate militarily together. That said, Member States of both organisations also appear to have an interest in an EU that draws upon its comparative strengths as a different strategic actor, and which utilises its inherent potential towards a Comprehensive Approach. However, similar to the findings in Chapter 4 a Huntingtonian separation of the civil–military interface is also evident throughout the capability dimension, which suggests again that the EU has yet to fully live up to its ambitions and potential as a comprehensive strategic actor.

6 | CSDP operations: learning through failure or failing to learn?

Without war, 'we' would hardly know who 'we' are.

Peter van Ham (2005)

Having addressed the capacity to generate relevant capabilities, this chapter directs attention to the operational dimension of strategy, which relates directly to our third and final criterion for a strategic actor, the resolve to engage in operations that promote common interests. This is also the ultimate test case for a collective purpose behind the CSDP, to recap the fifth and final feature of security governance. Ideally, an operation or a mission, whether military or civilian, as a strategic act, should answer to a clearly defined (set of) national and/ or collective interest(s). In reality, this is rarely the case. A decision to deploy military force or other instruments of external power to a foreign country, and especially so in a multilateral context, will often be subject to a range of factors, such as short-term political objectives, national agendas, peer pressure, media interest, etc. Moreover, it is always possible to link an operation or a mission to some broadly defined national or European interest(s), since these, as shown in the discussion of the European Security Strategy (ESS) in Chapter 2, are rarely very clear-cut.

This complexity reflects also the interconnectedness of Howard's four dimensions of strategy. Although a stated admirer and chronicler of Clausewitz, Howard, in fact, criticised him for his *preoccupation* with operational strategy, and thus his neglect of the other dimensions. Yet Howard also pointed out that 'the belief that technology has somehow eliminated the need for operational effectiveness is, in short, no more likely to be valid in the nuclear age than it was in the Second World War' (Howard 1983b: 112–113). The conventional conflicts, in which Western states have intervened in recent years, once again confirm the limits of technology, while highlighting the importance of the social dimension for mission success. Inter alia, the *resolve* to use capabilities, once you have them, is ultimately a question of political will. But it is also a matter of logistics, or the ability, financially and institutionally, to mobilise, deploy and sustain scarce resources in the field.

Moreover, as the ultimate proof of the pudding, operations or missions constitute a source of success or failure, pride or shame, and determine ultimately how a state or institution – whatever is considered to constitute the 'we' – is perceived both by its own constituents and its surroundings (see van Ham 2005). The failure to act in one instance, Kosovo being a prime example, may generate the will and pressure to act the next time. Indeed, the symbolic value of almost all CSDP operations has been significant, framed as they have been in an historical context: the return to the Balkans that Europe had seen in ruins less than ten years before; the responsibility taken in Africa, a continent tainted by Europe's colonial legacy; and a Europe assuming responsibility for its own destiny 50 years after its last devastating war, and at a time when the Americans have their hands full in other parts of the world. Mission success – and they are almost always framed in positive terms, even when failing – will, in turn, create confidence, and induce change within the organisation.

Operational experience is, therefore, deemed to feed back into the CSDP through two key mechanisms. The first one is a *narrative mechanism*, or the way in which a steadily expanding list of completed operations is purposively framed. This is perhaps best described as a premeditated *success narrative*, which confirms the image of a strategic actor that is gradually rising to the task, and which enhances the EU's confidence in pursuing a particular security and defence policy. It is, therefore, a key source of an emerging European strategic culture (see Chapter 2), and a powerful 'mover' for a more autonomous CSDP, insofar as it reinforces the elements that are deemed particular to the EU, perhaps best encapsulated by the Comprehensive Approach. However, given the purpose of the narrative, it is not necessarily or always rooted in real progress or accomplishments in the field, which may, in turn, distort a second feedback mechanism, which is a *lessons learned* mechanism. Challenges posed in theatre have, as this chapter shows, constituted a powerful incentive for changing existing practices or formalising ad hoc arrangements. This has taken the shape of a rapid and somewhat messy institutionalisation of the CSDP, as described in Chapter 4, while the general ad hoc nature of most CSDP operations has created precedents that have not always followed best practice – i.e. the lessons learned have not always been the 'right' ones.

This interplay between the two feedback mechanisms is traced in this chapter through a comprehensive breakdown of civilian and military CSDP operations carried out to date. The aim is to offer a total picture of how the operations affect the EU, as seen from the inside and the outside, rather than the snapshot images that in-depth cases studies of individual operations provide. However, this requires some ordering principles for how they ought to be presented, which are discussed first. Two ordering principles are proposed: geographical proximity conceptualised as three concentric circles around EU territory; and comprehensiveness understood as linkages between civilian and military operations in the same theatre of operations.

Categorising EU operations

The EU tends to make a great deal of the numbers of operations or missions it has carried out. And if we let numbers speak for themselves, a grand total of 24 CSDP operations since going operational on 1 January 2003 does, indeed, come across as an impressive accomplishment. If comparing the EU's ongoing 13 missions to the UN's 16, or NATO's meagre four, one may even be led to think that the EU is in league with the UN, or more active than NATO for that matter.[1] However, the picture changes when taking into account that NATO still deploys more personnel to Kosovo alone (ca. 8,500) than the EU does in all of its current 14 CSDP operations (ca. 6,500).

The EU's way of counting also does not discriminate between military and civilian operations.[2] All are, as such, presented as equally meriting, even though they differ significantly in numbers of deployed personnel, resources required, duration, financing, risk, etc. This has prompted some people to claim that 'In Brussels they are more interested in counting missions; how they are carried out does not earn political points' (interview with European Union Staff Group official, NATO-SHAPE, May 2006). A more positive reading suggests, on the other hand, that military operations are not considered more desirable or valued by the EU than civilian ones. The EU's portfolio of operations, which are not exactly 'of the masculine, heroic kind', to borrow Peter van Ham's somewhat ironic characteristic (2005: 40), has, nevertheless, often prompted scornful comments about the actual abilities of the EU. In any case, merely stating that the EU has undertaken more than 20 CSDP operations without some further qualification comes across as overselling its success.

The interchangeable use of the terms *operations* and *missions* is also in need of some clarification. Civilians are, on the one hand, usually reluctant to refer to what they do as operations because of the military connotations. To military personnel, on the other hand, a mission will often reflect something short of operations, while lacking the kind of instrumental ends–means quality that comes with operations, which corresponds with one of the traditional three levels of war (the strategic, the operational and the tactical). It is perhaps worth noting that the UN has traditionally referred to both its civilian and military deployments as *missions*.[3] When listing its CSDP deployments, the EU, on the other hand, and perhaps symptomatically, refers to all of them as *operations* in line with NATO terminology, although the term *mission* tends to be used in the actual name of civilian CSDP deployments. In the following, this chapter will use the term *operations* to stay in line with EU terminology, but also because there seems to be no principal reason for a functional division between civilian and military CSDP operations, never mind the *practical* division documented in the previous chapters. Rather, the Comprehensive Approach has become a central reference point for EU external activities (see Chapter 2), and will, therefore, be a central benchmark for operational evaluation too. This means that the existence of both military and civilian operations in the same theatre of operations has been used as a criterion for selecting certain operations for deeper discussion. Admittedly, this approach means that some operations, which are regarded important for other reasons, may receive shorter shrift in this book's analysis.

There are, indeed, a number of ways of grouping CSDP operations.[4] One is the functional approach in which military operations are presented as merely one of five types of CSDP operations (the other are military support missions, police missions, rule-of-law training missions, and peace-monitoring missions) and which downplays the military dimension somewhat (see e.g. Howorth 2007: ch. 7). Another is a straightforward chronology, which may tell us something about how the EU's operational dimension has evolved over time, but says little about coherence or consistency within one specific area of operations (Messervy-Whiting 2006: 32–37). A third is a classification of operations according to which (broad) objective of the European

Security Strategy (ESS) is served (i.e. support for the UN, support for the transatlantic relationship, regional stabilisation and the spread of good governance), which has a certain strategic quality, but, nevertheless, comes across as somewhat a posteriori or construed, in the sense that all operations may be framed to serve almost any interest(s) (Messervy-Whiting 2006: 40). A fourth option is the EU's own, in which operations are presented according to geographical zone, but without priority to any one specifically, which at first glance suggests perhaps a wider area of activities than is actually the case. However, this approach does lend focus to the geographical concentration of CSDP activities, while implicitly raising questions about comprehensiveness across operations in the same theatres.

In fact, the differentiated geographical approach, presented in a now dated report by the Dutch Clingendael Institute (van Staden *et al.* 2000), in which the (then) tentative CSDP area of operations was classified in three concentric circles, seems worthy of reconsideration now that the operational pattern has become more discernible. The first circle originally covered 'the arch stretching from the Baltic states over the Balkans to Europe's South Eastern (Turkey) and Southern flanks (Mediterranean and Northern Africa)', or the EU's immediate neighbourhood (van Staden *et al.* 2000: 29). This circle has after enlargement been widened, and should be seen to include the states listed as candidates or potential candidates for accession, and the countries that fall within the *European Neighbourhood Policy* (ENP), launched in 2004 (European Commission 2004).[5] The second circle is harder to delineate, but would incorporate roughly the rest of the African continent and the wider Middle Eastern region (van Staden *et al.* 2000: 30).[6] The third circle covers the rest of the world (van Staden *et al.* 2000: 32).

Europe and its Southern flanks: mastering your own backyard

Although CSDP operations are not explicitly or principally more likely the closer they get to the European mainland, the European Security Strategy (ESS) does state the need to 'promote a *ring* of *well governed* countries to the East of the European Union and on the borders of the Mediterranean', iterating, in the preceding paragraph (although separated by a headline), that 'In *failed* states, *military instruments* may be needed to restore order' (European Council 2003d: 7–8, emphasis added). Of course, having carefully to piece together and interpret such indicators from a strikingly un-military strategy document probably speaks for itself when it comes to the chances of deciding the where, when and how of the EU's use of force (see Chapter 2). But the tone of the ESS, nonetheless, suggests a sense of priority and likelihood of forceful intervention inside the immediate neighbourhood of the EU. Roughly half of all CSDP operations (11) have taken place here, including the largest to date in Bosnia and Herzegovina (BiH). In the Western Balkans, the EU has taken over, or plans to take over, all of NATO's military operations. In Eastern Europe, it has largely replaced the OSCE as the main civilian security actor, leaving the EU as (a) main player in, although perhaps not (yet) main *guarantor* of European security.

Operations in the Western Balkans

The CSDP operational portfolio was opened in the Western Balkans in 2003 with the launch of the European Union Police Mission (EUPM) in BiH on 1 January, and the military operation *Concordia* in FYROM (Former Yugoslav Republic of Macedonia) on 31 March. *Concordia* would have been the first had it not been for the full year it took to broker the Berlin Plus agreement, which for political but also operational reasons (see Chapter 4) had become a *sine qua non* for the operation to take place. However, despite the fanfare with which it was launched, operation *Concordia* involved a mere 400 troops, deployed in a comparatively benign environment. It was, therefore, first and foremost a test case for Berlin Plus, and an opportunity to take CSDP into the field (see Mace 2004; Howorth 2007: 231–233). Yet, within these parameters, the EU's military debut must be considered a success. It broke the psychological and political barrier of 'going operational', paving the way for more demanding operations to follow, and it set up a practical working relationship with NATO-SHAPE through the establishment of a nine-person-strong European Union Staff Group (EUSG), and the double-hatting of the roles of D-SACEUR and EU Operation Commander. On the practical side of things, the arrangements seemed to work out fine for the most part, despite the political blockage of the PSC–NAC channel described in Chapter 4.

Beyond the symbolic value of operation *Concordia*, the EU force was tasked to contribute to a secure and stable environment and to facilitate the implementation of the Ohrid Agreement, which had been brokered by Javier Solana together with NATO Secretary General George Robertson in August 2001. The EU and the OSCE already had monitors in FYROM under the protection of the some 1,000 NATO troops serving in operation *Amber Fox* since September 2001 (renamed operation *Allied Harmony* and downscaled to 400 troops in December 2002).[7] It seemed natural, therefore, that the EU would take over responsibility for their protection, while carrying forward the work that NATO had started. Although the North Atlantic Council (NAC) already in 2002 acknowledged that military operations in FYROM could be successfully finalised, it was agreed that a military presence seemed pertinent to minimise the risk of destabilisation. As such, operation *Concordia* could be seen as an example of the EU's strategy of *constructive engagement* (European Council 2003d: 11), eventually transitioning into less intrusive instruments, and finally status as accession country – the quintessential EU carrot-and-stick tool.

As operation *Concordia* was finalised in December 2003, it was quite obvious that the probability of armed conflict was almost non-existent, while a problem of organised crime, on the other hand, was on the rise. On 15 December 2003, the EU, therefore, replaced *Concordia* with a police mission – *Proxima* – the second of its kind. Consisting initially of some 200 international police personnel, the operation was replaced by an EU police advisory team (EUPAT), launched on 15 December 2005, and subsequently scaled down to 30 police officers in 2006. EUPAT was terminated on 15 December 2006 upon the request of the FYROM government who feared that its very presence would compromise the country's chance of speedy accession to the EU (Ioannides 2006; Howorth 2007: 228).

In the end, the FYROM case, as it is often portrayed, allowed for a rather neat, traditional *sequential* pattern of operations dealing with quite specific problems one at a time, although Michael Sahlin, previous EU Special Representative (EUSR) to FYROM, has pointed out that the failure to tackle organised crime, which he saw as a root cause of the conflict, at an earlier stage accentuated the problem and prolonged the international presence in FYROM (Sahlin 2005). The Comprehensive Approach was, as such, not really put to the test, whereas at least the more superfluous success criteria for these operations had only limited validity for subsequent operations, insofar as it was an untypical crisis – if that, indeed, is an appropriate term for the situation after NATO pulled out. The FYROM experience was, all the way, marked by the underlying assumption that military action was not really required, suggesting that the EU needed a more robust venture to earn the badge of military player in the Balkans.

The opportunity came with the takeover of NATO operation SFOR and the launch of operation EUFOR *Althea* in December 2004, which was, in fact, the EU's third military operation (we shall return to the second one below), but the first one of some size, involving 7,000–9,000 troops. Equally important, it was the EU's first experience of running *simultaneous* (as opposed to *integrated*) crisis management operations in the same theatre. The EU Police Mission (EUPM) had already been running for almost two years, earning a somewhat dubious track record (see below). Since this had implications for *Althea*, we shall briefly cover this operation first.

Launched on 1 January 2003, the EUPM counted, at its height, over 500 international police officers and civilian staff. The mission was renewed in November 2005 with a modified mandate and reduced size, making it the longest running CSDP operation to date. In addition, it comes across as a mostly positive source of lessons learned amongst EU personnel, who insist that the rearrangements in 2005 were the result of a thorough analysis of the first two years of operations, which consequently led to a heavier focus on organised crime and fighting corruption in EUPM II (interview with Council Secretariat official, May 2006). Further to this, the EU claimed a number of successes, including 'transformation' and 'solid development' of key state-level police institutions, and progress in implementing police reform with the EUPM playing a key advisory role (European Council 2009b). Unfortunately, as Jolyon Howorth points out, 'this self-congratulatory balance sheet is not shared by independent analysts of the EUPM record' (2007: 225).

One central point is that the mission represented an arguably premature step down from the more robust mandate of the UN International Police Task Force (IPTF), which it replaced. The launch of the EUPM was, in fact, followed by a steep rise in crime, according to the International Crisis Group (ICG 2005: 12–13).[8] Beyond the purely operational side of this latter issue, the EUPM suffered from Brussels' failure to put pressure on the Serb authorities to address the continued ethnic imbalances and presence of war criminals in parts of the police force (see Osland 2004). However, as regards the operational concept, the focus on *strengthening* through 'mentoring, monitoring and inspecting' rather than *substitution* of a fragmented and corrupt police force, led to criticism of the EUPM's failure to bring about essential public security and trust in the police at the community level (Merlingen and Ostrauskaite 2005, 2006). The focus on the high to medium police management levels also led to confusion about the respective roles of the Council and the Commission. Instead the EUPM seems to have fallen between two stools, neither having the mandate nor resources – nor appropriate operational concept in the first place – to make a significant impact through executive policing at the community level, nor having the right skills to manage major public administration reforms, since this, as has been remarked, requires 'highly experienced civilians', not police officers (ICG 2005: 13). The obvious dissonance between these criticisms, and the lessons that the EU, at least officially, has drawn from the EUPM record, as the critiques point out, did not augur well for future EU police operations.

Moreover, it was, in many respects, against the backdrop of a largely inefficient police operation that EUFOR *Althea* was launched in December 2004. In one of the strikingly few analyses of this operation, the first EU Force Commander David Leakey describes it as essentially a police support operation (Leakey 2006).[9] When prompted by Solana to make EUFOR 'new and distinct', and to ensure that it was to 'make a difference', Leakey, in his own words, 'looked in the High Representative's Mission Implementation Plan (MIP) for areas in which EUFOR's military capability could give "support", as ordered' (Leakey 2006: 61). As it turned out, 'supporting the fight against organised crime', which was in EUFOR's mandate, and Lord Ashdown's identification of crime and corruption as the main 'obstructionism' hindering BiH's progress, proved to be 'two sides of the same coin in the context of BiH' (Leakey 2006: 62).

However, as far as 'new and distinct' goes, the idea of including Integrated Police Units (IPUs) in a military operation to fill the so-called 'public security gap' between military peace enforcement and civilian reconstruction had already been identified by NATO in 1997 as a response to the challenges in BiH (Dziedzic and Stark 2006). Accordingly, as part of the objective of a 'seamless transition' from SFOR to EUFOR, the EU inherited a battalion of gendarmerie forces from NATO, which had been deployed as part of SFOR since 1998, in what amounted to little more than a re-badging of uniforms and equipment (Norheim-Martinsen 2005). The novelty and distinctiveness of the EU approach only eventually came to rest with the fact that it used the whole of EUFOR capabilities to support the fight against crime, after most of the contributing nations released their national caveats against the new operational tasks during 2005 (Leakey 2006: 63). The advantage of this 'whole of EUFOR' approach, as Leakey describes it, included: surveillance, intelligence, communications, a critical mass of soldiers (6,500) deployable throughout BiH at short notice, a protracted operational capacity, and 'the professional approach of the officers and soldiers to adapt military skills to unorthodox operations' (Leakey 2006: 63). Not to discredit the professionalism of European soldiers, gendarmerie forces represent an arguably unique capability that only a few EU Member States retain, which does call into question the appropriateness of having EUFOR engage in the kind of tasks it was given after the 2005 turnaround.

Of course, in their efforts merely to *support* the fight against organised crime, EU soldiers and officers were to stay well clear of specialised police work, such as handling evidence or investigating crimes, aiming rather to 'embolden' BiH law enforcement agencies to do their job. In retrospect, it appears that the line between the roles of the EUPM and EUFOR respectively eventually became clear enough, although initially, from the EUPM point of view, EUFOR exceeded its own mandate and interfered with that of the EUPM (see Knutsen 2008; Mustonen 2008). Despite this initial antipathy – as well as the more enduring principled resistance higher up in the system and amongst certain Member States – practical working relations have reportedly been good (Leakey 2006: 65–67; interview with Council Secretariat official, June 2009). Both Jolyon Howorth (2007: 236) and Giovanni Grevi (2007: 87) also underline that EUFOR was and remains far more of a civil–military mix than a traditional military operation, and that it became part of coordinated EU presence in BiH under the chairmanship and direction of the EUSR.

However, beyond the practical results EUFOR quite clearly illustrates the shortcomings of the 'glorified *ad hocery*' (see Everts and Keohane 2003) that appears such a fitting description of Leakey's somewhat personal narrative of how the operation was reformed and renewed in 2005.[10] First of all, the disconnectedness between both the EUPM and EUFOR's claims to success, especially insofar as the latter's success was in some way rooted in the relative failure of the former (although it did fulfil what it was *mandated* to do), inevitably comes across as odd. Leakey also probably did what he could with a rather fuzzy mandate, but could, as a result, potentially have set some unwarranted precedents, which is perhaps why EUFOR does not appear as a significant source of lessons learned for the CSDP, despite its size.[11]

Keeping in mind the *supporting* role that EUFOR was to have, using 'normal' soldiers to do policing inherently brings the danger of undermining the Comprehensive Approach, since it may be inferred that the military can be quite successful at doing this kind of work. This essentially goes against all conventional understanding of how contemporary crisis management ought to be carried out. That said, it was the BiH experience that, at the September 2004 Noordwijk Summit, prompted five EU Member States – France, Italy, the Netherlands, Portugal and Spain – to create the European Gendarmerie Force (Eurogendfor), following a G-8 initiative at the June 2004 Sea Island Summit to create a Centre of Excellence for Stability Police Units (CoESPE).[12] Both are co-located in Vicenza, Italy. Although a multilateral initiative outside the EU treaty framework, Eurogendfor is first and foremost at the disposal of the EU, but it can be used in the context of NATO, the OSCE or ad hoc coalitions. It consists of a rather unique compilation of hybrid police forces with *military status* and *full police powers*. Indeed, only the currently six signatory EU Member States have them. The key condition is that they can be readily deployed as Integrated Police Units (IPUs) under military command. As such, they are predominantly seen as an asset to be used to fill the public security gap in the immediate aftermath of armed conflict, although they are also able to operate as a stand-alone armed or unarmed police force with its own logistics and command and control (C2) capabilities. Herein lies also the challenge for fitting Eurogendfor into the CSDP conceptual framework.

It appears that such hybrid capabilities sit somewhat uncomfortably in the heavily compartmentalised civil–military CSDP set-up described in the previous chapters. The Eurogendfor took over the responsibility for the IPU HQ in BiH in November 2007, but has not deployed as IPUs in CSDP operations before or after. Some of the police officers that make up the Eurogendfor rapid reaction capacity, which are the same forces pledged to the Helsinki catalogue for civilian police forces (see Chapter 5), have been used in civilian CSDP police operations, but rarely in an executive role. It may be that there has been little need for IPUs in the kind of environments that the EU has intervened.

After all, the Balkans was way past the conflict stage when the EU got its act together, although some substitution of executive functions was obviously needed in BiH and later in Kosovo (see Merlingen and Ostrauskaite 2006). The EU has, quite understandably, pursued strengthening and local ownership as main principles for its civilian CSDP operations in the Balkans, presumably because if you do substitution, as one EU official put it, 'you shoot yourself in the foot' – i.e. you are forced to stay there forever (interview with Council Secretariat official, June 2009). The promise of speedy accession to the EU for these countries also fits badly with substitution or forceful intervention, which suggests perhaps that this ultimate EU 'carrot' represents something of a limiting factor for EU crisis management, in the sense that it creates what can be called an *executive gap* between the military and civilian-operational concepts.

In any case, the policing carried out as part of EUFOR *Althea* has not been, and is not likely to be, carried forward as a significant set of lessons learned for the CSDP. In addition, the fact that EUFOR *Althea* was carried out as a Berlin Plus operation seems to have further narrowed down the lessons that the EU could have drawn from it, insofar as, by the time a takeover of NATOs KFOR operation in Kosovo came up, the political winds had changed in favour of autonomous CSDP operations. Now, the Berlin Plus set-up seemed to work out fine on a practical level in BiH, and a few quite significant steps were made to streamline the arrangements introduced for operation *Concordia* in FYROM. Although a temporary arrangement at the time, the EU Staff Group (EUSG) at NATO-SHAPE was kept on for 'lessons learned' after Concordia ended in December 2003, in anticipation of the SFOR takeover, and a permanent EU Cell was soon established. However, as described in Chapter 4, it soon became clear that it was the EU that put the brakes on when it came to pursuing practical relations with NATO further. The message from NATO-SHAPE – that the EU got a great deal when it secured access to an operations HQ 'at the cost of 19 people' – was lost on people in Brussels, who came to regard Berlin Plus rather as an interim arrangement until the Union secured an operations HQ capacity of its own.[13] Accordingly, the takeover of KFOR, which has not yet left the prospective stage after several years of anticipatory rumours and fact-finding missions, is not likely to benefit much from the *Althea* record. This is, of course, a political decision more than anything else, but going for the autonomous option would also arguably involve an unnecessary duplication of command structure, which is already in place on the ground, since in case of autonomous CSDP operations elsewhere one would at least need to set up a new command structure anyway.

The political symbolism of taking over the last piece of Balkan peacekeeping was, nevertheless, significant, even though the EU has made quite a mess out of the Kosovo experience so far, starting with the refusal by a number of EU Member States, including Spain, Greece, Romania and Slovakia, to recognise it after independence was declared on 17 February 2008. This has, of course, been a controversial issue, but it is probably safe to say that there has been a perceived mismatch between the signals coming out of Brussels prior to the declaration of independence, and the decisiveness of EU concerted action in the period after. The respective roles of the civilian EU Rule of Law Mission in Kosovo, EULEX, launched on 16 February 2008, and the UN police mission, UNMIK, have also been far from clear. The objective of EULEX, which is the biggest civilian CSDP operation to date (1,950 at full operational capacity), is to support the Kosovo authorities by monitoring, mentoring and advising on all areas related to the rule of law, including police, but it also has *some* executive functions, as explained by EU Chief of Mission, Yves de Kermabon, upon deployment (*Koha Ditore Press* 2008). However, until the authorities are ready to execute these powers themselves, it remains chiefly the responsibility of UNMIK and KFOR. As the security situation in Kosovo is stabilised, the latter will be scaled down, starting with the reduction of the NATO forces from 14,000 to 10,000 in January 2010, and then to 2,000 over the next two years (*KosovoCompromise* 2009) – which should be about the right size for an autonomous CSDP operation, judging from previous experience (see below). In the end, it is hard to argue against the impression that Kosovo, which should have been a parade ground for the EU, has left a rather bitter taste in the mouth.

To sum up so far, the EU can somewhat reluctantly, and in a piecemeal fashion, be seen to have reclaimed its backyard, and it has today, with the notable exception of KFOR, become the main security actor in the Balkans. However, the record has been mixed, and the lessons learned limited, since all operations were already wrapped up in a web of different actors, mandates and institutional legacies, ultimately narrowing down the EU's wriggle room for putting its mark on these operations. Then again, it was arguably the lack of an institutional legacy that has allowed the Union to play a more independent operational role if we take a step further east.

Operations in the Caucasus and Eastern Europe

The EU has carried out a small number of civilian CSDP operations in the Caucasus and Eastern Europe, including the EU Rule of Law Mission in Georgia, EUJUST THEMIS, from July 2004 to July 2005, and the EU Border Assistance Mission to Moldova and the Ukraine (EUBAM), launched on 30 November 2005. Both have engaged in activities that have been the main responsibility of the OSCE, which retains an active presence in the region, but may be seen to have lost some of its influence to the EU. However, it is the European Union Monitoring Mission, EUMM, in Georgia, following the Russo-Georgian war in August 2008 that has been the most groundbreaking in several key respects. While all other CSDP operations have taken months, if not years, to plan, and frankly fall short of *crisis* management, at least in the narrowest sense of the term, the EUMM was the first operation to defuse a very real crisis in the immediate EU neighbourhood after the CSDP was created.

After the formal decision to launch the operation was made by the Council on 15 September 2008, some 200 monitors were deployed within two weeks, ready to implement their mandate from 1 October. This was only made possible by what comes across as a true exercise in Civil–Military Coordination (CMCO) in the *informal* meaning of the term, as described in Chapter 4. As an unarmed civilian, autonomous CSDP operation, it was planned and led from within the Civilian Planning and Conduct Capability (CPCC) and DGE VIII, but it was reinforced by 20 officers from the Civil–Military Strategic Planning branch of the CivMilCell. This 'double-secondment' of military staff has since become a semi-permanent arrangement to make up for the lack of strategic planning experience and personnel in the CPCC (interview with Council Secretariat official, June 2009). Moreover, as soon as the intention to launch a CSDP operation materialised over the course of the 12 August and 8 September agreements between Russian President Medvedev and French President Sarkozy, who held the Council Presidency at the time, and the 1 September extraordinary European Council, the EU sent off a seven-person-strong forward team of military planners to Georgia. Their task was to verify the

Operation Plan (OPLAN), and to prepare the deployment of the rest of the force. All of the monitors initially deployed were also either serving or ex-military officers or gendarmes operating as civilians. This was necessary to fulfil the EUMM mandate, a key element of which was the monitoring of the withdrawal of the Russian and Georgian armed forces to the positions held prior to the war, since this required familiarity with military equipment, tactics and procedures.

It is also worth mentioning that upon arrival of the forward team of planners, the EU Situation Centre (SITCEN) already had two to three people on the ground providing a reach-back capacity to relay intelligence information to and from Brussels. The information provided through this channel was reportedly of great help to the forward team (interview with Council Secretariat official, June 2009). The deployment of SITCEN personnel was another EU first, and although its budget is not geared towards such forward activities, the sentiments are that if needed, funds will be 'lobbied for' – and most likely secured – in future contingencies (interview with Council Secretariat official, June 2009). Similarly, the success of the forward team, an arrangement that was also used in the Aceh Monitoring Mission (see below), gave impetus to plans for a so-called Deployable Augmentee Cadre (interviews with Council Secretariat officials, June 2009). The idea of the DAC concept is to have a small team of dedicated personnel, prepared and deployable at short notice, who will arrive at the scene of a crisis at the earliest possible time, and then ensure that the initial political objectives are verified and carried forward from the Crisis Management Concept (CMC) down to the OPLAN (see Chapter 4).

As described by several EUMS officers, the EUMM did 'develop *a kind of* Comprehensive Approach at both the Brussels and theatre levels', and it has been deemed the 'most comprehensive of all CSDP operations so far' (interview with Council Secretariat official, April 2009, emphasis added). Yet others have pointed out that the operation ended up as a civilian monitoring mission chiefly 'to avoid a military confrontation with Russia' (comment by British officer, Brussels, June 2009). ICG has also, on the one hand, commended the EU for being 'quick to broker the ceasefire and dispatch monitors to Georgia', but, on the other hand, criticised it for its failure to 'react firmly when Russia did not fully comply with the terms of the agreement' (ICG 2009: 14). In any case, one should probably be careful not to exaggerate the EU's diplomatic victory – nor the subsequent launch of the EUMM – after the Russo-Georgian war. What the crisis did was, after all, to set in plain view the utter powerlessness of the Western world when faced with Russian aggression in those regions it deems remain inside its traditional sphere of influence. Under the French Presidency, the EU did, nevertheless, turn out to be the only player capable of doing something, whereas NATO's only option, the suspension of all military cooperation with Russia, effectively closed down any room for manoeuvre.

This effectively left the EU with a great responsibility for managing the crisis, a responsibility that it has carried alone after the UN observer mission (UNOMIG) and the OSCE mission were closed down.[14] This first and foremost represents another serious blow to the OSCE, which may please those proponents of the CSDP who see European security as a zero-sum game. Then again, it may be that Russia finds that it is better positioned to bargain with the EU, or sees it as less of a threat than both NATO and the OSCE (of which it is a member), which do not have trade or other issues to worry about in their dealings with Moscow. It is no secret that some 'member states do not always strongly represent core EU principles when it comes to Russia, hastening, for example, to restore ties that were briefly suspended due to the war in Georgia' (ICG 2009: 15). EU-Russia interdependence can, therefore, be seen as a double-edged sword for the CSDP, which allows the EU some leverage vis-à-vis Moscow, but which may also prevent it from acting resolutely if required. Indeed, it is a good example of how the different identities of the EU do not always come together.

Operations in the Middle East

As a final key area within our first circle, the Middle East has been regarded as a priority area for the EU, but one that has seen comparatively little CSDP activities, in terms of number of operations and personnel involved. The EU has run a small EU Border Assistance Mission at the Rafah Crossing Point, EUBAM Rafah, since November 2005, and a Police (strengthening) Mission for the Palestinian Territories, EUPOL COPPS, since January 2006. Although these operations may be interesting from a political point of view, no military CSDP operations have been carried out in this region. UNIFIL II, following the 2006 Israeli offensive in Lebanon, turned out to be a predominantly European affair. It can, as such, be put on the EU's 'strengthening of the UN' account, but few operational lessons learned can be drawn from it, save perhaps the difficulties of force generation for such an operation (see Chapter 3).

Africa and the wider Middle East: a testing ground for the CSDP

While most of the operations in Europe were handed over to the EU, leaving it with little room to put its own distinct stamp on them, CSDP operations on the African continent have allowed the EU to experiment more. A number of EU-specific force concepts and principles have been generated en route following experience gained in these operations, although the lessons learned, as we shall see, have perhaps not always been the 'right' ones. Being on the receiving end of five EU military operations, Africa has become a key CSDP area of operations. At the same time, the EU has become a vehicle for the revival of European peacekeeping in Africa, after a series of traumatic experiences in Somalia and Rwanda in the early 1990s led to 'an almost complete withdrawal from military engagement in Africa' (Ulriksen *et al.* 2004: 509). However, with France, which has remained an active unilateral intervener in its former colonies throughout the post-Cold War period, as the main engine of its African endeavour, the EU has had to navigate carefully between both accusations of legitimising national policies, and of inconsistency in the face of emerging crises.

Operations in the Democratic Republic of Congo (DRC)

Within three months of launching its first military operation in FYROM, the EU launched a second one, *Artemis*, in the Democratic Republic of Congo (DRC) on 12 June 2003. This was the first *autonomous* CSDP operation, the symbolic value of which was considerable insofar as it showed that the EU was able to operate independently and outside NATO's traditional area of operations. Despite its short duration (four months) and comparatively small force (1,400 troops), operation *Artemis* was immediately hailed as a success. However, it needs to be stressed from the start that much of what made it a success relied heavily on the French involvement throughout the operation (see Ulriksen *et al.* 2004).

First, the speed with which the operation was mounted was largely due to the fact that France started the operational planning at least a month before the Council formally launched it on 12 June, and also before the EU planning process was initiated by the joint action of 5 June. In response to the UN Secretary-General's request to the UN Member States to supply an interim force to stabilise the rapidly deteriorating security situation in Bunia pending reinforcement of the UN MONUC force in September, France had, in fact, indicated that it would be ready to take the lead of such a force already on 13 May. As Ståle Ulriksen *et al.* also point out, being highly experienced in operations of this kind in Africa, France would certainly have contingency plans that could be adapted to a comparatively small operation in the DRC (Ulriksen *et al.* 2004: 512). However, as the French made it clear that they would not intervene alone, the EU alternative was by no means a given at this point. That Britain somewhat surprisingly went along with the proposal from Paris for a French-led autonomous EU operation was arguably due to the fact that, in this case, both countries' desire to strengthen Europe's military credibility and reinforce the EU's role in Africa went hand in hand – and Europe needed to prove that it could still launch operations in spite of its divisions over the Iraq war.[15]

The claims to success in this particular operation have been largely undisputed. The usual criticism by NGOs and think tanks, that *Artemis* was too limited in time, scope and space, seemed to stem from a misperception of what it was actually tasked to do (Howorth 2007: 234; ICG 2003). In accordance with its UN Chapter VII mandate, the EU force actually managed to secure the city of Bunia, protect the airport and the refugee camps, and avoid further killings of civilians by the militias who had taken over the city. It did so by proactive and robust use of military force by seasoned French marine infantry troops, 'coherent, prepared and highly experienced in operations in Africa', reinforced by 70–80 Swedish Special Forces troops (Ulriksen *et al.* 2004: 516–517). This included serious clashes with the militias – one amounting to the 'the hardest fight for any Swedish unit since the UN campaigns in Katanga in the 1960s' – which ended in an ultimatum by the EU Force Commander Gen. Jean-Paul Thonier on 22 June to the militias to lay down their arms or leave the city (Ulriksen *et al.* 2004: 519). As it turned out, most of the militiamen left, continuing to massacre civilians in other parts of Ituri. It is this point that lies at the heart of the critique against *Artemis*, although the EU force can hardly by blamed for it, as Jolyon Howorth points out, since it only did what it was tasked to do, and could hardly have been expected to do more with the time and resources it was given (Howorth 2007: 234).

This sentiment was shared by the UN in a lessons learned report, which was generally positive towards how the EU Interim Emergency Multinational Force (IEMF) carried out its mandate (DPKO 2004). The report contends that 'the IEMF used the threat of the use of force in a convincing manner, managing quickly to establish its presence and stabilize the area of its deployment' (DPKO 2004: 12). Also, despite the French dominance on the ground, the report contends that 'the EU dimension added a significant strength to the IEMF' and that the 'employment of EU diplomacy was effective in obtaining cooperation by neighbouring states' (DPKO 2004: 12). This could hardly have been done by France alone, given its strained relations with Rwanda in particular (Ulriksen *et al.* 2004: 511). That said, the report also criticised the IEMF for its lack of communication with MONUC in the pre-deployment phase. In fact, MONUC was not even warned of the landing of the first EU troops. Also, once the EU force had left, MONUC could not benefit from such EU assets as the French and Swedish Special Forces, nor the overflight capability of eight French Mirage fighters operating out of Chad and Entebbe. As it turned out, 'even DPKO's request for the IEMF to make occasional visits was turned down by the EU' (DPKO 2004: 14).

However, despite the criticisms, *Artemis* could be and was portrayed as a genuine and shared EU commitment to the UN. It was undoubtedly a by-product of the Iraq war, but this did not, as Richard Gowan argues, overshadow the fact that it also showed that Western military interventions did not have to be about regime change. This won African support, while contributing to the image of Europe as the 'good interventionist', in contrast to the United States (Gowan 2009: 58). As such, *Artemis* reinforced the element of *otherness* so essential to a pending EU strategic culture, while at the same time, proving that the EU could, indeed, resort to robust military force without violating its identity as a benign or peaceful strategic actor (see Chapter 2). That it was, to all intents and purposes, a French operation was successfully defused as a (potential) problem, and it was instead taken forward as one among several positive lessons learned from *Artemis*. In the long run, these lessons may not necessarily have been the right ones.

First, the successful use of the framework nation command option worked as a catalyst for the establishment of the six national operations headquarters, which were later in 2003 identified as the preferred option for running autonomous EU operations (European

Council 2003c; see Chapter 4). As such, *Artemis* set a precedent for what has, by some, been referred to as a largely ineffective and expensive proliferation of headquarters for multinational operations in Europe, while putting work towards a truly integrated EU operations headquarters (see discussion in Chapter 4) on the backburner (see e.g. Witney 2008). It worked well in this instance – and perhaps better than the other option, i.e. NATO-SHAPE, would have in this particular case – because of France's unique experience in running operations in Africa, but this was exactly why it may also have set a false precedent for subsequent autonomous EU operations. Secondly, the 'bridging operation' concept proved to be a constructive way for the EU to support and reinforce its commitment to the UN (see e.g. Braud 2006). But setting specific force levels for these kinds of ventures was probably ill-conceived. As it has turned out, the EU Battlegroups (EUBGs), which built directly on the *Artemis* experience (France/Germany/UK 2004), have for both practical and political reasons not found their use to date (see below) – and have, therefore, arguably proved to be – from an operational, but perhaps not transformational, point of view – an irrelevant EU tool (see Chapter 5). Thirdly, as a traditional peace enforcement operation, *Artemis* did not add to the Comprehensive Approach. In fact, the success of the operation was not in any way linked to the EU's capabilities as a civil–military actor, but rather to French (and Swedish) military efficiency. According to an NGO report cited in Ulriksen *et al.*, there was no senior EU civilian representative working with the operation commander to link the operation to broader civilian activities in the region (Saferworld and International Alert 2004; Ulriksen *et al.* 2004: 515).[16] For example, the Commission was simultaneously supporting NGOs in Bunia to build capacity in the local police, but no direct contact was made.[17] Finally, the use of the framework nation idea as a way for individual Member States to 'step up' in CSDP worked out fine for the French who already had a clear national interest in taking the lead in *Artemis* and, at the same time, push the CSDP forward. However, it annoyed the Germans, who felt compelled by France to take the lead in a second short military venture in the DRC in 2006.

When, in December 2005, a new request came from the UN for an EU military force to assist MONUC in maintaining peace and security during the upcoming presidential elections, Europe's enthusiasm for another military operation in Africa and in the DRC had waned considerably. Britain, heavily engaged in Iraq and Afghanistan, made it clear that it would not contribute to the operation, whereas France, having taken the lead in *Artemis*, felt that it was time for another EU state to step up. Of course, the only other option was Germany, and the French made no secret of their desire to exploit this opportunity to (re-)establish the special Franco-German relationship inside the CSDP (Howorth 2007: 238). The Germans, on the other hand, had been sceptical of extending the CSDP area of operations to Africa all along, feeling that it was too far away from Europe (Martinelli 2008: 125). Accordingly, Germany was less than lukewarm towards taking the lead in a new operation in the DRC. This also dominated the whole process, from the protracted planning, to the composition of the force, and the premature withdrawal after only four months.

First, in stark contrast to the seven days it took for the EU to agree on *Artemis*, the EU first offered its initial reply to the UN in March 2006. What was offered was a small military force of 400 troops to be stationed in Kinshasa, but with the back-up of a battalion size 'over the horizon' force of 1,200 troops to be stationed in neighbouring Gabon. This set-up reflected roughly 'option III' of three intervention scenarios drawn up by the EU Military Committee (EUMC) in February (see Quille 2006: 9).[18] It was agreed that the force would deploy well in time before the first round of elections on 30 July, but the first troops did not arrive until mid-June, after a protracted force generation process, and the gearing-up of the EU Operations Headquarters (OHQ) in Potsdam, which – again in stark contrast with the French command in *Artemis* – was completely new to running a multinational operation of this sort. This could be seen as valuable experience for the Germans, but the costs of setting up a 400-person-strong headquarters to run a limited military operation in Africa 'only to make the French happy' were regarded by many Germans as higher than the gains (interviews with German diplomats, April 2009 and June 2009).

These tensions seem, in turn, to have been confirmed by the German Operation Commander, Gen. Karlheinz Viereck, and the French Force Commander on the ground, Gen. Christian Damay. The reported result was poor coordination between the OHQ and the FHQ, but this was also due to the late build-up of the FHQ (Ducastel 2007; Knutsen 2008). In addition, the German Bundestag (as usual) imposed strong caveats on its forces, which meant that of the 780 German troops only some 100 went to Kinshasa under

French command (see Howorth 2007: 238). However, potentially more disrupting was the strict end date set by German Defence Minister Franz-Josef Jung, who promised that the German troops would be home by Christmas (see Martinelli 2008: note 8). This meant that the operation would end at the time when the force was most needed – after the announcement of the election results on 29 October. Amongst other criticisms launched at EUFOR RD Congo was the fact that the EU troops were overwhelmingly based in the capital of Kinshasa, which had been pacified for some time. None were deployed to the eastern parts of the DRC, where trouble was more likely to occur. However, this would have required a vastly bigger force, and was never considered an option by the EUMC, whether this reflected the wishes of UN DPKO, or a realisation of the limits of the number of forces that Germany and the rest of the Member States would be willing to contribute. In any case, when discussing the three intervention scenarios in February, the PSC ambassadors emphasised that any EU role should be of a *preventive* and *deterrent* character, since the EU did not intend to substitute MONUC (Quille 2006: 9). A nationwide EU military presence in a country three times the size of France was arguably far beyond reasonable expectations anyway.

Instead Solana put the usual positive spin on the operation by underlining that by keeping the 'over the horizon' force on standby in Gabon, EUFOR avoided an unnecessarily heavy military presence in Kinshasa (Solana 2007). Whether the relative calm that attended the elections was due to the deterrent effect of the EU force is hard to say, but the few incidents that occurred were effectively defused.[19] The operation, therefore, fulfilled its mandate to support MONUC during a crucial phase of the transition of the DRC from civil war to functional democracy. As such, the striking dissonance between *Artemis'* largely undisputed claims to success, and the allegations of 'tokenism' that made it 'unlikely' for EUFOR RD Congo 'to go down in the annals as an CSDP success story', as concluded by Jolyon Howorth (2007: 239), appears a bit unfair (Giegerich and Haine 2006).

When evaluated as a purely military operation, EUFOR RD Congo received a fair amount of mostly appropriate criticism, but when compared with *Artemis*, EUFOR RD Congo fared better in at least two key respects. First, EU–UN cooperation on the ground was reportedly better than in *Artemis*, as close contacts were established between

EU Force Commander Gen. Damay and MONUC from the outset of the operation. Yet there were the usual problems associated with the exchange of intelligence, and the fact that EUFOR was allowed to act in support of MONUC only when explicitly requested by the UN, which led, for example, to some delays in EUFOR's reaction to the August riots (Martinelli 2008: 123).

Secondly, while *Artemis* was very much a traditional, isolated military endeavour, the collective EU efforts in support of the 2006 elections, including EUFOR, were, indeed, true to the Comprehensive Approach. In fact, the elections turned out to be a focal point around which the activities of the two parallel civilian CSDP operations, which had been launched in 2005, and the EU military force presence in DRC, finally came together. The small EU police operation, EUPOL Kinshasa, was, upon the recommendation of the Political and Security Committee (PSC), reinforced with 29 international staff to help secure order in and around the capital for the five months of the elections (European Council 2006c). These came in addition to some 20 police advisors, who had been deployed since February 2005 to guide and supervise the so-called Integrated Police Unit (IPU), a specialised unit within the Congolese police force, established to protect state institutions and reinforce the international security apparatus in the DRC (see Martinelli 2008: 118–120).[20] In addition, the EU Security Sector Reform (SSR) operation, EUSEC DRC, was involved in nationwide security efforts around the time of the elections. Under the guidance of some 50 EU officers deployed since June 2005, a number of so-called integrated brigades have been developed to unite some of the rebel factions into a single Congolese army. Of these brigades (of about 4,000 soldiers in each), 12 were deployed nationwide by July 2006.[21] Gerrard Quille reports that it was 'suggested' that these 12 brigades were enough to secure the elections, although Head of EUSEC DRC, Gen. Pierre Joana, had originally indicated that 18 would be necessary – never mind the concerns that most of the brigades were poorly trained, poorly managed, and lacked food, shelter and equipment (see Quille 2006: 8). Of course, if security was the real concern, many Congolese would probably have felt more reassured with more European troops instead.

Still, the fact that the EU did respond to a (second) specific request for military support by the UN in the DRC, albeit with a small and perhaps largely symbolic military operation, did prove that *Artemis* had not been a one-off, as projected by some analysts (see Gegout

2005). As such, it may also have reinforced perceptions in UN DPKO of 'CSDP as an instrument – or even a front – for the deployment of European armies in Africa' (Braud 2006: 77). However, as a new crisis mounted in the DRC in the autumn of 2008, the expectations – or at least hopes – that the EU would feel some kind of obligation to send troops again, since it had 'after all, sent troops to ensure stability in the Congo in 2003 and 2006', were soon crushed (Gowan 2009: 58). Although the 3,000 forces asked for by the UN Secretary-General did not seem an insurmountable number for the EU Member States, and the political pressure was considerable, they consistently failed to offer troops. It seemed as if over the course of five years of operations in the DRC, the Member States had grown wary of the whole venture one by one, such that by 2008, only Belgium seemed strongly in favour of a third EU military operation.[22] As summarised by Richard Gowan:

> Had the timing been better, or the security situation more promising, there is no way the Europeans would have stayed away. By this logic, the crisis was tragic and an embarrassment for the EU, but not really a turning point for European security cooperation. (Gowan 2009: 58)

If it was an embarrassment for the EU, it was not really held to account for it, as the Union's failure to act when faced with a new crisis in the DRC was overshadowed by the launch of two other EU military operations in Africa at the time, EUFOR Tchad/RCA and EU NAVFOR *Atalanta* off the coast of Somalia. This seems to confirm a maxim that permeates EU crisis management beyond that first concentric circle, and on the African continent in particular: *where* is less important, doing *something* is usually enough.

Operations in Central Africa

When a request from Paris was received through diplomatic channels by fellow Member States on 21 May 2007 to 'do something in eastern Chad', they were reminded of the notoriously bad conscience that had haunted Europe and the rest of the Western world over the failure to deal with the humanitarian crisis in Darfur from 2003 onwards (see Mattelaer 2008: 10). Despite persistent rumours in 2004 that the EU was preparing a military intervention, some seeing it as a perfect opportunity to test-run the EU Battlegroups (EUBGs), the challenge in Darfur, as

Jolyon Howorth concludes, 'proved too severe a politico-military test for the fledgling CSDP' (Howorth 2007: 215). Instead, the EU avoided direct involvement in the crisis by assuming a supporting role behind the African Union Mission in Sudan (AMIS) under the guise of 'effective multilateralism' through 'working with partners', while at the same time, respecting 'African ownership' (see Braud 2006; Howorth 2007). Between January 2004 and December 2007, the EU delivered what Solana eventually came to label a 'Consolidated EU package in support of AMIS', which, within the CSDP framework, included support for both the military and police components of AMIS II.[23] The absence of Western boots on the ground in Darfur, nevertheless, remained a source of persistent criticism against the EU, and it was, therefore, a key contextual factor for the decision to launch the EU operation in Chad and the Central African Republic (CAR) in 2008.

The original French proposal was presented amidst increasing armed activity amongst rebel groups in Eastern Chad and north-eastern CAR since 2006, which had, in turn, led to mass population displacement and worsening conditions for the some 230,000 Sudanese refugees in Eastern Chad.[24] In response to these developments, the UN sent a fact-finding mission to Chad and the CAR in June 2006, recommending a security presence to protect the refugees and displaced persons in the UN camps in Eastern Chad bordering Darfur. The Security Council subsequently supported the deployment of a UN force, but Chadian authorities refused (see Seibert 2009: 4). However, France was able to draw upon its close relations with Chad in obtaining the government's acceptance of a prospective EU military force as part of a multidimensional UN presence in Chad and the CAR. Paris taking the lead was, therefore, a precondition for an operation in the first place, but it also cast doubt on the impartiality and neutrality of an EU force. In contrast to more questionable concerns about the EU legitimising French national interests in operation *Artemis* in the DRC, French interests in Chad were well known to all parties and hard to argue against. France already had forces deployed in N'djamena as part of operation *Epervier* (since 1986), and had as late as in April 2006 – albeit only through *indirect* military logistics and intelligence support – helped the government led by General Idriss Déby fight back a rebel attack on the capital launched from Western Sudan and north-eastern CAR (Seibert 2007: 9). This led to the somewhat paradoxical situation in that the EU force needed to be *multinationalised* to avoid claims to partiality, while the other Member States, seeing it as a French venture from the start, expected it to also put up most of the troops and assets for the operation, and were, therefore, reluctant to offer the contributions that would ensure a convincing 'level of multinationality'.

The particular challenges associated with force generation, as well as the political and strategic planning for EUFOR Tchad/RCA, have received comparatively thorough coverage (see Mattelaer 2008; Seibert 2007). There is, therefore, little need to go into specific details, but rather look into some key points raised, as some of them also tie in with lessons (not) learned from the previous EU operations. First, with regard to force generation, the option of using one of the battlegroups came up early, and as an alternative to sending one to the DRC in response to the autumn 2008 riots (Mattelaer 2008: 15). Gen. Karl Engelbrektsson, commander of the Nordic Battlegroup (NBG) on standby at the time, said that 'the NBG would have absolutely been ready' had Chad been interpreted as a 'battlegroup situation' (*Jane's Defence Weekly* 2008). Insofar as it was not, this appeared as more of a political decision than an outcome of an objective needs assessment.[25] Deploying the NBG would have also complicated the relationship between a British-led EUBG with a Swedish Force Commander, and the French force presence already on the ground, although they were formally to be set up as two self-sustained forces each with their own mission description. The British, who had the dedicated OHQ responsibility for the NBG, were heavily engaged in Afghanistan. The French had the enablers and the know-how when it came to operating in Chad. Hence, the costs of sending in the NBG did not outweigh the gains in terms of signalling impartiality – nor the prospective prestige in going operational with the EUBGs. In the end, the Member States, therefore, opted for the usual force generation path.

According to one EU officer, 'Chad was calibrated according to what the force generation market could bear', rather than resulting from an estimation of force requirements from a mission objective, as is normal procedure (interview with Council Secretariat official, June 2009). But even then the force was lacking key assets – most importantly helicopters and aircraft – at the projected time of deployment (see Seibert 2009). It was only in a fifth (!) force generation conference (preceded by an informal indicative one), in January 2008, that France 'grudgingly provided the essential assets to be able to start the mission' (Mattelaer 2008: 24). Shortfalls in aircraft were covered by double-hatting French

Mirages and unmanned aerial vehicles (UAVs) from the *Epervier* contingent, while it was assumed – although formally no arrangements were made – that the *Epervier* forces would also provide a strategic reserve, which was still not provided for (Mattelaer 2008: 24).[26] This again brought up the question of the impartiality of the force. In fact, this appeared to be such a major concern that when it turned out that Irish troops had very similar battle fatigues to the French, Brussels reportedly insisted they get new uniforms (Gowan 2009: 59). Despite EUFOR Tchad/RCA being hailed by Brussels as 'the most multinational military operation carried out in Africa so far' then, it did almost by default once again end up as a predominantly French operation (European Council 2009a). Because of the protracted force generation, it also only reached its Full Operational Capacity (FOC) of 3,700 troops on 15 September 2008, almost halfway into the operation.

Because of the problems of force generation, the planning of EUFOR Tchad/RCA took place in a vacuum. This meant that the OPLAN had to be adjusted several times, while the final composition of the force deviated from the Strategic Option that had been adopted by the PSC on 4 October 2007 (interview with Council Secretariat official, June 2009).[27] In addition, there was the usual lack of continuity between the strategic planning, which takes place in the EUMS, while awaiting the OHQ in Paris to gear itself up and take on the operational planning, a process that was further complicated by the late appointment of Irish LtGen. Patrick Nash as Operation Commander (see Witney 2008: 48). Finally, planning was made difficult by the lack of a clear mission objective. The force received a UN Chapter VII mandate to: protect civilians in danger, particularly refugees and displaced persons; facilitate the delivery of humanitarian aid and the free movement of humanitarian personnel by helping to improve security in the area of operations; and protect UN personnel, facilities, installations and equipment, and ensure the security and freedom of movement of its staff and associated personnel (European Council 2009a). The EU force was to deploy alongside MINURCAT, whose chief task was to help maintain order in the camps for refugees and displaced persons through the training of Chadian police, who were to do the actual policing inside the camps (see Seibert 2007: 17). The EU force was, in other words, tasked to maintain a *condition* under which other instruments would be allowed to operate, but never really given a clear outcome or end-state.

Instead it was given an end-*date* exactly one year after the operation was launched, on which it was assumed that MINURCAT would also take over the responsibility for the military element. As such, it was conceived as a *bridging operation*, but it was far from clear at this point whether the UN would actually be able to launch a military operation by 15 March 2009. After operation EUFOR RD Congo in 2006, it was also concluded that setting strict end-dates was not advisable, which, as Alexander Mattelaer remarks, begs the question of why the EU went against its own recommendations (Mattelaer 2008: 30). A traditional fear of so-called 'mission creep', which stems from experiences with 'never-ending' operations such as UNIFIL in Lebanon (running since 1978) partly explains why EU Member States keep insisting on short timeframes. But an operational pattern of providing an initial entry force for a short period and then handing over the operation to the UN also comes across as appealing for those in Brussels who tend to resort to numbers of operations as indicative of how successful the CSDP has become.

Moreover, the mandate of maintaining secure *conditions* in which other actors, in this case the UN, engage with the actual humanitarian challenges *inside* the camps, although these challenges are admittedly merely a symptom of wider regional challenges, leaves very little room for failure. That is, with a comparatively small (3,700 troops) but robust force, drawing upon the historical presence of French forces in Chad to provide a credible deterrent, it was relatively easy for the EU to raise the level of security in the dedicated area(s) of operations. The only incident that occurred was a rebel incursion in 2009, which avoided the camps, as these were defended by EU forces. That the UN was not able to deploy as fast as the EU, such that by September, halfway into the operation, only some 300 Chadian police officers had received UN training, while none of them were even yet present on the ground inside the camps, did not end up on the EU balance sheet (see Mattelaer 2008: 29). It could, on the other hand, be argued that this should have been an EU responsibility as part of a parallel, or perhaps even *integrated*, civilian CSDP presence, although it is unclear whether this option was actually discussed. In any case, if using the Comprehensive Approach as a benchmark, EUFOR Tchad/RCA fared only marginally better than operation *Artemis*, and probably worse than EUFOR RD Congo.

However, from a military point of view, the EU successfully passed a considerable challenge by deploying and sustaining its forces in a land-locked country with almost no functioning infrastructure what-soever (see Seibert 2007). Despite the fact that France provided 'more than 50 per cent of the structure', LtGen. David Leakey, Director of the EUMS, stressed that 'the EUMS had been impressed by the per-formance of member states whose militaries were not accustomed to African deployments' and that accordingly a number of them could now take on such operations, 'not only with competence but with con-fidence' (*Jane's Defence Weekly* 2009b). Yet the problem appears to be that the political will to do so may seem to have waned correspond-ingly since the first EU military operation in the DRC in 2003.

The only way to avoid the embarrassment of pulling out of Chad and the CAR without a UN force in place in March 2009 was by re-hatting some 2,000 of the EU soldiers, which prompted an EU officer to admit that 'in reality, Chad was a predominantly French force re-hatted to EUFOR and then re-hatted again to a UN operation' (interview with Council Secretariat official, June 2009). The handover was essentially sold by the EU as a successful example of EU–UN cooperation, and a 'continuing EU commitment' to the Darfur crisis (European Council 2009a). But the fact of the matter is that much of the assets that pro-vided the EU force with a credible deterrent, including fighters and helicopters, were withdrawn, while the UN continues the struggle to fulfil the 5,200 troop target for MINURCAT II (*Jane's Defence Weekly* 2009a). In the end, the failure to engage militarily in the DRC when requested by the UN in 2008, even as it had a battlegroup ready to go, and the difficulties of force generation in Chad, even as European states should have been itching to send troops to ease their conscience over Darfur, seem to indicate a steadily growing fatigue when it comes to humanitarian operations in Africa.

Other EU operations in Africa and beyond

The comparative enthusiasm with which the anti-piracy operation EU NAVFOR *Atalanta* off the coast of Somalia was launched in December 2008 would seem to further harm the image of the EU as the 'good interventionist'. With this operation still running, it has become increas-ingly harder for the EU to distance itself from claims that it is legitimis-ing national interests in operations such as EUFOR Tchad/RCA, and even harder to escape the point that operation *Atalanta* restricts itself to treating only those symptoms of a web of interrelated problems in Somalia that directly threaten European economic interests, while the factors causing the symptoms are left largely untreated. In other words, operation *Atalanta*, to many, has signalled a shift in EU policy away from operations that could be at least *portrayed* as driven by humanitarian concerns rather than or in addition to self-interest.

The small military training mission EUTM Somalia, which was launched in Uganda in May 2010 to provide training for Somali security forces, is probably not enough to turn this image around. And insofar as no other operations seem to be in the pipeline yet, the current image is not likely to be challenged for some time, since at the moment, the CSDP is again reduced to a rather small active presence on the ground in Africa.[28]

The world is the stage: the EU's global ambitions

Among the few operations beyond the neighbourhood and Africa, the EU carried out the Aceh Monitoring Mission (AMM) in Indonesia between 15 September 2005 and 15 December 2006. Its mandate was to monitor the implementation of the peace agreement brokered by former Finnish President Martti Ahtisaari and signed by Indonesia and the Free Aceh Movement (GAM) in Helsinki in 2005. The mission was, as such, a forerunner for the Georgia Monitoring Mission (EUMM) launched in 2008 in terms of how it was composed (predominantly personnel with military background) and the tasks it carried out (monitoring demobilisation and relocation of military personnel and equipment).

Deployment of the 230-person-strong mission was preceded by an Initial Monitoring Presence (AMM-IMP), which filled the gap between the signing of the peace agreement and the launch of the AMM proper, and made preparations for the arrival of the main force, an arrangement which was later taken forward into the Georgia mission (Kirwan 2008: 132–133). In addition, the AMM managed to bypass some of the budgetary and procedural constraints that threatened to stall a rapid deployment, a feat that owes much to the presence of Pieter Feith, a seasoned Dutch diplomat and long-serving Director in the Council Secretariat, as Head of Mission. In terms of impact, the AMM was widely regarded as a success, and a perfect example of 'effective multilateralism', insofar as it was conducted in close association with ASEAN, which also supplied the force with monitors on the ground (see Feith 2007; Kirwan 2008). As expected, Brussels was also quick to announce the role of the AMM in giving the CSDP a global dimension. But insofar as the EU has only launched this one operation globally so far, it would be an exaggeration to say that the CSDP really has a global scope for its operations, at least for the moment.

Concluding remarks

An analysis of the more than 20 operations that the EU has carried out under the auspices of the CSDP confirms, at the very least, that the EU has developed the resolve to engage in operations, although the interests they serve are not always readily discernible. Nevertheless, the EU must be seen to fulfil our third criterion for a strategic actor. However, perhaps more than anything else, the CSDP operational portfolio reflects what Xymena Kurowska refers to as a 'strategic search for opportunities to convey an image of the EU as unique crisis manager' (Kurowska 2009: 25). As observed across all strategic dimensions, what the EU *does* tends to be framed in a way that confirms what it *is* (or ought to be), whereas appropriate benchmarks are often lacking. Because of what operations have become for the EU itself, a source of confidence and confirmation, they are naturally predisposed for success even before they are launched. Also in the research literature, even in the few edited volumes that cover the CSDP operations explicitly, operations tend to be treated in isolation from each other and subjected to different benchmarks (see Deighton and Mauer 2006; Grevi *et al.* 2009; Merlingen and Ostrauskaite 2008). Each individual operation naturally needs to be evaluated on the basis of what its purpose is/was, but given the role that operations play in relation to the overall perception of the EU as a strategic actor, they also need to be seen *in toto*.

This chapter again used the Comprehensive Approach as a reference point and criterion for the selection of the operations that are covered in depth, since, as argued in Chapter 2, this has become a central end in itself, and a defining feature of the CSDP. Geographical proximity was, in turn, chosen as an appropriate ordering principle for three concentric circles around Europe to highlight comprehensiveness across individual operations within each regional theatre of operations. Interestingly, the character of the operations and the lessons learned from them are often specific to each circle. For example, whereas operations in the first circle are framed inside a neighbourhood logic, according to which some kind of association or interdependence with the EU is always present and bilateral ties between individual Member States and host countries for deployment are downplayed, operations inside the second circle are almost always pushed by one (usually France) or a small group of Member States. This is a wholly uncontroversial point to be made, but it is worth pondering whether association or interdependence represents, in fact, a constraint on CSDP operations, which effectively limits it ability to act resolutely and in an executive manner if required. The promise of speedy accession to the EU for neighbouring countries, and the pursuit of strategic partnerships with countries like Russia, fit badly with forceful intervention. As such, there may seem to exist what can be referred to as an *executive gap* in between military and civilian operations concepts, in particular when it comes to policing, as reflected in the difficulties of accommodating hybrid forces, such as the Eurogendfor, into the heavily compartmentalised CSDP operational practices (see Merlingen and Ostrauskaite 2005, 2006).

As far as a Comprehensive Approach to operations is concerned, there is, therefore, a general point to be made about the lack of connectivity between civilian and military operations. No integrated operations have been carried out so far, while the most publicised ventures in Africa, such as *Artemis* and EUFOR Tchad/RCA, have been hailed as strictly *military* success stories. This, of course, raises the question: is something else going on in operational terms that does not correspond to the EU's strategic narrative? And if so, what does this mean for the credibility of the Comprehensive Approach narrative as a focal point around which to build a viable CSDP for the future? We shall return to this in the final chapter.

7 | Conclusion: a comprehensive strategic actor for the future?

> If capacity for informed strategic analysis – integrating political, economic, and military judgement – is not preserved and applied, decisions on the use of force will be uninformed and, therefore, irresponsible.
>
> Richard K. Betts (1997)

The aim of this book has been to develop a conceptual framework for analysing how a non-state actor such as the EU can purposefully prepare for and apply the use of military force. I wanted to present a way to understand the CSDP, how it has evolved and how it works in practice. More importantly, I wanted to offer a robust and inclusive conceptual framework for assessing how it will continue to evolve in the years to come.

The – in many ways – unlikely marriage between military force and a non-state civilian power such as the EU raises a number of issues. While security and defence have generally represented a last bastion of realist and intergovernmental theories, the rapid and far-reaching evolution of the CSDP has defied many of the inherent state and national constraints on cooperation that these theories predict. This book shows that the security governance approach may offer a third way of understanding a case like the CSDP, which is neither a function of integration in the traditional understanding of the term nor a function of intergovernmental bargaining. The concept of security governance has proved a valuable tool for identifying some of the alternative mechanisms that can help explain outcomes that are inconsistent with or only partly explained by intergovernmental approaches to the CSDP. By testing some of these theoretical mechanisms against empirical findings, this book has taken some significant steps towards a full-blown EU security governance research programme (Norheim-Martinsen 2010).

Another central question is: does the adoption of military force make the EU into a strategic actor, one that can be understood through the prism of strategy, the research trajectory normally applied to this field? Strategic actorness carries a certain appeal because as a concept it is parsimonious and reduces the analysis of a rather complex field to a question of whether the EU fulfils three more or less straightforward criteria or benchmarks – ends, means and resolve. Yet the very notion of being an *actor* requires intuitively the presence of something more, whether it be identity, or some shared normative or institutional features that induce a sense of collectiveness – or what in the strategic literature is often referred to as a strategic culture. As this book shows, this cultural element is, in fact, essential to our understanding of the EU as a strategic actor. A strategic actor devoid of a clear set of collectively shared security interests can still act in an interest-driven manner, insofar as the way in which to act in itself is perceived to be in the EU's stated interest. By placing a broad understanding of the Comprehensive Approach at the heart of an emerging European strategic culture, the EU as a collective found a commonly acceptable reference point for the evolving CSDP.

As a simple answer to the question this book set out to answer, therefore, the analysis shows that the EU is able to act in an interest-driven manner in its preparations for and application of military force as an inherent part of its foreign and security policy. The EU is inter alia a strategic actor. Yet merely bestowing such a label on the EU is in itself of limited value – as is arguably any other of the fleeting 'labels' that have been used to describe the EU's changing presence in international affairs. Being a strategic or international actor is not a matter of 'either/or' but of 'degree of', as Christopher Hill reminds us (1993, 1998; 2007; see Chapter 1).

However, the very acceptance of the idea that the EU can be perceived as a strategic actor normalises it as an actor in the military domain. There appears to be no obvious reasons for treating traditional high politics, including the CSDP, fundamentally differently from other EU politics. Despite the formal intergovernmental character of the CSDP, this book shows that a number of other factors need to be taken into account to fully explain how this policy area functions. As such, the book challenges deep-rooted assumptions about security and defence in International Relations and EU theory.

For some time, the CSDP has been allowed to develop in a sort of theoretical vacuum between EU studies, on the one hand, and the US-dominated strategic studies, on the other. The former tradition tends to view the EU as something that needs special attention empirically and theoretically. The mere existence of such a vast range of EU-specific integration theories and the constant need to (re-)label its changing 'uniqueness' testify to this. The inherent focus on integration as *process* – i.e. that the CSDP is going somewhere and continues to exist predominantly in its (vast) potentials – also fails to grasp that it has already become a fairly stable policy-making structure, the focus on which may help us explain actual outcomes (Raik 2006; Wallace 2005).

Strategic studies, on the other hand, tend to focus solely on the state and national constraints on the CSDP, and have, therefore, failed to pursue explanations for how it has, in fact, evolved. By reducing the theoretical lag between the fields of EU and strategic studies, the book adds a sense of normalcy to the EU. It also offers reparation to a field that has struggled to retain its relevance in, but also adapt to, a changing security environment (see Betts 1997; Strachan 2005). At the same time, the evolution of the CSDP challenges some traditional truisms of this field.

First, the prominence given to the national interest, which has represented almost a holy grail for many strategic scholars, must be modified to incorporate ideas of *normative fit* or *logic of appropriateness* (see Chapters 1 and 2). *How* to act has become all the more important in the modern world, as reflected in the massive opposition against some of the excesses of the US war on terror in the wake of 9/11, at a time when moral support should never have been higher. This opens up to more nuanced comparisons between the EU and the United States than the traditional weak/strong dichotomy. Ideas of normative fit also allow us to make more fruitful comparisons between the EU and NATO. Secondly, by drawing on recent developments in strategic culture theory, the book shows that the idea of strategic culture may be a particularly useful conceptual tool for studying actors for which ideational relationships can make up for the lack of more material factors, such as borders, language, political structure, national history, etc. Indeed, the idea of strategic narratives as an inherent part of a strategic culture, could even be useful for studying networks such as Al Qaeda (see e.g. Douglas 2007; Kepel 2008), or serve as a model for organisations like the African Union (AU). Finally, the book shows how classical models of organising the civil–military interface offer a useful backdrop for analysing concepts and strategies for dealing with the complex challenges of contemporary peace and stabilisation operations (Barnett 2004; Egnell 2009; Feaver and Kohn 2001; Nielsen and Snider 2009).

As a very basic yet pertinent point, then, the book confirms Michael Howard's (1983b) key message that strategy is not the simple 'science' it is sometimes made out to be. Strategy does, nevertheless, lend a particular focus to the *interconnectedness* between ends, means and resolve that allows us to critically examine and come up with some conclusions as to what has, in fact, been accomplished over the course of ten years of the CSDP.

A comprehensive strategic actor?

A key point raised in this book is that, like any strategic actor, the EU cannot and does not operate outside a fairly stable cultural context that constrains and facilitates certain actions. As argued in Chapter 2, the Comprehensive Approach has become an expression of, or an omnipresent reference point for, the EU's approach to security. Concepts such as *Civil–Military Coordination* (CMCO) and *broad interoperability* are all derived from and reiterate the centrality of the Comprehensive Approach for the CSDP and EU security policy in general. It is also worth noting that amidst all the general controversy that has characterised the jumps and starts mode in which the CSDP has evolved, ideas of civil–military coordination have attracted little resistance or discussion. Part of the reason for this is that the Comprehensive Approach as an idea fitted well with the conventional narrative of the European integration process as a project for peace, by underlining the military dimension's integrated and non-aggressive nature. It also showed that a European strategic culture could be perceived and nurtured without having to resort to the kind of negative stereotyping of an adversary that has often dominated national strategic cultures. As such, it could be both contrasted against and reconciled with an image of a US strategic culture, by showing that transatlantic differences lie not in who or what we *are* and *want*, but in what we *do* and *how* we do it. From being interpreted as a sign of weakness by Robert Kagan (2002, 2003) and others, civil–military approaches have rather become an ideal or potential EU asset, helped along by the complex challenges encountered in places such as Iraq, Afghanistan, Darfur and the DRC.

Accordingly, the Comprehensive Approach has, for reasons of both external and internal pressure, gradually gained a heavier momentum and deeper meaning in and outside of the EU. This has, in turn, created other and higher expectations of the EU as a strategic actor. At the same time, it has created an opportunity for the EU to set its own terms of reference as an *alternative* to the US or NATO approaches. Yet for the EU to remain credible, legitimate and relevant as a strategic actor in the long run, it is bound to deliver ways, means and results that are consistent with these expectations. This book shows that this has only partly been the case.

Nevertheless, Chapter 3 showed that the EU has proved itself as a far more potent security and defence policy-maker than having 27 veto-wielding Member States might suggest. By striking a balance between the influence of state, individual and institutional actors inside the Council structures, the EU has, in several areas, been able to lead a proactive and efficient foreign and security policy, without losing the legitimacy of the consensus mechanism.

By approaching the Council as an informal governance structure, we open up to alternative, more subtle forms of influence than traditional state sources of power. Several studies confirm that through their work in bodies such as the PSC, the COREPER and the Policy Unit, national representatives cease to be mere agents of national interests and develop a collective stake in reaching common grounds for agreement (Duke 2005; Howorth 2007; Juncos and Reynolds 2007; Meyer 2006). Drawing on central mechanisms for influence inside a networked governance structure, such as relative placement in the structure, direct or indirect access to decision-making, access to and control of information, control of and ability to set the agenda, independence, and trust received from other actors in the network, we are also able to start explaining how they influence policy (see also Justaert and Keukeleire 2010; Merand *et al.* 2010).

In addition to examining the largely decision-facilitating effects of institutionalised actors, Chapter 3 also addressed the more proactive role that some individuals have been given in the CFSP/CSDP. Solana in particular played a central role as a political entrepreneur and as an EU 'voice' whenever he was given room to act. Indeed, personalisation of responsibility in the hands of often high profile diplomats or political figures has been a rather successful way for the EU to deal with problems of coordination and leadership. The High Representative, the special coordinators and the EUSRs have given the EU considerable flexibility in terms of external representation and presence, while easing problems of coordination.

This insight was also carried on into the Lisbon Treaty. First, the creation of the joint European External Action Service (EEAS) may in time meet the ambition of giving the EU a stronger voice around the world, while improving consistency and coherence in EU external relations. However, a number of questions remain as to role (policy initiator or implementer), composition, accountability (to the Council, or to the Commission and the Parliament), financing, appointments, rotation schemes, etc. As the EU consolidates its own diplomatic service – and with it the inherent career paths, bureaucracy, norms, rules and procedures of the traditional national diplomatic services – there is a danger of losing some of the inherent dynamism and flexibility that characterised CFSP diplomacy under Solana.

Second, by merging the posts of Commissioner for External Relations and the old HR-CFSP into the new post of High Representative of the Union for Foreign Affairs and Security Policy, the idea was to improve coordination of foreign and security policy between the Council and the Commission. However, it is worth reiterating the fact that this formula did not really amount to a merger of the two positions, but attributed instead to one and the same person the exercise of two functions – i.e. a *personal union* (see Grevi *et al.* 2004: 4; Norheim-Martinsen 2008). It served, as such, largely as a substitute for institutional change. While formally expanding the powers of the High Representative, it also subjects this person to an inevitable conflict of interests and loyalty, as observed in practice in Lady Ashton's frantic shuttle diplomacy between the Commission, the Parliament and the Council in her first years as High Representative. This situation can, in fact, lead to a weakening of the essential trust received from the Member States, which allowed Solana to expand his informal influence, in spite of the limited formal powers that originally defined the post.

We see already that the institutional expansion of the 'Solana era' may have backfired in the sense that the more the formal powers of institutions are strengthened, the more the real influence of institutions over great power policy is undermined. Whereas until recently, the Member States have been careful to avoid the formation of big power directorates inside the EU, the possibility of taking cooperation outside has re-invoked the idea of a two-speed Europe when it comes to security and defence.

The institutional expansion of the Council Secretariat has, indeed, been one of the most striking features of the EU's move towards a security governance structure. From being a *secretariat* similar to those of other international organisations, the Council Secretariat has developed into an autonomous institutional capacity for contingency planning, intelligence analysis, strategic and operational planning, and a civilian and military OHQ for running operations. Part of the rationale for this vast institutional expansion has been the stated desire to develop structures that enable a Comprehensive Approach. However, Chapter 4 shows how the infusion of a military element into the EU bureaucracy was bound to – and has – run into challenges well known to and documented in the strategic studies literature.

On the one hand, the EU has sought a 'Janowitzian' integrated approach to the civil–military interface, perhaps best captured in its aim to develop a 'culture of coordination' as part of the Civil–Military Coordination (CMCO) initiative (European Council 2003b). But on the other hand, it has through the institutionalisation of its crisis management structures confirmed a 'Huntingtonian' separation of its civilian and military arms, which goes back to the lack of attention paid to the cultural and structural challenges of integrating the officers of the EUMS with the rest of the Council Secretariat back in 2000. These challenges were, in turn, accentuated by the lack of civilian structures to counteract military dominance, a strong NATO influence on EU civil–military thinking in the early years, and the influence of national agendas upon the institutionalisation process. The result has been a strong military bias throughout the strategic and operational planning process, which only recently has been 'evened out' by a strengthening of the civilian arm.

The strengthening of civilian institutional capabilities, including the establishment of a civilian 'OHQ' (the CPCC) in 2007, was, indeed, necessary to keep up with the steady growth in the civilian operational activities, but at the same time it cemented a classical stovepipe structure with parallel civilian and military chains of command. Linking work across the 'pipes' has also been difficult, insofar as the EU continues to branch out operational planning and command to the physically and doctrinally separate NATO-SHAPE. The creation of the CivMilCell and the OpCen gave rise to expectations of better coordination when planning operations, and even prospects for leading integrated civil–military operations through the OpCen. However, the cell did, on French insistence, receive a strong military bias, while the OpCen element, on British insistence, was not made a standing OHQ and was given a high threshold for activation.

For all means and purposes this stovepipe structure remains intact. This has made it hard for a 'culture of coordination' to take root, insofar as it would require extensive interaction in order to 'break down' heavily ingrained professional cultures. The non-binding EU Comprehensive Planning Initiative (CPI) did make some headway towards clarifying concepts and procedures, and may have served as a first step towards a 'culture of coordination'. The 'double second-ment' of 20 officers from the Civil–Military Strategic Planning branch of the CivMilCell in the run-up to the Georgia Monitoring Mission in 2008 indicated some flexibility in this regard (see Chapter 6). Other forms of ad hoc coordination, such as the Core Team Meetings (CTMs) and Crisis Response Coordinating Teams (CRCTs) described in Chapter 4, also point towards a gradual move towards a 'culture for coordination'.

If for a brief moment one could put political realities aside, one could imagine a more radical re-organisation of the whole Council Secretariat. Rather than having dedicated 'cells' for civil–military coordination, one could instead go for a model of functionally and/or geographically ordered 'cells' in which military officers and civilians work together on a daily basis. In practical terms, this would mean that the EUMS would represent merely the overall organisational entity comprising all military personnel, and not the physical section of the Kortenberg building where all the officers sit. Some contingency planning and doctrine development would also be carried out in inte-grated cells with a balanced representation of civilian and military per-sonnel, although it is to be expected that some parts of it would have to cater to the specific needs of both branches respectively.

The establishment of the Crisis Management and Planning Directorate (CMPD) has some potential for solving some of the exist-ing problems, insofar as it has lifted civil–military planning activities *out* of the EUMS, *up* to Deputy Director level, and *back* to the Crisis Management Concept (CMC) stage. However, this is a process that needs to be followed closely. Institutional reshuffling apart, it is the continued Huntingtonian *mindset* that seems to permeate the CSDP structures – and which has more to do with institutional culture than formal institutional structures – that needs to be broken. The somewhat impressive track record of institutional innovations in later years suggests that there is no quick fix to this problem.

This Huntingtonian mindset is also evident in the EU's capability initiatives. The capability question has, indeed, been a trump card for CSDP sceptics who have resorted to 'hard numbers' to show why it is bound to fail. Yet capabilities are not objective entities that can be measured or counted without regard to the strategic interests they serve, or the scenarios in which they are (to be) employed. In Chapter 5, this book, therefore, takes issue with the one-sided focus on Europe's military shortcomings that has followed from the notion of a transatlantic military gap. Instead it identifies the alternative concept of *broad interoperability* as a more appropriate benchmark for capability developments, insofar as it reflects better the civil–military focus of the EU's Comprehensive Approach.

By looking into issues of broad interoperability, Chapter 5 offers an alternative perspective on European capability developments. It does not free the EU of responsibilities for traditional *military* interoperability. Yet, by including civilian aspects of interoperability, the spectrum of relevant capabilities that can be 'counted' towards narrowing the transatlantic gap widens, insofar as the EU also has a potential *comparative advantage* in being able to offer capabilities that other states or institutions do not possess (see Howard 1983b: 104). Due to the growing acknowledgement – also in the United States – of the need for integrated civil–military approaches to complex peace operations (Barnett 2004; Feaver and Kohn 2001; Nielsen and Snider 2009), the EU aspires to fill a real gap in currently available integrated planning facilities (see also Chapter 4) and deployable civil–military force concepts. However, this is a gap that the EU has yet to fill. Although both the parallel civilian and military force generation processes have taken some significant steps towards a more capable CSDP, they have, nevertheless, developed largely separate from each other.

On the military side, the move towards small, rapid reaction force packages, as part of the Headline Goal 2010, signalled a qualitative shift in the force generation process. In addition, the development of the Battlegroup Concept has arguably helped consolidate ongoing trends towards some intra-European division of labour, helped along by the European Defence Agency's (EDA) work towards more collaborative defence acquisitions procedures, and attempts to break down protectionist national defence industrial regimes. By offering incentives for some states to change in order to *lead*, while rewarding other states for developing niche capabilities that increase their *influence* within the system, the Battlegroup Concept has, as illustrated with the Nordic Battlegroup (NBG) example, spurred transformation within and integration between some of the Member States. This is a point that has been somewhat lost amidst the more visible failures to deploy any of the EUBGs, and which reflects rather the *normative* transformation that has become an inherent part of the move towards an EU security governance structure. Chapter 5 showed that a variety of processes have emerged at the EU level that have started to change the normative frameworks within which perhaps most notably military capabilities are generated in Europe.

However, significant developments have also taken place on the civilian side. As initially a by-product of the adoption and development of military crisis management instruments, the EU started, with the first civilian Headline Goals in 1999, to fill an operational and conceptual vacuum, until then only partially occupied by the EU itself via first pillar activities and Member State involvement in UN and OSCE missions. By harvesting national experiences, and creating a normative and institutional space in which civilian instruments could be developed, the EU opened up the conceptual and operational area of civilian crisis management (CCM), eventually transcending the military support role for which it was first envisioned.

Through the identification of the civilian Headline Goal 2010, it has also started addressing some of the methodological and conceptual challenges associated with the initial subordination of CCM to military instruments, while creating an additional set of tools for the EU. The development of the concept of Civilian Response Teams (CRTs) in particular, and the launch of the integrated Rule of Law Mission in Kosovo EULEX in 2008 (see Chapter 6), demonstrate that the EU has taken a qualitative step away from the initial 'boxing' of civilian capabilities into separate areas, towards more flexible and integrated planning and deployment of civilian CSDP operations. Yet as CCM has evolved to become more of a proactive instrument of the EU, it has also accentuated challenges of civil–civil coordination between the Council and the Commission, which has traditionally been responsible for the conflict preventive elements of the EU's external relations portfolio. This so-called *security–development nexus* has to date received some attention in the literature (see e.g. Gourlay 2006; Klingebiel

2006). However, as the presence of military and civilian CSDP instruments grows in areas where the Commission has traditionally been the main or only actor it is natural that this aspect of *broad interoperability* receives more attention in future research.

But even as more connectivity across all civilian and military instruments is acknowledged as necessary to raise the *comparative advantage* of the EU, developing integrated capabilities or force concepts has appeared difficult for the EU. The solution has often been informal ad hoc coordination through one of the many EU Special Representatives (EUSRs) if or when the EU happens to be active with more than one type of instrument on the ground (see e.g. Grevi 2007). Even a typically European capability such as the Eurogendfor (described in Chapter 6), which can be fitted into, for example, the EUBGs as Integrated Police Units (IPUs), has been developed outside of the EU and remains to date a largely untapped asset for the Union. It appears that such hybrid capabilities are not easily accommodated in the heavily stovepiped civil–military CSDP framework. This confirms a main point of the book about the feasibility of developing a Comprehensive Approach inside the EU.

More importantly, it represents an opportunity lost for the EU to gain comparative advantage. Or, as pointed out by Boyer and Lindley-French (2007: 5): 'While the US military is beginning to "talk the talk" of the Comprehensive Approach, its lack of an imperial policing tradition prevents it from "walking the walk"'. The EU has many of the capabilities to 'walk the walk', but arguably fails to take full advantage of them in its operations.

As the ultimate proof of the pudding, operations constitute a source of success or failure, pride or shame, and determine how the EU is perceived both by its own constituents and its surroundings. This is also why each EU operation tends to be framed inside what can be best described as a premeditated *success narrative*. This is not unique to the EU. When losing a war, military history teaches us, one can always declare victory and pull out, as goes the quip about the US withdrawal from Vietnam. However, as a new actor in the military domain it has arguably been particularly important for the EU to prove that it is rising to the task – hence the preoccupation with counting operations and ticking off 'firsts' on the success list. For the EU, every new operation still represents an 'exam', a point that is reinforced by the repeated warning, at the outset of each new operation, that failure will be the end of the CSDP project as such. Ten years old, the CSDP remains very much a fragile child. This, in turn, affects the *lessons* that the EU has been able to draw from its operational portfolio, what it has been able to accomplish on the ground within the mandates and timeframes that have been given for each operation, and the image that it portrays to the outside world, irrespective of its own way of narrating or 'selling' each operation. Lessons learned represent an important feedback mechanism and key incentive for changing existing practices, so that past failures are not repeated.

Chapter 6 shows that the EU has been willing, if not eager, to change some of its practices, but that the process has been somewhat disorganised and selective. However, on the military side, the EU has, since 2003, been operating a formal *EUMS Lessons Learned Process* (ELPRO). The ELPRO includes a software tool called the *EUMS Lessons Learned Application* (ELMA), which allows everyone involved in CSDP operations, also civilians, to access and enter lessons learned as well as suggestions for improvement into the database. However, the ELPRO relies on there being a 'clever mind' at the end of the chain that may draw the appropriate conclusions and implement the lessons (interview with Council Secretariat official, June 2009). The ELPRO involves two to three meetings at Director level each year, in which the ELMA record is evaluated and central elements fed back into concept development, but there is no guarantee that lessons are implemented, or taken account of, at lower levels. There is also no civilian equivalent to the ELPRO, nor a systematic way of dealing with lessons learned. Reports rather point towards a severe lack of institutional memory of concepts and procedures for things such as training, procurements, equipment, etc. (interviews with Council Secretariat officials, June 2009). This hampers the possibility of synthesising even lessons derived from the same theatre of operations, as illustrated with the Bosnia case (see Chapter 6).

In addition, many of the lessons implemented have been driven by political rather than practical concerns, as reflected in the controversy surrounding the establishment of the CivMilCell and the OpCen, described in Chapter 4. This reflects also a general tendency in which the EU, driven by Member States such as France, Germany and the Benelux states, is seeking autonomy from NATO, without necessarily putting this to use in better coordination between civilian and military instruments.

Without some kind of auditing mechanism for civilian and military operations, a task that, on the national level, is often performed by parliaments, proper evaluation in accordance with agreed standards ('success' should not be one of them) will be hard to achieve. A heavier role for the European Parliament Subcommittee on Security and Defence (SEDE), including giving it access to the ELPRO, could improve the lessons learned process. Yet to date, the scrutiny of EU operations has been left largely to the academic community. But the academic literature on operations, which tends to take the shape of more or less coherent edited volumes (Grevi *et al.* 2009; Merlingen and Ostrauskaite 2008; Nowak 2006) or singular in-depth case studies (Mattelaer 2008; Seibert 2007; Ulriksen *et al.* 2004), has also been prone to treating each operation in isolation, not taking account of how they interrelate. By seeing them *in toto*, on the other hand, Chapter 6 describes some emerging patterns in the EU's operational portfolio, and some challenges that the Union will need to confront.

In its immediate neighbourhood, the EU has gradually assumed a more dominant role. It has largely replaced NATO in the Western Balkans, although the remaining takeover of KFOR in Kosovo has yet to move beyond the planning stage. In the rest of Eastern and Southern Europe, the EU has challenged the OSCE's presence in several (potential) areas of operations, after a number of blowbacks for the latter organisation. The EU's role during and after the 2008 Russo-Georgian war, in particular, comes across as a turning point for the CSDP in Europe. It was a first display of crisis management proper, and it was admittedly able to play a rather constructive role vis-à-vis Russia, at a time when NATO lacked appropriate instruments to do so. Yet the EU Monitoring Mission (EUMM) in Georgia illustrated also a general lack of resolve, or capacity, to enter into the more robust and/or executive operations that are still needed in parts of Europe, where a real or latent public security gap still exists (see Merlingen and Ostrauskaite 2006). It appears that the EU, despite its unique development of Civilian Crisis Management (CCM) instruments, is often unable to fill the *executive gap* in between the crisis and the reconstruction stage.[1] Part of the reason for this can somewhat paradoxically be found in expectations created by what is generally agreed to be the ultimate EU power tool, i.e. the prospect of membership in, or at least some form of (economic) association with, the Union. Substitution of state executive functions fits badly with the image of a future EU Member or Partner State.

In Africa, the presence of Western boots on the ground in operation *Artemis* in the DRC in 2003 marked a welcome return of European peacekeepers to the continent. The EU has subsequently sought to make a difference in several conflicts by typically engaging in military 'bridging' operations, seeking to empower the UN. This proves that robust military intervention is feasible and, indeed, reconcilable with the peaceful image of the EU. However, a problem has been that the EU, through its short-term bridging operations, tends to increase the strains on the UN. The handover of EUFOR Tchad/RCA to MINURCAT II in 2009 was only possible due to the re-hatting of 2,000 predominantly French troops, but subsequent contingents have only aggravated the UN's problems of putting up the required force numbers for its simultaneous operations in Africa. To put it bluntly, when the EU looks good in Africa, it often makes the UN look bad.

Notwithstanding the fact that looking good, at least from a military point of view, has throughout the CSDP military record in Africa almost exclusively relied on French leadership and military clout. Member States such as Sweden and Ireland have played an important role in these operations, and the positive impact of participation on these Member States' military forces has undoubtedly been significant. Also, channelling French interventions through the CSDP probably increases multilateral control over and legitimacy of these operations. But the controversy over EUFOR Tchad/RCA in particular shows that the EU needs to take care when balancing between the need for military efficiency, on the one hand, and allegations of national interventionism in EU disguise, on the other.

Finally, the EU's military operations in Africa have been largely isolated ventures, and have, therefore, not tested the Comprehensive Approach. Indeed, no integrated EU civil–military operations have been carried out so far. It seems that the EU is constantly drawn into a discourse where military robustness in itself is treated as the only or most important benchmark for successful intervention, while the EU often fails to 'sell' the point about the 'upsurge in civilian crisis management' as the *real* 'success of the CSDP' (Kurowska 2009: 34).

Despite the appropriateness of and considerable drive behind developing into a comprehensive strategic actor, therefore, the EU has only partly lived up to these expectations. Whether it will in the future is, of course, yet to be seen. However, the gradual move towards a security governance structure suggests that there are a number of more fundamental processes going on that have started to shift the very dynamics that shape European security today.

EU security governance revisited: a strategic actor for the future?

Amongst these ongoing security governance processes, there is a tendency towards further fragmentation of the relative role that various actors play in the European security framework. In addition to the 'Brusselsization' thesis discussed in Chapter 3, certain attention has also been given to the alleged 'Berlinization' of the CSDP, following a tendency for *all* EU politics to be formally and/or informally, influenced, formulated and, to some extent, driven from an ever more influential Germany. NATO, on the other hand, is seemingly becoming more 'Parisified', following France's re-entry into NATO's integrated military structure and its key role in the NATO operation in Libya in 2011. By some referred to as a new Iraq crisis for the CSDP, Libya was the first time Germany would be seen to openly go against Europe, as it abstained from the vote on UN Security Resolution 1973. This was quickly cast by Eurosceptics as an expression of German resistance towards not only the intervention itself, but the European security and defence project per se. Or as one commentator is reported to have said: 'The CFSP died in Libya – we just have to pick a sand dune under which we can bury it' (quoted in Koenig 2011: 3).

However, in hindsight it may seem that German Defence Minister Karl-Theodor zu Guttenberg, at the time, misread the political climate for an intervention, and failed to anticipate the subsequent reaction towards its abstention from the vote: Germany did not vote *against* the operation, but ended up being portrayed as siding with China and Russia against the rest of the EU/NATO community. A less dramatic reading of the situation suggests that German decision-makers did not want to vote for an operation that Germany could not be a part of, and were concerned about the upcoming elections. The decision did not, therefore, necessarily signal a conscious break with the norms that have come to shape and underpin the European security framework. Recasting the CSDP as an intergovernmental bargain, where Germany now has become the veto power, comes across as premature.

However, it may be that operations, which have, as demonstrated in Chapter 6, so far played a key role in giving the CSDP a sense of collective purpose and direction, will play a lesser role in defining the future CSDP. The global financial crisis, and the ensuing crisis of the Eurozone, represents as such a key factor behind the relative slump in CSDP operational activities – with Germany posing as a gatekeeper for further expensive CSDP ventures into Africa, where the EU, for a while, was set to become a prominent security actor. It is no secret that Germany has been sceptical of these kinds of operations all along, while France and the UK have been pushing for an extended operational role for the EU in Africa. Nevertheless, it is economic realities rather than political infighting between the EU-3 that is going to set the tone for the future CSDP. This will pose challenges, but also new opportunities.

A key challenge is the expected cuts in European defence budgets, which will make it hard for European states to sustain their military commitments to both NATO and the EU. However, this is also an area that, as demonstrated in Chapter 5, has been subject to an incremental shift in the ideational relations that shape it. A principally important development in this regard has been the EU Defence and Security Procurement Directive 2009/81EC, adopted in 2009. With this decision, the Commission took yet another step in its long-standing quest against protectionist national defence acquisitions regimes (see e.g. Edwards 2011). The last time the Commission tried something similar, ten years ago, the proposal was resolutely revoked. Something has apparently changed.

As argued in Chapter 5, the European Defence Agency (EDA) has served as a catalyst for this change through *soft law* initiatives such as the voluntary Code of Conduct on defence procurement. It has also acted as an agent for a 'consolidate or perish' line of argument that has gradually weakened the legitimacy of the once so strong norm of the protection of a national defence technological and industrial base. Again, this putative normative change away from a state focus to a European focus on security and defence is arguably more significant in the long run than the more symbolic victories that the CSDP has been about so far. Now defence is gradually making its way into the realm of EU *hard law*. But as with previous contested areas that have been moved into the single market, the Commission will rely on slowly building up case law before the directive will have any major impact on state practices. This will take some time.

In the meantime, the 2010 German-Swedish Ghent initiative on pooling and sharing may facilitate more bottom-up collaboration on defence capabilities. However, this also appears to be a slow train coming. Two defence treaties signed between France and Britain on 2 November 2010, amongst other areas covering cooperation on nuclear testing, sharing of aircraft carriers and a Franco-British expeditionary force, gave rise to hopes for a new push for the CSDP. However, British Prime Minister David Cameron did make it explicitly clear that this cooperation was to take place *outside* of the EU framework (see *BBC News* 2010). More capability cooperation between the two largest military powers in Europe is probably a good thing in the long run. But the November 2010 London meeting was certainly no new Saint-Malo.

It is still somewhat unclear what impact the current British position towards the EU, and France's re-entry into NATO's integrated military structure, will have on the CSDP in the longer term. But the way that Libya turned out may suggest that the military operational dimension of the CSDP is being toned down. Rather the EU was able to play a constructive, yet less visible role, before, during and after the NATO campaign through the Frontex Joint Operation *Hermes* (mandated to assist Italian authorities to cope with migratory flows) and the Commission emergency instruments deployed under the civil protection and humanitarian assistance mechanisms. By focusing on mainly civilian instruments for crisis management, the EU arguably played up to its strengths. However, it received little praise for its efforts. NATO, in turn, was generally hailed for its ability to quickly carry out a high-end military operation, without too much help from the United States, and for getting out before the end of the year.[2]

The collective sigh of relief over how Libya turned out seems to reflect a general sentiment spreading from the experiences in Iraq and Afghanistan over the last decade: from being seen as the solution to all crises, the Comprehensive Approach – in all its forms and expressions – may gradually be losing its appeal. The appetite amongst European state leaders and home electorates for yet other expensive and protracted stability operations in faraway countries has waned considerably. It may also be that the ambition of the Comprehensive Approach has been too high, as it has gradually dawned on military and civilian planners just how difficult civil–military coordination is in practice.

However, while it may be convenient to think that the Libya-type of operation is the shape of things to come for European out-of-area military crisis management, there will still be a need to do stability operations and prevention in the future. European security governance can also cover more ground – politically and practically – by having two institutional and political frameworks through which to channel its security efforts. But then the Member States of both organisations need to continue to cultivate the inherent differences between the two. For the EU, this means that it has to up its game in areas where it has a comparative advantage.

As discussed in several chapters in this book, the Lisbon Treaty offers some remedies for many of the problems of coordination and leadership that have permeated the CSDP so far. For better or for worse, institutionalisation remains a distinctive and important feature of EU security governance. Most of the institutional changes, though many of them are still not optimal, were long overdue, and they were, for the most part, not merely cosmetic. They will hopefully improve the EU's often poor coordination of its civilian and military crisis management operations with its other instruments once (or if) it gets back on track after the many problems that have dominated the political agenda since 2008–2009.

However, if the EU does not improve its track record in the areas where it is expected to make a difference, there is a danger that the Comprehensive Approach narrative will lose its appeal. As warned in Chapter 3, a strategic narrative, as any narrative, is ultimately reliant on its credibility and legitimacy as such. Indeed, the EU's strategic narrative may already be losing its appeal for other reasons mentioned above, which may suggest that the window of opportunity for the CSDP to consolidate itself and become a major force for change also outside of Europe is already closing. This does not necessarily mean that the CSDP will go away. But we will perhaps see a very different CSDP more in line with the economic and market dynamics that have dominated other areas of European integration, as Europe is forced into more cooperation on defence capabilities by economic realities. If that was to happen, it would be most welcome, but it could also represent a unique opportunity lost for Europe to take the original peace rationale behind the European integration project one step further.

Notes

1 Introduction: CSDP, strategic actorness and security governance

1 The *European* Security and Defence Policy (*ESDP*) was re-baptised the *Common* Security and Defence Policy (CSDP) by the Lisbon Treaty. To avoid confusion the book uses the latter abbreviation throughout.

2 Original quote by previous Foreign Minister of Belgium, Mark Eyskens, in the run-up to operation *Desert Storm* in Iraq in 1991.

3 The term 'European Union' is used consistently throughout the book, and refers to the European integration project, which started out as the European Coal and Steel Community (ECSC) in 1952, as a whole.

4 Maull's often cited definition of a civilian power refers to: (1) the centrality of economic power in national foreign policy; (2) the primacy of diplomacy in solving international problems; and (3) the willingness to use supranational institutions to achieve international progress (Maull 1990: 92–93).

5 A similar notion is found in the term 'transformative power', which suggests that the EU can induce change by actively seeking to export its own political, social and economic model (Dannreuther and Peterson 2006). 'Ethical power' represents a latest addition to the 'forest' of terms (Aggestam 2008).

6 The original phrase is, of course: 'Anarchy is what states make of it' (Wendt 1992).

7 For a useful overview of alternative definitions, see Gray (1999a: 17–20).

8 In a similar vein, Basil Liddell-Hart has also argued that Clausewitz has been consistently misinterpreted as encouraging the subordination of politics to the object of war. Strategy should be interpreted rather as 'the art of distributing and applying military means to fulfil the ends of policy' (Liddell-Hart 1967: 335).

9 As such, it mirrors Gunnar Sjöstedt's traditional definition of an *international actor* as one that has the capacity for goal-oriented behaviour towards other international actors (Sjöstedt 1977).

10 Hallenberg proposes an alternative definition of a strategic actor, adding two criteria: 'an independent capability to assess intelligence' and

'an ability to assess what has happened in a given situation and to learn from that experience' (Hallenberg 2008). Rather than treating them as independent criteria, these are seen as inherent to the other three, and accommodated in the analysis by tracing strategic actorness across the four dimensions of strategy outlined below.

11 The status of culture vis-à-vis behaviour has been subject to much debate. We return to this in Chapter 2.

12 Some of the main ideas presented in this section are also discussed in a previous article in the *Journal of Common Market Studies* (Norheim-Martinsen 2010).

13 A common interpretation is that the Iraq crisis was a setback for the CFSP, because it, at the time, revealed serious differences between key Member States, but not necessarily for the CSDP, which in fact saw the launch of the first EU military operation in Macedonia at the height of the crisis.

14 Due to British resistance, the OpCen was never established as a permanent operational headquarters. The CivMilCell has been replaced by a new Crisis Management and Planning Directorate (CMPD). These developments are covered in depth by Chapter 4 of the book.

15 The relationship between the CJTF and Battlegroup concepts in particular, and the general role of innovation and adaptation in capability building, are discussed in Chapter 5.

16 The desire to act 'European' is arguably a key element of an emerging European strategic culture, which is discussed in Chapter 2.

17 The EDA and the European defence industry's role in capability developments under the CSDP are discussed in Chapter 5.

18 These different bodies' roles and functions are discussed in detail in Chapter 3.

19 The *process* behind the ESS is discussed in detail in Chapter 3, while the document's impact as a *strategic narrative* is analysed in Chapter 2.

20 Individual agency in the CSDP is discussed and contrasted with state and institutional agency in Chapter 3.

21 The Brusselsization thesis is put to the test in Chapter 3.

22 The relationship between collective and national interests in the carrying out of CSDP operations is discussed in Chapter 6.

23 See Chapter 2.

24 The ability of the EU to produce lessons learned from experiences is discussed in Chapter 6.

25 The EU is often referred to as a 'tightly coupled security community' (see e.g. Rieker 2003: 54).

26 The EDA is covered in Chapter 5, while SITCEN, whose legal status remains unclear, is discussed in Chapter 4.

27 Institutions as strategic enablers are discussed in Chapter 4.

28 The sociological or 'constabulary' model of civil–military relations (Janowitz 1960) is contrasted with what is often referred to as the 'normal' or separate model of civil–military relations (Huntington 1957). This is discussed further in Chapter 4.

29 Most often referred to as more an approach than a theory, constructivism is commonly portrayed as occupying the middle ground between rationalist and reflectivist theories (Adler 1997: 322; Checkel 1998: 327; Katzenstein *et al.* 1998: 678; Walt 1998: 44). Some offer a further classification into several sub-categories (see Smith 1999). A line of division is often drawn against critical or postmodernist theories, sometimes referred to as 'thick' or 'critical' constructivism (Campbell 1992; Klein 1989; Kratochwil 2000; Wyn Jones 1999).

30 Wendt (1999) cautiously presents constitutive theorising as explicitly non-causal, and as a scientifically valid alternative to causal explanations. However, Colin Wight (2006: 117) argues that constitutive theorising is 'perfectly compatible' with causation (see also Kurki 2008). The key point is that constitutive theorising is a valid part of scientific inquiry, which, in our particular case, grasps better the perceived epistemological relationship between security governance and strategic actorness.

2   European strategic culture and the Comprehensive Approach

1 The most notorious account of differing perceptions of security and power on either side of the Atlantic has been offered by Robert Kagan (2002, 2003).

2 Some of these questions are picked up in Chapter 5.

3 According to Johnston (1995: 48), behaviour (dependent variable) may causally follow from strategic culture (independent variable), defined as 'a limited ranked set of strategic preference'. In that case, the validity of strategic culture as an explanatory variable is verified, whereas in cases of non-compliance between strategic culture and behaviour, the theory must be discarded.

4 See also Johnston and Gray's subsequent replies and replies to replies. Johnston's definition of culture has been generally discredited, since it represents a sharp departure from definitions in sociological and anthropological literature (see Neumann and Heikka 2005 for a detailed discussion).

5 In contrast, NATO's 1999 *Strategic Concept* never got the same symbolic stature as the ESS. Interestingly, NATO's new *Strategic Concept*, adopted in Lisbon on 19 November 2010 – and particularly the process that led to it – was quite remarkable in terms of transparency and outreach (NATO 2010). In some ways, it resembled the process that led to the ESS (see Chapter 3).

6 The exception was the accession of Greece, Spain and Portugal, which was a testing ground for the EU's ability to promote stability and democracy in the region. The success of this venture later became an important reference point for Eastern enlargement (see Raik 2006: 78).

7 This point is picked up in Chapter 6, where the effects upon the EU as a strategic actor of engaging in operations, even those of a less 'masculine, heroic kind', as goes van Ham's description of EU operations to date, are analysed in depth.

8 The fact that neither the Cold War nor the 'war on terror' were wars in the conventional meaning of the term makes referring to them as such appear all the more conspicuous in the sense that they create a feeling of urgency and lack of safety, as well as commanding a certain way of dealing with the problem.

9 The 'war against terror' was re-baptised 'the long war' in the 2006 NSS, which signified a somewhat reluctant acceptance of the fact that it was going to be protracted *struggle* rather than a war, with all the costs (the Iraq war was and remains the most expensive ever fought by the United States) and suffering it is bound to incur.

10 Commentators differed on what to make of the frequent use of the term 'global' in the ESS. Bailes (2005: 15) saw a 'truly global approach' as a feature it shared with the NSS, while Duke (2004: 464) and Berenskoetter (2004: 6) recognised the global outlook of the ESS, but concluded that it was, nonetheless, primarily concerned with regional security.

11 See the discussion in Chapter 1 of the impact of militarisation upon different conceptions of the EU as actor or power.

12 According to Asle Toje (2005), the EU acts in accordance with what Max Weber refers to as *wert rationalitet*, or value rationality rather than traditional ends-rationality.

13 The ESS adds organised crime and regional conflicts to the list. Note also the difference between 'rogue' and 'failed' states. While a failed state is in the ESS seen as a catalyst for other threats to emerge, a rogue state is in the NSS seen as a threat in itself, either by its own direct actions, its sponsorship of terrorists, or failure to prevent these from hurting US interests. Each term anchors fundamentally different opinions about when forceful intervention is considered legitimate.

14 This point is taken up in Chapter 6, in which the CSDP operational portfolio is evaluated.

15 The Petersberg tasks were originally set out at the Hotel Petersberg near Bonn at the Western European Union (WEU) Summit in June 1992. They were adopted from the WEU and incorporated into the Treaty on European Union (TEU) by the 1997 Amsterdam Treaty (entered into force in 1999). For the role that the Petersberg tasks have played in capability planning in particular, see the discussion in Chapter 5.

3   In pursuit of the EU interest: state, individual and institutional agency in the CSDP

1 *Efficiency* is here understood as the ability to make effective decisions, whether in normalcy or crises, that are coherent and consistent over time. *Legitimacy* is understood as the general compatibility of decisions with the Member States' and their constituents' views, as expressed, for example, through popular consent and parliamentary scrutiny at the national and EU levels.

2 Decisions on CSDP operations are covered in Chapter 6.

3 For a thorough discussion of the various options, see Diedrichs and Jopp (2003) or Stubb (1996).

4 The trade-off was also reflected in the creation of an autonomous (albeit non-permanent) operational HQ in Brussels, despite the fact that the British were initially against it. This is covered in Chapter 4. The capability criteria for 'enhanced structured cooperation' are discussed in Chapter 5.

5 A similar view is presented by Mathias Koenig-Archibugi (2004), who uses the CFSP to corroborate Klaus Dieter Wolf's claim that sometimes national governments use the appeal of international cooperation to overcome domestic opposition to their preferred policies (Wolf 1999).

6 Given the relatively thorough coverage of the workings of the PSC in present literature, I have concentrated my interviews on other parts of the institutional apparatus.

7 The MILREPs are in most cases double-hatted with each state's NATO representative.

8 One diplomat describes the Policy Unit as a deliberately small and fully integrated group, where one tries 'to get all the [27] people around the table as often as possible' (interview with Council Secretariat official, May 2003).

9 Indeed, in the *Quartet*, established in May 2002, which was created in order to press for negotiations between the main parties to the conflict, and which consists of the United States, Russia, the UN and the EU, the EU has found it necessary to have three voices speaking for it (the HR, the Commissioner for External Relations and the President of the Council).

10 Whereas Lord Ashdown was seen as a typical 'fixer', his successor, Christian Schwarz-Schilling, was described as more of an 'administrator'.

11 Indeed, the reputation Lord Ashdown earned in Bosnia subsequently prompted Afghan authorities to prevent his appointment as new UN envoy to Afghanistan (*BBC News* 2008).

12 It is, of course, hard to know the extent to which Solana, in fact, kept other Member States informed, but there were few official objections to the way the 'EU-3+1' dealt with the Iran issue.

13 'Variable geometry' means that not every country need take part in every initiative but some can cooperate more closely, taking advantage of individual foreign policy interests, existing diplomatic relations and historic ties (see Grant 2005; Grant and Leonard 2006).

14 As we shall see in Chapter 5, this is also evident in an emerging role specialisation between framework nations and niche providers, which may over time lead to heavier small state dependency on the bigger states.

4 The institutional link: creating a civil–military organisation fit for purpose

1 For detailed comparison of Huntington and Janowitz, see Robert Egnell (2006, 2009).

2 The idea of militaries as constabulary forces or cosmopolitan law enforcers has received renewed attention in the post Cold War context (see e.g. Elliot and Cheeseman 2004; Kaldor 1999).

3 Information obtained in interviews. See also Solana's early speeches as HR-CFSP.

4 Operations are covered in depth in Chapter 6.

5 Since 1 January 2007, the OpCen has been allocated permanent facilities (premises and equipment) in Brussels. It has a permanent staff of eight officers. At full operational capacity, it will be manned by a total of 89 officers and civilians (European Council 2008a).

6 In addition to the OpCen Permanent Staff, the CMC consists of a Strategic Planning Branch of eight military and seven civilian experts, including two permanent Commission representatives.

7 This point is further substantiated in Chapter 6.

8 For a detailed breakdown of the planning process, consult Lindström (2007: 19–21). See also Ehrhart and Quille (2007: 9).

9 In the Club of Berne, Italy and Spain are represented by the Heads of their external intelligence services. The Heads of national external intelligence services have also, since around 2000, come together for annual meetings in a low-profile, informal grouping referred to as 'Club de Madrid'. It has no official link to SITCEN, but only EU Member States are involved.

10 The CTG is tasked with coordinating the anti-terrorist activities of the 17 participating states' internal security services. The security services of the ten EU accession states joined the CTG on 1 May 2004, but were not included in the original Club of Berne.

11 Information on the composition of SITCEN has not been available to the public since 2004 (Duke 2006: note 49). However, it has been suggested that, amongst the new Member States, for example, Poland and/or Hungary are likely to have been invited to second national officials, due to the general high quality of their intelligence services.

5 Building European capabilities: beyond the transatlantic gap

1 Quoted in Howorth (2007: 62).
2 The International Institute for Strategic Studies' *Military Balance* defines capabilities as 'forces or resources giving a country or a state the ability to undertake a particular kind of military action'. As such, 'they comprise the assets and skills that nations can bring to bear to counter identified threats and to meet responsibilities' (Giegerich and Nicoll 2008: 9).
3 The United States also experienced a drop in defence spending after the end of the Cold War, reaching a low point of less than 3 per cent of GDP in 1999. But, while Europe has experienced a continued downward trend, with figures falling from 2.17 per cent of GDP in 1995 to 1.77 per cent and a total of US$283bn spent on defence in 2006 (the UK and France account for 40 per cent), US spending on defence had risen to 3.94 per cent of GDP and a total of US$617bn in 2006 (Giegerich and Nicoll 2008: 93).
4 The only time Article five has been invoked to date was after the 11 September 2001 terrorist attacks.
5 Note that the extension of tasks by the Lisbon Treaty does not significantly change this, although it can be argued that they now express more explicitly the combined civil–military approach that is envisioned for future CSDP operations. See the discussion in Chapter 2.
6 Force numbers and composition were largely influenced by the Kosovo campaign.
7 The origins of the Battlegroup Concept are covered in depth by Gustav Lindström (2007: ch. 1).
8 Britain originally wanted the battlegroups to be made up of predominantly single nations, since this would ease challenges of interoperability and deployability.
9 For discussions of the feasibility of alternative transport by sea, see von Weissenberg (2002) or Lindström (2007: 40–45).
10 The Swedish C-130 aircraft would have been able to cover some of the tactical airlift requirements, but they would have been limited to areas with appropriate airfields. The problem is rather one of a general lack of suitable helicopters, which significantly reduces the tactical mobility of a combat force. As the NBG entered into standby mode, Sweden was still

awaiting delivery of its new NH90. As a temporary solution, it initiated the conversion of three civilian Puma helicopters into tactical transport helicopters, but these were not delivered in time. As it stands, Europe faces continued shortfalls in tactical transport helicopter capabilities, but these problems will be reduced when the NH90, which has been purchased by 11 European states, enters into service after several delays.

11 *Strategic airlift* refers to the ability of aircraft to carry so-called out-sized equipment, such as helicopters, armoured vehicles and boats, and/or large numbers of personnel over long distances *into* theatres of oper-ation; i.e. between two airbases that are not in the same vicinity. Defining characteristics are, as such, payload, troop-carrying capacity and range, but also size of cargo doors, dimension and geometry of cargo compart-ment and floor loading restrictions. See Lindström (2007: 31–40) for a detailed discussion.

12 It has also been pointed out that since the A-400-M is significantly smaller than the Antonov or the C-17, it will only reduce, not solve, the problem (Andersson 2006: 31).

13 It is worth noting that Luxembourg, for example, could and would hardly have purchased *one* A-400-M had it not been for the prospect of being able to offer a highly valued capability to NATO and the CSDP.

14 There is no absolute reserve force requirement, but it remains a basic military principle (Lindström 2007: 53).

15 The political context for CSDP operational deployments (as well as fail-ures to deploy) is covered in more depth in Chapter 6.

16 The initiative was introduced by US Secretary of Defence Donald Rumsfeld and loosely based on a concept put forward in an article by Hans Binnendijk and Richard Kugler (2002). The final NRF concept was then agreed at the 2004 NATO Istanbul summit. For more details, see Kaitera and Ben-Ari (2008: 2–3).

17 Although not deployed for military purposes, the NRF was used for security purposes in the 2004 Summer Olympics in Athens and the 2004 presidential elections in Afghanistan, and to carry out disaster relief after hurricane Katrina in the United States and the earthquake in Pakistan, both in 2005.

18 Exceptions from the CoC are allowed in cases of pressing operational urgency, for follow-on work or supplementary goods and services, and for extraordinary and compelling reasons of national security. In these cases, an explanation must be provided to the EDA. Excluded from the Code altogether are procurement of chemical, bacteriological and radiological goods and services, nuclear propulsion systems and crypto-graphic equipment.

19 For a more detailed account of these developments, see Nowak (2006).

6   CSDP operations: learning through failure or failing to learn?

1 **UN:** Africa (7 operations), Americas (1), Asia (2), Europe (3) and Middle East (3). **NATO:** International Security Assistance Force (ISAF) in Afghanistan, Kosovo Force (KFOR), NATO Training Mission in Iraq (NTM-I), Operation *Active Endeavour* (OAE) monitoring the Mediterranean Sea, and Operation *Allied Protector* off the Horn of Africa.

2 See the list at the Council Secretariat website, www.consilium.europa.eu/showPage.aspx?id=268&lang=En.

3 The use of terms is not consistent in the UN, and with the rise in Chapter VII interventions in later years, the UN seems to favour the term *Peacekeeping Operations*, as reflected in the title of the new capstone doctrine (UN 2008).

4 See Howorth (2007: 208) for a brief account of the broader academic discussion on how to analyse the international actions of the EU.

5 The list of candidates for accession includes Turkey, Croatia, Serbia, Iceland, Montenegro and FYROM. Potential candidates are Albania, Bosnia and Herzegovina and Kosovo (see the list at the Commission website, http://ec.europa.eu/enlargement/countries/index_en.htm, accessed 20 July 2012). The states covered by the ENP are Algeria, Armenia, Azerbaijan, Belarus, Egypt, Georgia, Israel, Jordan, Lebanon, Libya, Moldova, Morocco, the Palestinian Territories, Syria, Tunisia and the Ukraine. Russia is not covered by ENP, but its relations with the EU are covered by a *Strategic Partnership*. I return to this below.

6 Including Iran, Iraq, Saudi Arabia, Afghanistan, Pakistan and the former Soviet Republics in Central Asia.

7 These operations followed, in turn, operation *Essential Harvest*, which was carried out in August 2001 to disarm Albanian insurgents in the regions bordering Serbia and Kosovo.

8 However, it must be noted that, despite its unquestioningly more robust mandate, many would argue that the IPTF was rather part of the problem of organised crime in BiH than a solution to it due to widespread corruption amongst UN police officers, who were mostly coming from non-Western countries. The rise in crime could also reflect systematic under-reporting up until the takeover by EUPM (interview with Council Secretariat official, June 2009).

9 Of course, one explanation for the lack of analyses of *Althea* is that it is still ongoing, and that the news value of taking over a ten-year-old NATO operation was and remains comparatively low. As such, *Althea* was trumped by the success in operation *Artemis* in the DRC, which was an *autonomous* operation, while the former was *only* Berlin Plus.

10 The somewhat heavy-handed personal touch that Lord Ashdown as High Representative turned EUSR also put on EU activities in BiH, is described in Chapter 3.

11 EUFOR was reduced to around 2,200 in February 2007. Full withdrawal has been discussed, but not confirmed (see Chapter 4).

12 Eurogendfor was declared fully operational on 20 July 2006. Romania joined in 2008. Poland and Turkey have been granted partner and observer status respectively.

13 These sentiments were shared by both EU and NATO officials consulted at NATO-SHAPE in 2006, whereas EUMS and other Council officials seemed generally disinterested in discussing current or future EU–NATO relations. Somewhat surprisingly, contacts between the EUMS and the EUSG at NATO-SHAPE appeared to be virtually non-existent.

14 Russia vetoed the extension of UNOMIG on 15 June 2009, signalling, at the same time, that it wanted to remove the OSCE mission (ICG 2009).

15 Ulriksen *et al.* describe a consistent focus on Africa throughout French–British summit declarations since 1994, including the Saint-Malo declaration that established the CSDP in 1998 (2004: 513).

16 The EU Special Representative (EUSR) for the Great Lakes Region, Mr Aldo Ajello, who was appointed already in 1996, had no formal role in the military chain of command, and appears not to have been consulted, at least not in any regularised manner, by the French commanders on the ground or in Paris.

17 The Commission had reportedly by 2006 used 24 million euro to support the training of up to 60,000 police officers throughout the DRC, in addition to the funds allocated to the police operations carried out under the CSDP (see below) (Martinelli 2008: 117).

18 The three options resulted from liaisons with UN DPKO in New York, aiming to draw out what the UN expected from an EU force, and a civil-military fact-finding mission, which went to the DRC to facilitate the EU's analysis and needs assessment for an operation. The exact details of the three options have not been reported, but they all included troops stationed in and outside of the DRC, advance deployment before the election, and duration of three to four months.

19 After the announcement of the results of the first round of elections, riots broke out in Kinshasa from 20 to 22 August, but tensions were successfully curbed by the EU force. The remainder of the elections went by practically without incident.

20 EUPOL Kinshasa was replaced by a nationwide police operation, EUPOL RD Congo, in July 2007. The operation is made up of some 50 international staff.

21 The mandate of EUSEC DRC is to provide direct advice and assistance to the Congolese military authorities with a view to rebuilding an army that will ensure peace and facilitate economic growth. In addition to the integrated brigades, projects include reforming payments structures to avoid corruption, and the development of a biometric census aimed at the complete and reliable identification of Congolese army troops.

22 France, Germany and Britain wanted to reinforce MONUC rather than send in a separate EU force, but none of the EU Member States committed extra troops (see Davis 2009: 14).

23 AMIS was deployed in May 2004 and expanded, becoming AMIS II, in October 2004, and again in April 2005. It was terminated and replaced by the joint EU/AU operation in Darfur (UNAMID) in December 2007. On the military side, EU support included: provision of equipment and assets (including strategic airlift together with NATO), planning and technical assistance, military observers, and training of African troops. Police support included: support for AMIS CIVPOL chain of command, training of personnel, and assistance in setting up a police unit within the AU Secretariat. EU personnel deployed on average consisted of 30 police officers, 15 military experts and two military observers. The support package also included financial assistance channelled through the Commission, but the operation was led by the Council (for more information, see European Council 2006b, 2008b).

24 The crisis in Darfur is, as such, not contained to Sudan, but the result of a web of interrelated domestic and regional factors that involve all the states in the Central African region. See Bjoern Seibert's detailed case study of EUFOR Tchad/RCA for more information (2007: 8–11).

25 In fact, Gen. Engelbrektsson is reported to have 'lobbied heavily' for using the NBG in Chad, but was met with little enthusiasm since most of the Member States had made up their minds – EUFOR Tchad/RCA was a French initiative and, thus, perceived as a French responsibility from start to finish (interviews with Norwegian MoD official, December 2008 and Council Secretariat official, June 2009).

26 In addition, a helicopter pool was established with French, Polish, Irish and Russian helicopters. It is perhaps worth mentioning that it could, in the words of Alexander Mattelaer, be seen as somewhat embarrassing that the EU should accept military support from Russia at the same time that it was sending observers to monitor a Russian withdrawal of troops in Georgia (see above) (Mattelaer 2008: note 25). It could, on the other hand, also be put on the ESS' 'constructive engagement' account. In any case, the Russian helicopters were a much-needed asset that the EU could not have turned down without a significant loss of operational effectiveness.

27 Notwithstanding doubts about the level of ambition, the PSC went for option 3 (all at once rapid deployment of four battalions), while the final composition of the force resembled more option 2 (step-by-step deployment of three battalions and gradual geographical expansion (see Mattelaer 2008: 16–17).

28 In addition to the two small civilian operations in the DRC, it has been running a small Security Sector Reform operation in Guinea-Bissau, EU SSR Guinea-Bissau, since February 2008. With respect to other operations in what is regarded as relative proximity to Europe, i.e. still within our second concentric circle, two small civilian CSDP operations are currently still running: the Rule of Law Mission in Iraq, EUJUST Lex Iraq (since July 2005), and the Police Mission in Afghanistan, EUPOL Afghanistan (since June 2007). However, in conclusion, the EU cannot be said to have left a very notable operational footprint beyond the African continent.

7   Conclusion: a comprehensive strategic actor for the future?

1 Note that these 'stages' need not follow chronologically, but can exist at the same time in a given area of operations.

2 At the time of writing, the situation in Libya is still far from consolidated.

References

Adler, Emanuel. 1997. Seizing the Middle Ground: Constructivism and World Politics. *European Journal of International Politics* 3: 319–363.

Adler, Emanuel and Michael Barnett. 1998. *Security Communities.* Cambridge University Press.

Aggestam, Lisbeth. 2005. *A European Foreign Policy?* Paper presented at ARENA, Centre for European Studies, University of Oslo. 22 February.

2008. Introduction: Ethical Power Europe? *International Affairs* 84 (1): 1–11.

Allen, David. 2004. So Who Will Speak for Europe? The Constitutional Treaty and Coherence in EU External Relations. *CFSP Forum* 2 (5).

2008. *European Foreign Policy in the Solana Era.* Paper presented at ISA's 49th Annual Convention, Bridging Multiple Divides. San Francisco.

Allen, David and Michael Smith. 1990. Western Europe's Presence in the Contemporary International Arena. *Review of International Affairs* 16 (1): 19–37.

2005. External Policy Developments. *Journal of Common Market Studies* 43 (Annual Review).

Andersson, Jan Joel. 2006. *Armed and Ready? The EU Battlegroup Concept and the Nordic Battlegroup.* Stockholm: Swedish Institute for European Policy Studies. Report no. 2, March 2006.

Andréani, Gilles, Christoph Bertram and Charles Grant. 2001. *Europe's Military Revolution.* London: Centre for European Reform.

AngusReid Global Monitor. 2007. Many Danes Willing to Switch to Euro. 30 November.

Arquilla, John and David Ronfeldt. 2001. *Networks and Netwars: The Future of Terror, Crime and Militancy.* Santa Monica: RAND Corporation.

Asmus, Ronald D. 2002. *Opening NATO's Door: How the Alliance Remade Itself for a New Era.* New York: Columbia University Press.

Austin, John L. 1955. *How to Do Things with Words: The William James Lectures delivered at Harvard University in 1955.* Oxford: Clarendon.

Avant, Deborah. 2004. The Privatization of Security and Change in the Control of Force. *International Studies Perspectives* 5 (2): 153–157.

Ayoob, Mohammed. 1995. *The Third World Security Predicament: State Making Regional Conflict and the International System*. Boulder: Lynne Rienner.

Bailes, Alyson J.K. 2004. *EU and US Strategic Concepts: A Mirror for Partnership and Difference? The International Spectator* XXXIX (3): 19–33.

2005. *The European Security Strategy. An Evolutionary History*. Stockholm: SIPRI. Policy Paper no.10, February 2005.

Barcelona Report. 2004. *A Human Security Doctrine for Europe*. Report of the Study Group on Europe's Security Capabilities, Barcelona, 15 September.

Barnett, Thomas P.M. 2004. *The Pentagon's New Map: War and Peace in the Twenty-First Century*. New York: Putnam.

Barrinha, André. 2008. *The European Defence Agency and the Discourse on the European Defence Agency*. Paper presented at the ISA Annual Convention. New York, 15–18 February.

2010. Moving towards a European Defence Industry? The Political Discourse on a Changing Reality and its Implications for the Future of the European Union. *Global Society* 24 (4): 467–485.

BBC News. 2008. Kabul Against Ashdown Envoy Role. 26 January.

2010. Cameron and Sarkozy Hail UK-France Defence Treaties. 2 November.

Berenskoetter, Felix. 2004. *Mapping the Mind Gap: A Comparison of US and EU Security Strategies*. Unpublished paper, London: London School of Economics and Political Science.

Betts, Richard K. 1997. Should Strategic Studies Survive? *World Politics* 50: 7–33.

Bigo, Didier. 2001. The Möbius Ribbon of Internal and External Security(ies). In *Identities, Borders, Orders: Rethinking International Relations Theory*, edited by Mathias Albert, David Jacobsen and Yosef Lapid. Minneapolis: University of Minnesota Press.

Binnendijk, Hans and Richard L. Kugler. 2002. Transforming European Forces. *Survival* 44 (3): 117–132.

2003. Dual-Track Transformation for NATO. *Defense Horizons* 35 (October issue).

Biscop, Sven. 1999. The UK's Change of Course: A New Chance for the ESDI. *European Foreign Affairs Review* 4: 253–268.

2004. *The European Security Strategy. Implementing a Distinctive Approach to Security*. Brussels: Royal Defence College (IRSD-KHID). Paper no. 82, March.

2006. *NATO, ESDP and the Riga Summit: No Transformation without Re-Equilibration*. Brussels: IRRI-KIIB. Egmont Paper no. 11.

2007. *The ABC of European Security Strategy: Ambition, Benchmark, Culture*. Brussels: Egmont Royal Institute of International Relations. Egmont Paper 16.

2008. The European Security Strategy in Context: A Comprehensive Trend. In *The EU and the European Security Strategy: Forging a Global Europe*, edited by S. Biscop and J.J. Andersson. London: Routledge, pp. 5–20.

Biscop, Sven and Jan Joel Andersson, eds. 2008. *The EU and the European Security Strategy: Forging a Global Europe*. London: Routledge.

Biscop, Sven and Jo Coelmont. 2011. *Pooling & Sharing: From Slow March to Quick March?* Brussels: Egmont Royal Institute of International Relations. Security Policy Brief #23, May.

Bitzinger, Richard. 2003. *Towards a Brave New Arms Industry?* London: IISS. Adelphi Paper no. 356.

Bono, Giovanna. 2004. The EU's Military Doctrine: An Assessment. *International Peacekeeping* 11 (3): 439–456.

2005. National Parliaments and EU External Military Operations: Is there any Parliamentary Control? *European Security* 14 (2): 203–229.

Booth, Ken. 1979. *Strategy and Ethnocentrism*. New York: Holmes and Meier.

Borchert, Heiko. 2006. Homeland Security and Transformation: Why It Is Essential to Bring Together Both Agendas. In *Transforming Homeland Security: U.S. and European Approaches*, edited by Esther Brimmer. Washington, DC: Centre for Transatlantic Relations, Johns Hopkins University.

Boyer, Yves and Julian Lindley-French. 2007. *Euro-Interoperability: The Effective Military Interoperability of European Armed Forces*. Report requested by European Parliament's Sub-Committee on Security and Defence.

Braud, Pierre Antoine. 2006. Implementing ESDP Operations in Africa. In *Securing Europe? Implementing the European Security Strategy*, edited by A. Deighton and V. Mauer. Zurich: ETH Center for Security Studies, pp. 69–78.

Bretherton, Charlotte and John Vogler. 2006. *The European Union as a Global Actor*. 2nd edn. London: Routledge.

Bull, Hedley. 1982. Civilian Power Europe: A Contradiction in Terms? *Journal of Common Market Studies* 21 (1–2): 149–164.

1983. European Self-Reliance and the Reform of NATO. *Foreign Affairs* 61 (4): 874–892.

Bulmer, S., D. Dolowitz, P. Humphreys and S.A. Padgett. 2007. *Policy Transfer in European Union Governance: Regulating the Utilities*. London: Routledge.

Bunse, S. 2006. *The Value of the Rotating Council Presidency: Small State Entrepreneurship in the European Union*. PhD Thesis. University of Oxford.

Bunse, S., P. Magnette and K. Nicolaïdis. 2005. Shared Leadership in the EU: Theory and Reality. In *The EU Constitution: The Best Way Forward?*, edited by D. Curtin, A.E. Kellermann and S. Blockmans. The Hague: Asser Press, pp. 275–296.

Burley, Anne Marie and Walter Mattli. 1993. Europe Before the Court: A Political Theory of Legal Integration. *International Organization* 41: 41–76.

Buzan, Barry, Jaap de Wilde and Ole Waever. 1998. *Security: A New Framework for Analysis*. Boulder: Lynne Rienner.

Campbell, David. 1992. *Writing Security: United States Foreign Policy and the Politics of Identity*. Minneapolis: University of Minnesota Press.

Carbonell, Belén Martinez. 2004. EU Policy towards Iran. In *Iran and Its Neighbours: Diverging Views on a Strategic Region, Vol. II*, edited by J. Reissner and E. Whitlock. Berlin: Stiftung Wissenschaft und Politik, pp. 17–23.

Carrington, Peter J., John Scott and Stanley Wasserman. 2005. *Models and Methods in Social Network Analysis*. New York: Cambridge University Press.

Checkel, Jeffrey. 1998. The Constructivist Turn in International Relations Theory. *World Politics* 50 (2): 324–348.

2005. *It's the Process Stupid! Process Tracing in the Study of European and International Politics*. Oslo: ARENA Centre for European Studies. Working Paper no. 26.

2008. *Causal Mechanisms and Civil War*. Paper presented at the Annual Convention of the American Political Science Association. Boston, August 2008.

Christiansen, Thomas. 2001. Intra-Institutional Politics and Inter-Institutional Relations in the EU: Towards Coherent Governance? *Journal of European Public Policy* 8 (5): 747–769.

Christiansen, Thomas and Simona Piattoni. 2003. *Informal Governance in the European Union*. Cheltenham: Edward Elgar Publishing.

Clausewitz, Carl von. 1976 [1832]. *On War*. Princeton University Press. Translation by Michael Howard and Peter Paret.

Cogan, Charles. 2001. *The Third Option: The Emancipation of European Defense, 1989–2000*. Westport: Praeger.

Coletta, Damon. 2005. Managing the Transatlantic Gap. *Foreign Policy Analysis* 1 (2): 229–247.

Cornish, Paul. 1997. *Partnership in Crisis: the US, Europe and the Fall and Rise of NATO*. London: Cassell.

Cornish, Paul and Geoffrey Edwards. 2001. Beyond the EU/NATO Dichotomy: The Beginnings of a European Strategic Culture. *International Affairs* 77 (3): 587–603.

2005. The Strategic Culture of the European Union: A Progress Report. *International Affairs* 81 (4): 801–820.

Cowles, Maria, James Caporaso and Thomas Risse. 2001. *Transforming Europe. Europeanization and Domestic Change.* London: Cornell University Press.

Cronin, Bruce. 1999. *Community Under Anarchy: Transnational Identity and the Evolution of Cooperation.* New York: Columbia University Press.

Crowe, Brian. 2003. A Common Foreign Policy after Iraq? *International Affairs* 79 (3): 533–546.

2005. *Foreign Minister of Europe.* London: Foreign Policy Centre, February.

Dannreuther, Roland and John Peterson. 2006. Conclusion: Alliance Dead or Alive? In *Security Strategy and Transatlantic Relations*, edited by R. Dannreuther and J. Peterson. London: Routledge, pp. 161–173.

Davidson, Elisabeth, Arita Eriksson and Jan Hallenberg. 2002. *Europeanization of Security and Defence Policy.* Stockholm: The Swedish National Defence College.

Davis, Laura. 2009. *Small Steps, Large Hurdles: The EU's Role in Promoting Justice in Peacemaking in the DRC.* Brussels: Initiative for Peacebuilding, May.

Deighton, Anne and Victor Mauer, eds. 2006. *Securing Europe? Implementing the European Security Strategy.* Zurich: ETH Centre for Security Studies.

Desch, Michael C. 1998. Culture Clash: Assessing the Importance of Ideas in Security Studies. *World Politics* 50 (2): 141–170.

Deudney, Daniel. 1990. The Case against Linking Environmental Degradation and National Security. *Millennium* 19 (3): 461–476.

Deutsch, Karl W. 1957. *Political Community in the North Atlantic Area.* Princeton University Press.

Deutsche Welle. 2006. G6 Ministers Debate Terrorism behind Closed Doors. 25 October.

Diedrichs, Udo and Mathias Jopp. 2003. Flexible Modes of Governance: Making CFSP and ESDP Work. *The International Spectator* 3 (2003): 15–30.

Dijkstra, Hylke. 2008. The Council Secretariat's Role in the Common Foreign and Security Policy. *European Foreign Affairs Review* 13 (2): 149–166.

DiMaggio, Paul J. and Walter W. Powell. 1991. *The New Institutionalism in Organizational Analysis.* University of Chicago Press.

Dinan, Desmond. 1994. *Ever Closer Union*. New York: Palgrave.

Douglas, Frank 'Scott'. 2007. Waging the Inchoate War: Defining, Fighting, and Second-guessing the 'Long War'. *Journal of Strategic Studies* 30 (3): 391–420.

DPKO. 2004. *Operation Artemis: The Lessons of the Interim Emergency Multinational Force*. New York: UN Department of Peacekeeping Operations, Best Practices Unit, Military Division, October.

Ducastel, Clemence. 2007. Roles and Lessons Learned from European Union's Military Operations. *Doctrine#*. Available at: www.cdef. terre.defense.gouv.fr/publications/doctrine/doctrine13/us/retx/art1. pdf.

Dûchene, F. 1972. Europe in World Peace. In *Europe Tomorrow*, edited by R. Maine. London: Fontana/Collins, pp. 32–49.

Duke, Simon. 2002. CESDP and the EU Response to 11 September: Identifying the Weakest Link. *European Foreign Affairs Review* 7 (2): 153–169.

2004. The European Security Strategy in a Comparative Framework: Does it make for Secure Alliances in a Better World? *European Foreign Affairs Review* 9: 459–481.

2005. *The Linchpin COPS: Assessing the Workings and Institutional Relations of the Political and Security Committee*. Maastricht: European Institute for Public Administration. Working Paper 2005/W/05.

2006. Intelligence, Security and Information Flows in CFSP. *Intelligence and National Security* 21 (4): 604–630.

2008. *The Lisbon Treaty and External Relations*. Maastricht: European Institute of Public Administration. EIPASCOPE 2008/1.

Duke, Simon and Sophie Vanhoonhacker. 2006. Administrative Governance in the CFSP: Development and Practice. *European Foreign Affairs Review* 11 (2): 163–182.

Dziedzic, Michael and Christine Stark. 2006. *Bridging the Public Security Gap*. Washington, DC: USI Peace Briefing, June.

The Economist. 2006. The European Union in the World: Abroad Be Dangers. 26 November.

2008. The State of NATO. A Ray of Light in the Dark Defile. 27 March.

EDA. 2008. *Report on Implementation of EDA Code of Conduct on Defence Procurement*. Brussels: European Defence Agency, 11 July.

Edwards, Jay. 2011. *The EU Defence and Security Procurement Directive: A Step Towards Affordability?* London: Chatham House, International Security Programme Paper 2011/05.

Egnell, Robert. 2006. Explaining US and British Performance in Complex Expeditionary Operations: The Civil-Military Dimension. *The Journal of Strategic Studies* 29 (6): 1041–1075.

2009. *Complex Peace Operations and Civil-Military Relations: Winning the Peace*. London: Routledge.

Ehrhart, Hans-Georg and Gerhard Quille. 2007. *Civil-Military Co-Operation and Co-Ordination in the EU and in Selected Member States*. Report requested by European Parliament Sub-Committee on Security and Defence.

Eide, Espen Barth, Anja T. Kaspersen, R. Kent and K. van Hippel. 2005. *Report on Integrated Missions: Practical Perspectives and Recommendations*. New York: UN Office for the Co-ordination of Humanitarian Affairs, May.

Elgström, Ole. 2003. *European Union Council Presidencies: A Comparative Perspective*. London: Routledge.

Eliassen, Kjell A. and Nick Sitter. 2006. *Arms Procurement in the European Union: Achieving Mission Impossible*. Oslo: Norwegian School of Management. Report 4/2006.

Elliot, Lorraine and Graeme Cheeseman, eds. 2004. *Forces for Good. Cosmopolitan Militaries in the Twenty-First Century, New Approaches to Conflict Analysis*. Manchester University Press.

Engelbrekt, Kjell and Jan Hallenberg, eds. 2008. *The European Union and Strategy. An Emerging Actor*. London: Routledge.

European Commission. 2003. *Towards and EU Defence Equipment Policy*. Commission Communication COM 2003/113, 11 March.

2004. *European Neighbourhood Policy. Strategy Paper*. Commission Communication, COM 2004/373, 12 May.

2007. *A Strategy for a Stronger and More Competitive European Defence Industry*. Commission Communication, COM 2007/764, 5 December.

European Council. 1995. *The Stability Pact for Central and Eastern Europe*. Adopted by the European Council, Paris, 20–21 March.

1999. *Action Plan for Non-military Crisis Management of the EU*. Adopted by the European Council, Helsinki, 10–11 December. Annex IV to the Presidency Conclusions.

2002. *CIMIC Concept for EU-led Crisis Management Operations*. Council Doc. 7106/02, 18 March.

2003a. *Defining the Capability Development Mechanism (CDM)*. Council Doc. 6805/03, 26 February.

2003b. *Civil-Military Co-ordination (CMCO)*. Council Doc. 14457/03, 7 November.

2003c. *European Defence: NATO/EU Consultation, Planning, and Operations*. Endorsed by the European Council, Brussels, 12–13 December.

2003d. *A Secure Europe in a Better World: European Security Strategy*. Endorsed by the European Council, Brussels, 11–12 December.

2003e. *Suggestions for Procedures for Coherent, Comprehensive EU Crisis Management.* Council Doc. 7116/03, 6 March.

2004a. *Action Plan for Civilian Aspects of ESDP.* Adopted by the European Council, Brussels, 17–18 June.

2004b. *Civilian Headline Goal 2008.* Council Doc. 15863/04, 7 December.

2004c. *Headline Goal 2010.* Endorsed by the European Council, Brussels, 17–18 June.

2005a. *Draft EU Concept for Comprehensive Planning.* Council Doc. 13983/05, 3 November.

2005b. *EU Special Representatives (EUSRs): A Voice and Face of the EU in Crucial Areas.* Council Secretariat Factsheet.

2006a. *Civil-Military Co-ordination: Framework Paper of Possible Solutions for the Management of EU Crisis Management Operations.* Council Doc. 89226/06, 2 May.

2006b. *Darfur – Consolidated EU Package in Support of AMIS II.* Council Secretariat Factsheet, March 2006.

2006c. *EUPOL-KINSHASA: The First European Police Mission in Africa.* Council Secretariat Press document, October 2006.

2007. *Civilian Headline Goal 2010.* Adopted by GAERC, 19 November. Council Doc. 14823/07.

2008a. *The EU Operations Centre.* Council Secretariat Factsheet.

2008b. *EU Support to the African Union Mission in Darfur – AMIS.* Council Secretariat Factsheet, January 2008.

2008c. *Report on the Implementation of the European Security Strategy – Providing Security in a Changing World.* Adopted by the European Council, 11 December, S407/08.

2009a. *EU Military Operation in Eastern Chad and North Eastern Central African Republic (EUFOR Tchad/RCA).* Council Secretariat Factsheet, March 2009.

2009b. *European Police Mission in Bosnia and Herzegovina (EUPM).* Council Secretariat Factsheet.

2011. *Council Conclusions on Pooling and Sharing of Military Capabilities.* Adopted by FAC, 23 May.

Everts, Steven and Daniel Keohane. 2003. The European Convention and EU Foreign Policy: Learning form Failure. *Survival* 45 (3): 167–186.

Everts, Steven, Lawrence Freedman, Charles Grant, Francois Heisbourg, Daniel Keohane and Michael O'Hanlon. 2004. *A European Way of War.* London: Centre for European Reform.

Fägersten, B. 2008. *European Intelligence Cooperation: Drivers, Interests and Institutions.* Stockholm: Swedish Institute of International Affairs. SIIA Working Papers no. 6.

Farrell, Theo. 2002. Constructivist Security Studies: Portrait of a Research Program. *International Studies Review* 4: 49–72.

Featherstone, Kevin and George Kazamias. 2001. *Europeanization of the Southern Hemisphere*. London: Frank Cass.

Feaver, Peter D. and Richard H. Kohn, eds. 2001. *Soldiers and Civilians. The Civil Military Gap and American National Security*. Cambridge, MA: MIT Press.

Feith, Pieter. 2007. *The Aceh Peace Process: Nothing Less than Success*. Washington, DC: United States Institute of Peace. Special Report no. 184.

The Financial Times. 2004. Ashdown Sackings Anger Bosnian Serbs. 20 December.

2007. Sarkozy in Drive to Give EU a Global Goal. 27 August.

Foot, Rosemary, S. Neil MacFarlane and Michael Mastanduno, eds. 2003. *US Hegemony and International Organizations: The United States and Multilateral Institutions*. Oxford and New York: Oxford University Press.

Forster, Anthony. 2006. *Armed Forces and Society in Europe*. Houndmills: Palgrave Macmillan.

France/Germany/UK. 2004. *The Battlegroups Concept*. Food for thought paper, 10 February.

Freedman, Lawrence. 1998. International Security: Changing Targets. *Foreign Policy* 110: 48–63.

2006. *The Transformation of Strategic Affairs*. IISS, Adelphi Paper 379. London: Routledge.

Freeman, Linton C. 2004. *The Development of Social Network Analysis: A Study in the Sociology of Science*. Vancouver: Empirical Press.

Gegout, Catherine. 2002. The Quint: Acknowledging the Existence of a Big Four–US Directoire at the Heart of the European Union's Foreign Policy Decision-Making Process. *Journal of Common Market Studies* 40 (2): 331–344.

2005. Causes and Consequences of the EU's Military Intervention in the Democratic Republic of Congo: A Realist Explanation. *European Foreign Affairs Review* 10: 427–443.

George, Alexander L. and Andrew Bennett. 2005. *Case Studies and Theory Development in the Social Sciences*. Cambridge, MA: MIT Press.

Germany/Sweden. 2010. *Pooling and Sharing, German-Swedish Initiative*. Food for thought paper. Berlin and Stockholm, 10 February.

Gerring, John. 2007a. *Case Study Research: Principles and Practices*. Cambridge University Press.

2007b. The Mechanismic Worldview: Thinking Inside the Box. *British Journal of Political Science* 38: 161–179.

Giegerich, Bastian and Jean-Yves Haine. 2006. In Congo, a Cosmetic EU Operation. *International Herald Tribune.* 13 June.

Giegerich, Bastian and Alexander Nicoll, eds. 2008. *European Military Capabilities: Building Armed Forces for Modern Operations.* London: IISS Strategic Dossier.

Gilbert, Mark. 2008. Narrating the Process: Questioning the Progressive Story of European Integration. *Journal of Common Market Studies* 46 (3): 641–662.

Ginsberg, Roy H. 1989. *Foreign Policy Actions of the European Community: The Politics of Scale.* Boulder: Lynne Rienner.

1999. Conceptualising the European Union as an International Actor: Narrowing the Theoretical Capability-Expectations Gap. *Journal of Common Market Studies* 37: 429–454.

2001. *The European Union in International Politics: Baptism by Fire.* Lanham: Rowman & Littlefield.

Gompert, David C., Richard L. Kugler and Martin C. Libicki. 1999. *Mind the Gap: Promoting a Transatlantic Revolution in Military Affairs.* Washington, DC: National Defense University Press.

Gordon, Stuart. 2006. Exploring the Civil-Military Interface and Its Impact on European Strategic and Operational Personalities: 'Civilianisation' and Limiting Military Roles in Stabilisation Operations? *European Security* 15 (3): 339–361.

Gourlay, Catriona. 2004. *Feasibility Study on the European Civil Peace Corps.* Brussels: International Security Information Service. ISIS Europe Report.

2006. Civil-Civil Co-ordination in EU Crisis Management. In *Civilian Crisis Management the EU Way*, edited by A. Nowak. Paris: EU-ISS. Chaillot Paper no. 90, pp. 103–122.

Gowan, Richard. 2009. *Good Intentions, Bad Outcomes* 2009 [cited January–February 2009]. Available at: www.esharp.eu/issue/2009–1/Vi ewpoint-Good-intentions-bad-outcomes.

Granholm, Niklas and Pål Jonson. 2006. *EU-Battlegroups in Context. Underlying Dynamics, Military and Political Challenges.* Stockholm: Swedish Defence Research Agency. FOI Report no. 1950, March.

Grant, Charles. 2000. *Intimate Relations: Can Britain Play a Leading Role in European Defence, and Keep its Special Links to US Intelligence.* London: Centre for European Reform.

2005. *Variable Geometry.* London: Centre for European Reform.

Grant, Charles and Mark Leonard. 2006. *How to Strengthen EU Policy.* London: Centre for European Reform. Policy Brief.

Gray, Colin. 1981. National Styles in Strategy: The American Example. *International Security* 6 (2): 21–47.

1999a. *Modern Strategy*. New York: Oxford University Press.

1999b. Strategic Culture as Context: The First Generation of Theory Strikes Back. *Review of International Studies* 25: 49–69.

2006. *Out of the Wilderness: Prime Time for Strategic Culture*. Fort Belvoir: Defence Threat Reduction Agency.

Grevi, Giovanni. 2007. *Pioneering Foreign Policy: The EU Special Representatives*. Paris: EU-ISS. Chaillot Paper no. 106.

2009. *Institutional Change and Continuity in the CFSP and ESDP*. Paper presented at the 50th Annual ISA Convention. New York, 15–18 February.

Grevi, Giovanni, Damien Helly and Daniel Keohane, eds. 2009. *European Security and Defence Policy. The First Ten Years (1999–2009)*. Paris: EU-ISS.

Grevi, Giovanni, Daniela Manca and Gerhard Quille. 2004. *A Foreign Minister for the EU – Past, Present and Future*. CFSP Forum Working Papers. Available at: www.fornet.info/CFSPforumworkingpapers.html

Haas, Ernst. 1958. *The Uniting of Europe*. Stanford University Press.

Haftendorn, Helga. 1991. The Security Puzzle: Theory-Building and Discipline-Building in International Security. *International Studies Quarterly* 35 (1): 3–17.

Hall, Peter A. and Rosemary C. R. Taylor. 1996. Political Science and the Three New Institutionalisms. *Political Studies* 44: 936–957.

Hall, Rodney Bruce. 1999. *National Collective Identity: Social Constructs and International Systems*. New York: Columbia University Press.

Hallenberg, Jan. 2008. Introduction. In *The European Union and Strategy. An Emerging Actor*, edited by K. Engelbrekt and J. Hallenberg. London: Routledge, pp. 1–6.

Hansen, Annika S. 2006. *Against All Odds – The Evolution of Planning for ESDP Operations. Civilian Crisis Management Operations from EUPM Onwards*. Berlin: Centre for International Peace Operations. Study 10/06.

Hedström, Peder and Richard Swedberg. 1998. *Social Mechanisms: An Analytical Approach to Social Theory*. Cambridge University Press.

Heisbourg, Francois. 2000. Europe's Strategic Ambitions: The Limits of Ambiguity. *Survival* 42 (2): 5–15.

2004. The 'European Security Strategy' is not a Security Strategy. In *A European Way of War*, edited by S. Everts. London: Centre for European Reform.

Heiselberg, Stine. 2003. *Pacifism or Activsim: Towards a Common Strategic Culture within the European Security and Defence Policy?* Copenhagen: Danish Institute for International Studies. IIS Working Paper 2003/4.

Hermann, Margaret G., Thomas Preston, Korany Baghat and Timothy M. Shaw. 2001. Who Leads Matters: The Effects of Powerful Individuals. *International Studies Review* 3 (2): 83–131.

Hewson, Martin and Timothy J. Sinclair. 1999. *Approaches to Global Governance Theory*. Albany: State University of New York Press.

Hill, Christopher. 1993. The Capability–Expectations Gap, or Conceptualising Europe's International Role. *Journal of Common Market Studies* 31: 305–328.

1996. *The Actors in Europe's Foreign Policy*. London: Routledge.

1998. Closing the Capability–Expectations Gap. In *A Common Foreign Policy for Europe?*, edited by J. Peterson and H. Sjursen. London: Routledge.

2004. Renationalizing or Regrouping? EU Foreign Policy Since 11 September 2001. *Journal of Common Market Studies* 42 (1): 143–163.

2007. The Future of the European Union as a Global Actor. In *Managing a Multilevel Foreign Policy: The EU in International Affairs*, edited by P. Foradori, P. Rosa and R. Scartezzini. Lanham: Lexington, pp. 3–22.

Hill, Christopher and Michael H. Smith, eds. 2011. *International Relations and the EU*. 2nd edn. Oxford University Press.

Hix, Simon. 1998. The Study of the European Union II: The 'New Governance' Agenda and its Rival. *Journal of European Public Policy* 5 (1): 38–65.

Hollis, Martin and Steve Smith. 1990. *Explaining and Understanding International Relations*. Oxford University Press.

Holsti, Kalevi J. 1995. *International Politics: A Framework for Analysis*. New Jersey: Prentice Hall.

Hooghe, Lisbeth and Gary Marks. 2001. *Multi-Level Governance and European Integration*. Oxford: Rowman & Littlefield.

Hopf, Ted. 1998. The Promise of Constructivism in International Relations Theory. *International Security* 23 (1): 171–200.

House of Commons. 2005. *Third Report from the Foreign Affairs Committee: The Western Balkans: Session 2004–05: HC 87-II*. London: House of Commons.

Howard, Michael. 1983a. The Strategic Approach to International Relations. In *The Causes of Wars*. London: Temple Smith.

1983b. The Forgotten Dimensions of Strategy. In *The Causes of Wars*. London: Temple Smith.

Howorth, Jolyon. 2000. Britain, France and the European Defence Initiative. *Survival* 42 (2): 33–55.

2002. The CESDP and the Forging of a European Security Culture? *Politique Européenne* 8: 88–109.

2004. Discourse, Ideas, and Epistemic Communities in European Security and Defence Policy. *West European Politics* 27 (2): 211–234.

2005. The Euro-Atlantic Security Dilemma: France, Britain and the ESDP. *Journal of Transatlantic Studies* 3 (1): 39–54.

2007. *Security and Defence Policy in the European Union*. Houndmills: Palgrave.

Huntington, Samuel. 1957. *The Soldier and the State: The Theory and Politics of Civil-Military Relations*. Cambridge, MA: Harvard University Press.

Huysmans, Jef. 1995. Migrants as a Security Problem: Dangers of 'Securitising' Social Issues. In *Migration and European Integration: The Dynamics of Inclusion and Exclusion*, edited by R. Miles and D. Thränhardt. London: Pinter, pp. 53–72.

1998. Security! What do you mean? From Concept to Thick Signifier. *European Journal of International Relations* 4 (2): 229–258.

Hyde-Price, Adrian. 2004. European Security, Strategic Culture and the Use of Force. *European Security* 13 (4): 323–343.

2006. 'Normative' Power Europe: A Realist Critique. *Journal of European Public Policy* 13 (2): 217–234.

ICG. 2001. *EU Crisis Response Capability*. International Crisis Group Issues Report no. 2.

2003. *Congo Crisis. Military Intervention in Ituri*. International Crisis Group Africa Report no. 64.

2005. *Bosnia's Stalled Police Reform: No Progress, No EU*. International Crisis Group Report no. 164.

2009. *Georgia-Russia: Still Insecure and Dangerous*. International Crisis Group Europe Briefing no. 53.

Immergut, Ellen. 1998. The Theoretical Core of the New Institutionalism. *Politics and Society* 26 (1): 5–34.

International Herald Tribune. 2006. Solana, EU's 'Good Cop' Takes Stage. 12 November.

Ioannides, Isabelle. 2006. EU Police Mission Proxima: Testing the 'European Approach' to Building Peace. In *Civilian Crisis Management the EU Way*, edited by A. Nowak. Paris: EU-ISS. Chaillot Paper no. 90, pp. 69–86.

Jachtenfuchs, Markus. 2001. The Governance Approach to European Integration. *Journal of Common Market Studies* 39 (2): 245–264.

Jachtenfuchs, Markus and Beate Kohler-Koch. 2004. Governance and Institutional Development. In *European Integration Theory*, edited by A. Wiener and T. Diez. Oxford University Press.

Jakobsen, Peter Viggo. 2009. Small States, Big Influence: The Overlooked Nordic Influence on the Civilian ESDP. *Journal of Common Market Studies* 47 (1): 81–102.

James, Andrew D. 2006. The Transatlantic Defence R&D Gap: Causes, Consequences and Controversies. *Defence and Peace Economics* 17 (3): 223–238.

Jane's Defence Weekly. 2008. Interview: Brigadier General Karl Engelbrektson, Commander of the EU Nordic Battle Group. 12 March.

———. 2009a. EUFOR Mission in Chad/CAR Ends Amid MINURCAT Vulnerability Fears. 13 March.

———. 2009b. EUFOR Operations Prove EU Capabilities, says Military Head. 9 April.

Janowitz, Morris. 1960. *The Professional Soldier: A Social and Political Portrait.* New York: The Free Press.

Jervis, Robert. 1982. Security Regimes. *International Organization* 36 (2): 357–378.

Jessop, Bob. 1999. The Changing Governance of Welfare: Recent Trends in its Primary Functions, Scale and Modes of Coordination. *Social Policy & Administration* 33 (4): 348–359.

Joergensen, Knut Erik. 1997. Western Europe and the Petersberg Tasks. In *European Approaches to Crisis Management,* edited by K.E. Joergensen. The Hague: Kluwer Law International, pp. 131–152.

Johnston, Alastair Iain. 1995. Thinking About Strategic Culture. *International Security* 19 (4): 32–64.

Juncos, Ana E. and Christopher Reynolds. 2007. The Political and Security Committee: Governing in the Shadow. *European Foreign Affairs Review* 12 (2): 127–147.

Justaert, Arnout and Stephan Keukeleire. 2010. Network Governance in ESDP: The Case of the Democratic Republic of Congo. *European Integration Online Papers* 14 (Special Issue 1).

Kagan, Robert. 2002. Power and Weakness – Why the United States and Europe see the World Differently. *Policy Review* 113: 3–28.

———. 2003. *Of Paradise and Power: America and Europe in the New World Order.* New York: Knopf.

Kaitera, Juha and Guy Ben-Ari. 2008. *EU Battlegroups and the NATO Response Force: A Marriage of Convenience?* Washington, DC: Center for Strategic and International Studies. Euro-Focus, April.

Kaldor, Mary. 1999. *New and Old Wars: Organized Violence in a Global Era.* Cambridge: Polity Press.

Kaldor, Mary, Mary Martin and Sabine Selchow. 2007. Human Security: A New Strategic Narrative for Europe. *International Affairs* 83 (2): 273–288.

Karns, Margaret P. and Karen A. Mingst. 2004. *International Organizations: The Politics and Processes of Global Governance.* Boulder: Lynne Rienner Publishers.

Katzenstein, Peter J. 1996a. *Cultural Norms and National Security: Police and Military in Postwar Japan*. Ithaca: Cornell University Press.

    1996b. *The Culture of National Security. Norms and Identity in World Politics*. New York: Columbia University Press.

Katzenstein, Peter J., Robert O. Keohane and Stephen D. Krasner. 1998. International Organization and the Study of World Politics. *International Organization* 52 (4): 645–685.

Keohane, Robert O. 1984. *After Hegemony: Cooperation and Discord in the World Political Economy*. Princeton University Press.

Keohane, Robert O. and Lisa L. Martin. 1995. The Promise of Institutionalist Theory. *International Security* 20: 39–51.

Kepel, Gilles. 2008. *Beyond Terror and Martyrdom: The Future of the Middle East*. Cambridge, MA: Harvard University Press.

Khol, Radek. 2006. Civil-Military Co-ordination in EU Crisis Management. In *Civilian Crisis Management the EU Way*, edited by A. Nowak. Paris: EU-ISS. Chaillot Paper no. 90.

Kier, Elizabeth. 1997. *Imagining War: French and British Military Doctrine Between the Wars*. Princeton University Press.

King's College. 2001. *Achieving the Helsinki Headline Goals*. London: King's College, Centre for Defence Studies. Discussion Paper.

Kirchner, Emil J. 2006. The Challenge of European Union Security Governance. *Journal of Common Market Studies* 44 (5): 947–968.

Kirchner, Emil J. and James Sperling. 2007a. *EU Security Governance*. Manchester University Press.

    eds. 2007b. *Global Security Governance: Competing Perceptions of Security in the 21st Century*. London: Routledge.

Kirwan, Paul. 2008. From European to Global Security Actor. The Aceh Monitoring Mission in Indonesia. In *European Security and Defence Policy. An Implementation Perspective*, edited by M. Merlingen and R. Ostrauskaite. London: Routledge, pp. 128–142.

Klein, Bradley S. 1988. Hegemony and Strategic Culture: American Power Projection and Alliance Defence Politics. *Review of International Studies* 14 (2): 133–148.

    1989. The Textual Strategies of the Military: Or, Have You Read Any Good Defence Manuals Lately? In *International/Intertextual Relations: Postmodern Readings of World Politics*, edited by J. Der Derian and J. Shapiro. Lexington: Lexington Books, pp. 97–112.

Klingebiel, Stephan, ed. 2006. *New Interfaces between Security and Development: Changing Concepts and Approaches*. Bonn: Deutsches Institut für Entwicklungspolitik.

Knutsen, Bjørn Olav. 2008. *The EU and the Challenges of Civil-Military Coordination at the Strategic Level*. Kjeller: Norwegian Defence Research Establishment, FFI Report 2008/01463.

Koenig, Nicole. 2011. *The EU and the Libyan Crisis: In Quest of Coherence.* Rome: Istituto Affari Internazionali, IAI Working Papers 11/19.

Koenig-Archibugi, Mathias. 2004. International Governance as New Raison d'Ètat? The Case of the EU Foreign and Security Policy. *European Journal of International Relations* 10 (2): 147–188.

Koha Ditore Press. 2008. EULEX will Cover all the Territory of Kosovo. 12 March.

Kohler-Koch, Beate and Rainer Eising. 1999. *The Transformation of Governance in the European Union.* London: Routledge.

Kolodziej, Edward A. 2000. Security Studies for the Next Millennium: Quo Vadis? In *Critical Reflections on Security and Change*, edited by S. Croft and T. Terriff. London: Frank Cass, pp. 18–38.

KosovoCompromise. 2009. NATO Cuts Kfor to 10,000 Troops, Aims Cuts to 2,000. 24 June.

Krahmann, Elke. 2003a. Conceptualising Security and Governance. *Cooperation and Conflict* 38 (1): 5–26.

2003b. National, Regional and Global Governance: One Phenomenon or Many? *Global Governance* 9: 323–346.

2005. Security Governance and Networks: New Theoretical Perspectives in Transatlantic Security. *Cambridge Review of International Affairs* 18 (1): 15–30.

Krasner, Stephen D. 1983. *International Regimes.* Ithaca: Cornell University Press.

1984. Approaches to the State: Alternative Conceptions and Historical Developments. *Comparative Politics* 16: 223–246.

Kratochwil, Friedrich. 2000. Constructing a New Orthodoxy? Wendt's 'Social Theory of International Politics' and the Constructivist Challenge. *Millennium* 29 (1): 73–101.

Krause, Keith and Michael Williams. 1997. *Critical Security Studies.* Minneapolis: University of Minnesota Press.

Kristiansen, Dag. 2008. Nordic Battlegroup – Dr. Solana's First Choice. *Norsk Militært Tidsskrift [Norwegian Military Journal]* 178 (5): 29–33.

Kurki, Milja. 2008. *Causation in International Relations: Reclaiming Causal Analysis.* Cambridge University Press.

Kurowska, Xymena. 2009. The Role of ESDP Operations. In *European Security and Defence Policy. An Implementation Perspective*, edited by M. Merlingen and R. Ostrauskaite. London: Routledge, pp. 25–42.

Layne, Christopher. 2000. US Hegemony and the Perpetuation of NATO. *Journal of Strategic Studies* 23 (3): 59–91.

Leakey, David. 2006. ESDP and Civil/Military Cooperation: Bosnia and Herzegovina, 2005. In *Securing Europe? Implementing the European*

Security Strategy, edited by A. Deighton and V. Mauer. Zurich: ETH Center for Security Studies.

Legro, Jeffrey. 1995. *Cooperation Under Fire: Anglo-German Restraint during World War II*. Ithaca: Cornell University Press.

Liddell-Hart, Basil. 1967. *Strategy: The Indirect Approach*. London: Faber.

Lindberg, Leon. 1963. *The Political Dynamics of European Economic Integration*. Stanford University Press.

Lindley-French, Julian. 2002a. The Capabilities Development Process post-September 11. What Kind of Operational Needs for Which Purposes? Speech given to the WEU seminar on Equipping our Forces for Europe's Security and Defence Priorities and Shortcomings. Madrid, 5–6 March.

2002b. *Terms of Engagement. The Paradox of American Power and the Transatlantic Dilemma Post-11 September*. Paris: EU-ISS. Chaillot Paper no. 52.

Lindström, Gustav. 2007. *Enter the EU Battlegroups*. Paris: EU-ISS. Chaillot Paper no. 97.

Longhurst, Kerry. 2000. Strategic Culture. In *Military Sociology: The Richness of a Discipline*, edited by G. Kümmel and A.D. Prüfert. Baden Baden: Nomos, pp. 301–310.

Longhurst, Kerry and Marcin Zaborowski. 2004. The Future of European Security. *European Security* 13 (4): 381–391.

Lord, Carnes. 1985. American Strategic Culture. *Comparative Strategy* 5 (3): 269–293.

Mace, Catriona. 2004. Operation *Concordia*: Developing a 'European' Approach to Crisis Management. *International Peacekeeping* 11 (3): 474–490.

Manners, Ian. 2002. Normative Power Europe: A Contradiction in Terms? *Journal of Common Market Studies* 40 (2): 235–258.

2006. Normative Power Europe Reconsidered: Beyond the Crossroads. *Journal of European Public Policy* 13 (2): 182–199.

Manners, Ian and Richard G. Whitman. 2000. *The Foreign Policies of the European Union Member States*. London: Macmillan.

March, James and Johan P. Olsen. 1984. The New Institutionalism: Organizational Factors in Political Life. *The American Political Science Review* 78: 734–749.

1989. *Rediscovering Institutions: The Organizational Basis of Politics*. New York: Free Press.

1995. *Democratic Governance*. New York: Free Press.

2005. The Institutional Dynamics of International Political Orders. *International Organization* 52: 943–969.

Marks, Gary, Fritz W. Scharpf, Phillipe C. Schmitter and Wolfgang Streeck. 1996. *Governance in the European Union*. London: Thousand Oaks.

Markusen, Ann R. 2003. The Case against Privatizing National Security. *Governance* 16 (4): 471–501.

Marquina, Antonio and Xira Ruiz. 2005. A European Competitive Advantage? Civilian Instruments for Conflict Prevention and Crisis Management. *Journal of Transatlantic Studies* 3 (1): 71–87.

Martinelli, Marta. 2008. Implementing the ESDP in Africa: The Case of the Democratic Republic of Congo. In *European Security and Defence Policy. An Implementation Perspective*, edited by M. Merlingen and R. Ostrauskaite. London: Routledge, p. 111–127.

Martinsen, Per Martin. 2004. Forging a Strategic Culture – Putting Policy into the ESDP. *Oxford Journal on Good Governance* 1 (1): 61–66.

Matlary, Janne Haaland. 2006. When Soft Power Turns Hard: Is an EU Strategic Culture Possible? *Security Dialogue* 37 (1): 105–121.

2009. *European Union Security Dynamics. In the New National Interest*. London: Palgrave Macmillan.

Mattelaer, Alexander. 2008. *The Strategic Planning of EU Military Operations – The Case of EUFOR Tchad / RCA*. Brussels: Institute for European Studies. IES Working Paper 5/2008.

Maull, Hans. 1990. Germany and Japan: The New Civilian Powers? *Foreign Affairs* 69 (5): 91–106.

2000. Germany and the Use of Force: Still a Civilian Power? *Survival* 42 (2): 56–80.

Mawdsley, Jocelyn, Marta Martinelli and Eric Remacle, eds. 2004. *Europe and the Global Armament Agenda: Security, Trade and Accountability*. Baden Baden: Nomos.

Merand, Frederic. 2008. *European Defence Policy: Beyond the Nation State*. Oxford University Press.

Merand, Frederic, Stephanie Hofman and Bastien Irondelle. 2010. Formal and Informal Decison-Makers in ESDP: A Network Analysis. *European Integration Online Papers* 14 (Special Issue 1).

Merlingen, Michael and Rasa Ostrauskaite. 2005. ESDP Police Missions: Meaning, Context and Operational Challenges. *European Foreign Affairs Review* 10 (2): 215–235.

2006. *European Union Peacebuilding and Policing: Governance and the European Security and Defence Policy*. London: Routledge.

eds. 2008. *European Security and Defence Policy. An Implementation Perspective*. London: Routledge.

Merom, Gil. 2003. *How Democracies Lose Small Wars: State Society, and the Failures of France in Algeria, Israel in Lebanon, and the United States in Vietnam.* New York: Cambridge University Press.

Merton, Robert. 1957. *Social Theory and Social Structure.* New York: Free Press.

Messervy-Whiting, Graham. 2006. ESDP Deployments and the European Security Strategy. In *Securing Europe? Implementing the European Security Strategy,* edited by A. Deighton and V. Mauer. Zurich: ETH Center for Security Studies, pp. 31–41.

Mevel, Jean-Jacques. 2009. Van Rompuy, l'horloger des compromis impossibles. *Le Figaro,* 19 November.

Meyer, Christoph O. 2006. *The Quest for a European Strategic Culture: A Comparative Study of Strategic Norms and Ideas in the European Union.* Basingstoke: Palgrave Macmillan.

Missiroli, Antonio. 2002. Ploughshares into Swords? Euros for European Defence. *European Foreign Affairs Review* 8 (1): 5–33.

Mölling, Christian. 2007. *EU-Battlegroups: Stand und Probleme der Umsetzung in Deutschland unf für die EU.* Berlin: Stiftung Wissenschafft und Politik. Discussion Paper, March.

Moore, Wendela C. 2003. *Stability Operations: A Core Warfighting Cabability.* Washington, DC: National War College.

Moravcsik, Andrew. 1993. Preferences and Power in the European Community: A Liberal Intergovernmentalist Approach. *Journal of Common Market Studies* 31: 473–524.

  1998. *The Choice for Europe: Social Purpose and State Power from Messina to Maastricht.* Ithaca: Cornell University Press.

  1999. Is Something Rotten in the State of Denmark? Constructivism and European Integration. *Journal of European Public Policy* 65: 669–681.

Mörth, Ulrika. 2003a. Competing Frames in the European Commission – the Case of the Defence Industry and Equipment Issue. *Journal of European Public Policy* 7 (2): 173–189.

  2003b. *Organizing European Co-operation: The Case of Armaments.* Oxford: Rowman & Littlefield.

Müller-Wille, Björn. 2002. EU Intelligence Cooperation: A Critical Analysis. *Contemporary Security Policy* 23 (2): 61–86.

  2006. Improving the Democratic Accountability of EU Intelligence. *Intelligence and National Security* 21 (1): 100–128.

  2008. The Effect of International Terrorism on EU Intelligence Co-operation. *Journal of Common Market Studies* 46 (1): 49–73.

Mustonen, Jari. 2008. Coordination and Cooperation on tactical and Operational Levels. Studying EU-ESDP Crisis Managment Instruments in Bosnia and Herzegovina. *CMC Finland Crisis Management Studies* 1 (1).

NATO. (1999). Strategic Concept for the Defence and Security of the Members of the North Atlantic Treaty Organisation. Adopted by the Heads of State and Government, Washington, DC, 24 April.

2004. *The Alliance's Strategic Vision: The Military Challenge.* Mons/ Norfolk: ACO/ACT.

2010. *Strategic Concept for the Defence and Security of the Members of the North Atlantic Treaty Organisation.* Adopted by the NATO Heads of Government in Lisbon, 19 November.

Naumann, Klaus. 2000. *Europe's Military Ambitions.* London: Centre for European Reform. June/July Bulletin.

Neumann, Iver B. and Henrikki Heikka. 2005. Grand Strategy, Strategic Culture, Practice. The Social Roots of Nordic Defence. *Cooperation and Conflict* 40 (1): 5–23.

Nielsen, Suzanne and Don M. Snider, eds. 2009. *American Civil-Military Relations. The Soldier and the State in a New Era.* Baltimore: Johns Hopkins University Press.

Norheim-Martinsen, Per Martin. 2005. Operation EUFOR in BiH: Europe's Backyard Reclaimed. In *Third Report from the Foreign Affairs Committee: The Western Balkans.* London: House of Commons. Session 2004–05: HC 87-II.

2007. European Strategic Culture Revisited: The Ends and Means of a Militarised European Union. *Defence and Security Studies* 1 (3): 1–56.

2008. Who Speaks for Europe While We Wait for the EU Foreign Minister? In *The Rise and Fall of the EU's Constitutional Treaty,* edited by F. Laursen. Leiden: Martinus Nijhoff, pp. 105–120.

2010. Beyond Intergovernmentalism: European Security and Defence Policy and the Governance Approach. *Journal of Common Market Studies* 48 (5): 1351–1365.

Nowak, Agnieszka. 2006. Civilian Crisis Management within ESDP. In *Civilian Crisis Management the EU Way,* edited by A. Nowak. Paris: EU-ISS. Chaillot Paper no. 90, pp. 15–37.

Nuttall, Simon. 1992. *European Political Co-operation.* Oxford: Clarendon Press.

2000. *European Foreign Policy.* Oxford University Press.

Nye, Joseph H. 1990. *Bound to Lead: The Changing Nature of American Power.* New York: Basic Books.

2004. *Soft Power: The Means to Success in World Politics.* New York: Public Affairs.

Nye, Joseph H. and Robert O. Keohane. 2001. *Power and Interdependence.* New York: Longman.

O'Dwyer, Gerard. 2008. Sweden Pushes for More Nordic Cooperation. *Defence News*. Available at: www.defensenews.com/story.php?i=3557831

Oikonomou, Iraklis. 2006. *The EU Politico-Military-Industrial Complex: A New Research Agenda*. Paper presented at the BISA Annual Conference. University College Cork, 20 December.

Ojanen, Hanna. 2006. The EU and Nato: Two Competing Models for a Common Defence Policy. *Journal of Common Market Studies* 44: 57–76.

Olsen, Johan P. 2002. *The Many Faces of Europeanization*. Oslo: ARENA Centre for European Studies. Working Papers no. 1.

Onuf, Nicholas. 1998. The New Culture of Security Studies. *Mershon International Studies Review* 42: 132–134.

Osland, Kari M. 2004. The EU Police Mission in Bosnia and Herzegovina. *International Peacekeeping* 11 (3): 544–560.

Parsons, Craig. 2002. Showing Ideas as Causes. The Origins of the European Union. *International Organization* 56 (1): 47–84.

Pastore, Ferrucio. 2001. *Reconciling the Prince's Two Arms: Internal-External Security Policy Coordination in the European Union*. Paris: WEU Institute for Security Studies, Occasional Paper no. 30.

Peters, B. Guy. 1999. *Institutional Theory in Political Science: The New Institutionalism*. London: Pinter.

Peterson, John and Helene Sjursen. 1998. *A Common Foreign Policy for Europe? Competing Visions of the CFSP*. London: Routledge.

Piening, Christopher. 1997. *Global Europe: The EU in World Affairs*. Boulder: Lynne Rienner.

Pierre, Jon and B. Guy Peters. 2000. *Governance, Politics and the State*. Basingstoke: Macmillan.

Pierson, Paul. 2000. Increasing Returns, Path Dependence, and the Study of Politics. *American Political Science Review* 94 (2): 251–267.

2004. *Politics in Time: History, Institutions, and Social Analysis*. Princeton University Press.

Pipes, Richard. 1977. Why the Soviet Union Thinks It Could Fight and Win a Nuclear War. *Commentary* 1: 21–34.

Powell, Walter W. 1990. Neither Market nor Hierarchy: Network Forms of Organization. *Research in Organizational Behaviour* 12: 295–336.

Putnam, Robert. 1988. The Logic of Two-Level Games. *International Organization* 42: 427–460.

Quille, Gerard. 2006. *Note on ESDP Mission 'EUFOR R.D. Congo': In Support of UN Mission (MONUC) in the Democratic Republic of Congo (DRC) during the Election Expected in July 2006*. Brussels: European Parliament, Directorate General for External Policies of the Union, Directorate B, Policy Department, 2 May.

Quille, Gerard, Giovanni Gasparini, Roberto Menotti and Nicoletta Pirozzi. 2006. *Developing EU Civil Military Co-ordination: The Role of the New Civilian Military Cell.* Brussels: Joint Report by ISIS Europe and CeMiSS.

Raik, Kristi. 2006. The EU as a Regional Power: Extended Governance and Historical Responsibility. In *A Responsible Europe? Ethical Foundations of EU External Affairs*, edited by H. Mayer and H. Vogt. London: Palgrave Macmillan, pp. 76–97.

Rieker, Pernille. 2003. *Europeanisation of Nordic Security. The EU and the Changing Security Identities of the Nordic States.* PhD Thesis. Institutt for Statsvitenskap, University of Oslo.

2005. Power, Principles and Procedures: French Foreign Policy towards the USA (2001–2003). *Journal of International Politics* 42 (2): 264–280.

2006. *Europeanisation of National Security Identity: The EU and the Changing Identities of the Nordic States.* London: Routledge.

Risse, Thomas. 2000. 'Let's Argue!' Communicative Action in World Politics. *International Organization* 54 (1): 71–82.

Risse-Kappen, Thomas. 1994. Ideas Do Not Float Freely: Transnational Coalitions, Domestic Structures, and the End of the Cold War. *International Organization* 48 (2).

Rittberger, Volker. 1995. *Regime Theory and International Relations.* Oxford: Clarendon Press.

Rogers, Everett, M. 2003. *Diffusion of Innovations.* 5th edn. New York: Free Press.

Roper, John. 2000. Strategic Implications of the End of the Cold War. In *Critical Reflections on Security and Change*, edited by S. Croft and T. Terriff. London: Frank Cass, pp. 102–115.

Rosenau, James M. 1995. Governance in the Twenty-First Century. *Global Governance* 1 (1): 13–43.

Rosenau, James N. and Ernst-Otto Czempiel. 1992. *Governance without Government: Order and Change in World Politics.* Cambridge University Press.

Rummel, Reinhardt. 1990. *The Evolution of an International Actor: Western Europe's New Assertiveness.* Boulder: Westview Press.

Rynning, Sten. 2003. The European Union: Towards a Strategic Culture? *Security Dialogue* 34 (4): 479–496.

Saferworld and International Alert. 2004. *Strengthening Global Security through Addressing the Root Causes of Conflict: Priorities for the Irish and Dutch Presidencies in 2004*, downloadable at http://www.international-alert.org/sites/default/files/publications/strengthening_global_securi.pdf.

Sahlin, Michael. 2005. *Speech given to the Seminar on Rapid Deployment Capability in EU Civilian Crisis Management*. Folke Bernadotte Academy, Stockholm, 13–14 April.

Schadlow, Nadia and Richard A. Lacquement Jr. 2009. Winning Wars, Not Just Battles. Expanding the Military Profession to Incorporate Stability Operations. In *American Civil-Military Relations*, edited by S. Nielsen and D.M. Snider. Baltimore: Johns Hopkins University Press, pp. 112–132.

Schake, Kori. 2002. *Constructive Duplication: Reducing EU Reliance on US Military Assets*. London: Centre for European Reform.

Scharpf, Fritz W. 1993. *Games in Hierarchies and Networks: Analytical and Empirical Approaches to the Study of Governance Institutions*. Frankfurt: Campus Verlag.

Schatzki, Theodore M., Karin Knorr Cetina and Eike von Savigny. 2001. *The Practice Turn in Contemporary Theory*. London: Routledge.

Schimmelfenning, Frank. 1999. *The Double Puzzle of EU Enlargement. Liberal Norms, Rhetorical Action, and the Decision to Expand to the East*. Oslo: ARENA Centre for European Studies. Working Paper 15.

   2003. *The EU, NATO and the Integration of Europe: Rules and Rhetoric*. Cambridge: Polity Press.

Schmitter, Phillipe. 1969. Three Neo-Functional Hypotheses About International Integration. *International Organization* 23: 161–166.

Schneckener, Ulrich. 2002. Theory and Practice of European Crisis Management: Test Case Macedonia. *European Yearbook of Minority Issues* 1 (2001/02): 131–156.

Schneider, Gerald and Claudia Seybold. 1997. Twelve Tongues, One Voice: An Evaluation of European Political Cooperation. *European Journal of Political Research* 31: 367–396.

Schroeder, Ursula C. 2006. *Coping with Complexity: An Organizational Perspective on European Security Governance*. European University Institute. Working Paper SPS no. 9.

   2011. *The Organization of European Security Governance: Internal and External Security in Transition*. London: Routledge.

Scott, John. 1991. *Social Network Analysis: A Handbook*. London: Sage.

Seibert, Bjoern. 2007. *African Adventure? Assessing the European Union's Military Intervention in Chad and the Central African Republic*. MIT Security Studies Program. Working Paper, November.

   2009. *Ready for Action? Evaluating the European Union's Ability to Undertake Crisis Management Operations*. Paper presented at the European Security Strategy Revisited Conference. Jesus College, Cambridge, 22–23 May.

Shapcott, William. 2004. *Minutes of Evidence taken before the Select Committee on the European Union*. London: House of Lords.

Sjöstedt, Gunnar. 1977. *The External Role of the European Community*. London: Saxon House.

Smith, Karen. 2000. The End of Civilian Power EU: A Welcome Demise or a Cause for Concern? *International Spectator* XXXV (2): 11–28.

Smith, Michael E. 2004. *Europe's Foreign and Security Policy. The Institutionalization of Cooperation*. Cambridge University Press.

Smith, Michael H. 2001. The European Union as an International Actor. In *European Union: Power and Policy-Making*, 2nd edn, edited by J. Richardson. London: Routledge, pp. 283–302.

Smith, Rupert. 2007. *The Utility of Force: The Art of War in the Modern World*. New York: Knopf.

Smith, Steve. 1999. Social Constructivisms and European Studies: A Reflectivist Critique. *Journal of European Public Policy* 6 (4) Special Issue: 682–691.

Snyder, Jack L. 1977. *The Soviet Strategic Culture: Implications for Limited Nuclear Operations*. Santa Monica: Rand Corporation, R-2154-AF.

   1990. The Concept of Strategic Culture: Caveat Emptor. In *Strategic Power USA/USSR*, edited by C.G. Jacobsen. London: Basingstoke, pp. 3–9.

Solana, Javier. 2007. The Democratic Republic of Congo/EUFOR. Presentation to the United Nations Security Council. New York, 9 January.

Spence, David and Phillip Fluri, eds. 2008. *The European Union and Security Sector Reform*. London: John Harper Publishing.

Statewatch Bulletin. 2004. EU: 'Anti-Terrorism' Legitimises Sweeping New 'Internal Security' Complex. 14 May.

Stavridis, S. 2001. Militarising the EU: The Concept of Civilian Power Revisited. *International Spectator* XXXVI (4): 43–50.

Stoltenberg, Thorvald. 2009. *Nordic Cooperation on Foreign and Security Policy*. Report presented to the extraordinary meeting of Nordic foreign ministers. Oslo, 9 February.

Strachan, Hew. 2005. The Lost Meaning of Strategy. *Survival* 47 (3): 33–54.

Stubb, Alexander. 1996. A Categorization of Differentiated Integration. *Journal of Common Market Studies* 34 (2): 283–295.

Sundberg, Anna and Claes Nilsson. 2009. *Swedish Presidency Ambitions and ESDP*. Madrid: Elcano Royal Institute for International and Strategic Studies, ARI 156/2009.

Swedish Armed Forces. 2008. *Nordic Battlegroup Force Headquarters Sweden: Lessons Learned 2008*. Enköping: NBG Force Headquarters.

Swedish EU Presidency. 2009. *Important Defence Policy Issues during the Presidency.* Stockolm: Ministry of Defence, July.

Swidler, Ann. 2001. What Anchors Cultural Practices. In *The Practice Turn in Contemporary Theory*, edited by T.M. Schatzki, K.K. Cetina and E. von Savigny. London: Routledge, pp. 74–92.

Szigeti, Andràs. 2006. The Problem of Institutional Responsibility and the Europan Union. In *A Responsible Europe? Ethical Foundations of EU External Affairs*, edited by H. Mayer and H. Vogt. Houndmills: Palgrave Macmillan, pp. 17–35.

Tallberg, Jonas. 2003a. The Agenda-Shaping Powers of the EU Council Presidency. *Journal of European Public Policy* 10 (1): 1–19.

   2003b. *European Governance and Supranational Institutions: Making States Comply.* London: Routledge.

   2004. The Power of the Presidency: Brokerage, Efficiency and Distribution in EU Negotiations. *Journal of Common Market Studies* 42 (5): 999–1022.

   2006. *Leadership and Negotiation in the European Union.* Cambridge University Press.

   2008. Bargaining Power in the European Council. *Journal of Common Market Studies* 46 (3): 685–708.

Taylor, Phillip. 1979. *When Europe Speaks with One Voice: The External Relations of the European Community.* Westport: Greenwood Press.

Telo, Mario. 2006. *Europe: A Civilian Power? European Union, Global Governance, World Order.* Basingstoke: Palgrave.

Thompson, Robert. 2008. The Council Presidency in the European Union: Responsibility with Power. *Journal of Common Market Studies* 46 (3): 593–617.

The Times. 2010. Baroness Ashton under Fire for Missing European Defence Summit. 26 February.

Toje, Asle. 2005. The 2003 European Union Security Strategy: A Critical Appraisal. *European Foreign Affairs Review* 10: 117–133.

   2008a. *The EU, NATO and Strategic Culture: Renegotiating the Transatlantic Bargain.* London Routledge.

   2008b. The Consensus-Expectations Gap: Explaining Europe's Ineffective Foreign Policy. *Security Dialogue* 39 (1): 121–141.

Tranholm-Mikkelsen, Jeppe. 1991. Neo-Functionalism: Obstinate or Obsolete? A Reappraisal in the Light of the New Dynamism of the EC. *Millennium* (Spring): 1–22.

Ulriksen, Staale. 2003. Det Militære Europa. In *En annerledes supermakt? Sikkerhets- og forsvarspolitikken i EU*, edited by S. Ulriksen and P. Rieker. Oslo: Norwegian Institute of International Affairs, pp. 127–160.

Ulriksen, Staale, Catriona Gourlay and Catriona Mace. 2004. Operation Artemis: The Shape of Things to Come? *International Peacekeeping* 11 (3): 508–525.

UN. 2008. *United Nations Peacekeeping Operations. Principles and Guidelines*. New York: UN Department of Peacekeeping Operations.

Underdal, Arild. 1983. Can we, in the Study of International Politics, do without the Model of the State as a Rational, Unitary Actor? *Internasjonal Politikk* 1: 63–79.

United Press International. 2006. Lebanon Exposes EU Policy Flaws. 26 November.

US Government. 2002. *The National Security Strategy of the United States of America*. Washington, DC: The White House.

2006. *The National Security Strategy of the United States of America*. Washington, DC: The White House.

2010. *The National Security Strategy of the United States of America*. Washington, DC: The White House.

Valasek, Tomas. 2011. *Governments need Incentives to Pool and Share Militaries*. London: Centre for European Reform

van Ham, Peter. 2001. Europe's Postmodern Identity: A Critical Appraisal. *International Politics* 38 (1): 229–252.

2005. Europe's Strategic Culture and the Relevance of War. *Oxford Journal of Good Governance* 2 (1): 39–43.

van Staden, Alfred, Kees Homan, Bert Kreemers, Alfred Pijpers and Rob de Wijk. 2000. *Towards a European Strategic Concept*. The Hague: The Clingendael Institute.

Vlachos Dengler, Katia. 2002a. *From National Champions to European Heavyweights. The Development of European Defense Industrial Capabilities Across Market Segments*. Santa Monica: RAND Corporation. Documented Briefing.

2002b. *Getting There: Building Strategic Mobility into ESDP*. Paris: EU-ISS. Occasional Paper no. 38.

von Weissenberg, Jon. 2002. *Strategic Sealift Capacity in the Common European Security and Defence Policy*. Helsinki: National Defence College.

Waever, Ole. 1995. Securitization and Desecuritization. In *On Security*, edited by R.D. Lipschutz. New York: Columbia University Press, pp. 46–86.

1998. Insecurity, Security and Asecurity in the West European Non-war Community. In *Security Communities*, edited by E. Adler and M. Barnett. Cambridge University Press, pp. 69–118.

2005. European Integration and Security: Analysing French and German Discourses on State, Nation and Europe. In *Discourse Theory* in *European Politics: Identity, Policy and Governance*, edited by D. Howarth and J. Torfing. London: Palgrave, pp. 33–67.

Wagnsson, Charlotte, James Sperling and Jan Hallenberg, eds. 2009. *European Security Governance: The European Union in a Westphalian World*. London: Routledge.

Wall Street Journal. 2010. Catherine Ashton Presents the New EU Diplomatic Service. 27 July.

Wallace, William. 2005. Post-Sovereign Governance. In *Policy Making in the European Union*, edited by H. Wallace and M.A. Pollack. Oxford University Press, pp. 483–503.

Walsh, James I. 2006. Intelligence-Sharing in the European Union: Institutions Are Not Enough. *Journal of Common Market Studies* 44 (3): 625–643.

Walt, Stephen. 1991. The Renaissance of Security Studies. *International Studies Quarterly* 35 (2): 211–239.

  1998. International Relations: One World, Many Theories. *Foreign Policy* 110 (Spring): 29–45.

Webber, Mark. 2007. *Inclusion, Exclusion and the Governance of European Security*. Manchester University Press.

Webber, Mark, Stuart Croft, Jolyon Howorth, Terry Terriff and Elke Krahmann. 2004. The Governance of European Security. *Review of International Studies* 30: 3–26.

Wellman, Barry and S.D. Berkowitz. 1988. *Social Structures: A Network Approach*. Cambridge University Press.

Wendt, Alexander. 1992. Anarchy Is What States Make of It: The Social Construction of Power Politics. *International Organization* 46 (2): 391–425.

  1995. Constructing International Politics. *International Security* 20 (1): 71–81.

  1998. On Constitution and Causation in International Relations. *Review of International Relations* 24 (Special Issue): 101–117.

  1999. *Social Theory of International Politics*. Cambridge University Press.

Whitman, Richard G. 2006. Road Map for a Route Match? (De-)civilianizing through the EU's Security Strategy. *European Foreign Affairs Review* 11 (1): 1–15.

Wight, Colin. 2006. *Agents, Structures and International Relations: Politics as Ontology*. Cambridge University Press.

Williams, Michael and Iver B. Neumann. 2000. From Alliance to Security Community: NATO, Russia and the Powers of Identity. *Millennium* 29 (2): 357–387.

Witney, Nick. 2008. *Re-energising Europe's Security and Defence Policy*. London: European Council on Foreign Relations. Policy paper.

Wiwel, Anders. 2005. The Security Challenges of Small EU Member States: Interests, Identity and the Development of the EU as a Security Actor. *Journal of Common Market Studies* 43 (2): 393–412.

Wolf, Klaus Dieter. 1999. The New Raison d'Ètat as a Problem for Democracy in World Society. *European Journal of International Relations* 5 (3): 333–363.

Wyn Jones, Richard. 1999. *Security, Strategy and Critical Theory*. Boulder: Lynne Rienner.

Yost, David S. 2000. The NATO Capabilities Gap and the European Union. *Survival* 42 (4): 97–128.

Zegart, Amy B. 1999. *Flawed by Design. The Evolution of the CIA, JCS, and NSC*. Stanford University Press.

Zielonka, Jan. 1998. *Explaining Euro-Paralysis: Why Europe is Unable to Act in International Politics*. Basingstoke: Macmillan.

Index